MASTERING PYTHON

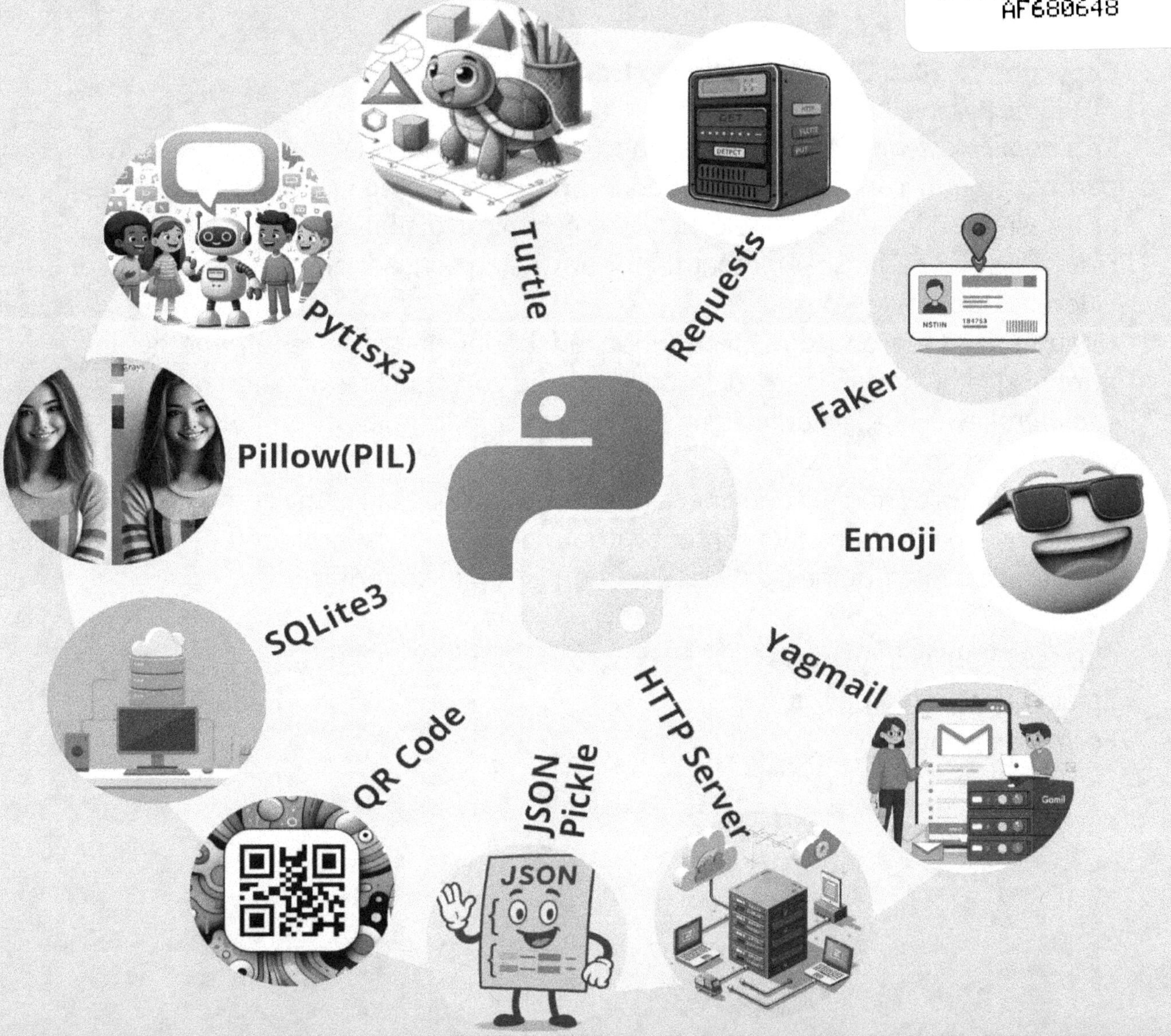

A Comprehensive Approach for Beginners and Beyond

Williams Asiedu

Mastering Python

A Comprehensive Approach for Beginners and Beyond

Ouereila Publishing House
Email: ouereila@gmail.com
Forms: ouereila?

Ouereila Publishing House EN_OP0003
Mastering Python
2025

Author: Williams Asiedu

MASTERING PYTHON
A Comprehensive Approach for Beginners and Beyond

Brief Contents

Table of Contents

Preface

Programming has rapidly evolved into a fundamental part of modern computing culture. Whether driven by passion or profession, individuals across the globe are embracing the art of designing, creating, and developing through code. The number of programmers has grown exponentially, especially as programming languages become more accessible and easier to learn.

From the early days of foundational languages like Assembly, COBOL, Fortran, BASIC, and Pascal—often referred to as the pioneers of programming—we've arrived at a new era where modern languages like Python dominate the landscape. Python, in particular, is celebrated for its simplicity, clean syntax, and beginner-friendly nature. It is an object-oriented language with a massive global community, rich library support, and unmatched versatility.

Python's real-world applications are vast. It powers critical innovations in fields such as:

- Artificial Intelligence (AI)
- Machine Learning (ML)
- Web Development
- Mobile and Desktop App Development
- Data Science and Analytics
- Automation and Scripting
- Game Development
- Image and Video Processing
- Graphic Design and Animation
- Internet of Things (IoT)
- Robotics
- Cybersecurity

... and more.

Who Is This Book For?

This book is designed for aspiring programmers and computer enthusiasts who are eager to learn Python from scratch and apply it across a variety of domains. Whether you aim to become a mobile or web developer, a data analyst, a game designer, or explore AI and machine learning, this book will serve as your springboard.

If you are:

- A beginner with no prior coding experience
- A student starting a computer science or IT program

- A tech-savvy professional exploring new skills
- A hobbyist interested in creating your own applications
- An experienced developer seeking to strengthen Python foundations

...then this book is for you.

It's written in a friendly, conversational tone with plenty of hands-on examples and exercises. You'll learn the core concepts of Python programming through clear explanations and real-world applications, all while building the confidence to take on more advanced topics.

Structure of the Book

This book is written in simple, clear English for easy comprehension. Each concept is explained with relatable examples and practical exercises, allowing readers to try their hands on real Python code—whether or not they are currently working on a computer.

Key Features

1. Code Snippets
Each chapter contains thoroughly tested code samples. These snippets serve as mini-simulations of real-world programming, making it easier for readers to understand and visualize how code works—even without access to a computer or development environment.

2. Notes
Scattered throughout the chapters are helpful notes that highlight key facts, tips, and best practices. These notes are designed to strengthen your mastery of essential Python concepts and make them memorable.

3. Deep Dives
This feature encourages readers to go beyond the basics. "Deep" sections provide additional insights, techniques, or extended examples that help deepen understanding and encourage independent exploration.

4. Think About It
These are thought-provoking questions posed at the end of certain sections. They challenge the reader to reflect on what they've learned, apply the concepts logically, and think critically—strengthening both retention and problem-solving skills.

Chapter Overview

Every chapter begins with a clear **overview**, introducing the topics to be covered. This prepares readers for what to expect and sets clear learning objectives, so they know what they will gain by the end of the chapter.

Chapters

The book is divided into **26 chapters**, each focusing on a distinct topic in Python programming. Some chapters build directly upon previous ones, allowing for a progressive, cumulative learning experience. Foundational chapters lay the groundwork, while later ones explore more advanced and applied topics.

From basic syntax and variables to file handling, OOP, web automation, APIs, and data visualization—this book guides readers through a structured journey to Python mastery.

Book Matter

The final section of the book is the **Book Matter**, which includes the **Author's Remarks**, **Acknowledgements**, and **Author's Bio**. Here, the author expresses gratitude to individuals who contributed to the creation of the book in any capacity and shares a brief professional background.

Chapter 1

Introduction to Programming

After you have studied this chapter, you should be able to:

- Understand what a programming language is
- Explain how programming languages work
- Identify different types of programming languages
- Recognize common programming languages used in the industry

Introduction

Understanding the underlying mechanisms of computers and modes of communication has underscored the necessity for efficient programming. Today, programming permeates our daily lives, accessible to all without the need for formal certification. It has become an integral aspect of digital market dynamics, with software proliferation driving industry growth.

Programming languages serve as the cornerstone of software development, representing the gateway to becoming a programmer or app developer. Over the years, these languages have evolved significantly, transitioning from complex structures to user-friendly interfaces. This century's programming languages are notably more intuitive, facilitating easier comprehension and application in development processes.

Credit is due to the inventors of modern programming languages for their tireless efforts and contributions to software development. Their innovations have not only democratized programming but also empowered individuals from diverse backgrounds to participate in the digital economy.

Programming Languages

Just as the name implies, language serves as a means of communication between two parties. Similarly, programming languages facilitate communication between users and computers through the use of symbols and objects, known as mnemonics. Since the inception of computers, programmers have continuously introduced new languages into the fold, each building upon or slightly altering the structure or syntax of its predecessors.

Programming languages are distinguished by their unique syntax, semantics, and intended applications. These languages range from low-level assembly languages, which directly interact with hardware, to high-level languages like Python and Java, which prioritize readability and ease of use. Despite their diversity, all programming languages share the common goal of enabling humans to instruct computers to perform specific tasks efficiently and accurately.

How the Programming Languages work

The fundamental language of computers is binary code, consisting of sequences of ones (1) and zeroes (0). For example, the binary code 101 is interpreted by the computer as the digit 5. Known as machine language, this binary code is the sole language that computers inherently understand. However, communicating with computers through binary code directly is arduous and impractical for users.

To bridge this gap, programming languages are utilized to facilitate communication between users and computers. These languages are designed to be more human-readable and intuitive, allowing users to express instructions in a familiar syntax. When a user writes code in a high-level programming language, a special software called a compiler or interpreter translates this code into machine language that the computer can execute.

In essence, programming languages act as an intermediary, enabling users to convey instructions to computers in a more accessible manner, while compilers and interpreters serve as translators, converting these instructions into the binary code that computers comprehend. This process streamlines the programming workflow, making it feasible for individuals to develop software and interact with computers effectively.

Kinds of Programming Languages

Low-Level Programming Languages:
Also known as machine language, low-level languages directly interact with hardware and consist of binary code represented by 0s and 1s. They are the most basic form of programming languages and are specific to the architecture of the computer's processor.

High-Level Programming Languages:
High-level languages are designed to be more user-friendly and abstracted from hardware specifics. They use natural language elements, symbols, and objects to make programming easier and more intuitive for humans. These languages are then compiled or interpreted into machine code.

Language	Year	Origin	Inventor
Fortran	1950	-	IBM
Cobol	1960	-	Grace Hopper
Lisp	1958	-	John McCarthy
Pascal	1970	-	Niklaus Wirth
C	1970	BCPL	Denis Ritchie
C++	1980	C	Bjarne Stroustrup

Perl	1987	C	Larry Wall
Python	1991	C, ABC	Guido Van Rossum
Java	1991	C	James Goslin (Oracle)
JavaScript	1995	ECMAScript	Netscape
C#	2000	Java, C++, Delphi	Anders Hejisberg
Kotlin	2011	Java	JetBrains
Dart	2011	C++	Google

Table 1.0: High-Level Programming Languages

Chapter 2

Starting Python

After you have studied this chapter, you should be able to:

- Understand the origin and history of Python
- Appreciate the importance and relevance of learning Python
- Install Python on your computer
- Set up a Python development environment
- Identify and use popular code editors
- Run Python scripts from different platforms
- Understand Python modules and libraries

Python

Python is a versatile and powerful programming language renowned for its readability, simplicity, and broad applicability across various domains. Developed by Guido Van Rossum in the late 1980s at the National Research Institute in the Netherlands, Python officially debuted in 1991. Since then, it has gained widespread adoption and popularity, becoming one of the most widely used programming languages globally.

Python's distinguishing features include being high-level, object-oriented, interactive, interpreted, and general-purpose. Its flexibility makes it suitable for a wide range of applications, including app development, data science, robotics, artificial intelligence, machine learning, web development, and game development.

One of Python's key strengths lies in its readability and simplicity. Python code is designed to resemble plain English, with keywords and syntax that are easy to understand and remember. This high-level scripting language allows developers to write concise and elegant code, facilitating rapid development and prototyping.

Moreover, Python boasts a vibrant and supportive community of developers and enthusiasts. This extensive community support ensures a wealth of resources, libraries, and frameworks readily available for developers to leverage in their projects, further enhancing Python's appeal and utility.

In essence, Python's combination of readability, versatility, and community support makes it an excellent choice for both beginners and experienced developers seeking to tackle a diverse range of programming challenges. Whether you're building web applications, analyzing data, or developing machine learning algorithms, Python offers the tools and resources necessary to bring your ideas to life effectively and efficiently.

Installing Python

Python is an open-source programming language, which means it is free to use and modify. It can be freely downloaded from the Python software Foundation's website at https://www.python.org

#Windows

Installing Python on Windows is indeed straightforward and hassle-free. Here's a concise guide:

1. Download Python: Visit the Python Software Foundation website (https://www.python.org/) and download the Python installer suitable for your Windows version.

2. Run the Installer: Once the download is complete, navigate to the location of the downloaded executable file (.exe) and double-click on it to launch the Python installer.

3. Installation Wizard: The installation wizard will guide you through the setup process. You can customize the installation by selecting optional features or changing the installation directory if desired.

4. Configure Environment Variables: During the installation process, ensure that you check the box labeled "Add Python to PATH." This option automatically configures the system environment variables to include the Python executable, making it accessible from any command prompt or PowerShell window.

Figure : 2.0

5. Complete Installation: Follow the prompts in the installation wizard to complete the installation process. Once the installation is finished, you can verify that Python is correctly installed by opening a command prompt and typing python --version. You should see the installed Python version displayed.

#Linux

Indeed, Linux distributions often come with Python pre-installed. However, users may wish to install a different version or manage Python installations themselves. Here are the steps to install Python on Linux:

1. Update Package Lists: Open a terminal and update the package lists to ensure you have the latest information about available packages. Use the command:

```
$ sudo apt update
```

2. Install Python: Use the package manager to install Python. The package name might vary slightly depending on your distribution. For Python 3, you can use:

```
$ sudo apt install python3
```

3. Verify Installation: After the installation is complete, verify that Python is installed correctly by running:

```
$ python --version
```

4. Optional: Install **pip** (Python Package Manager): Pip is a package manager for Python that allows you to install and manage additional libraries and packages. You can install pip using the following command:

```
$ sudo apt install python3-pip
```

#MacOS

1. Check Python Version (Optional): macOS usually comes with a pre-installed version of Python 2.x. You can check the version by opening the Terminal and running:

```
python --version
```

2. Install Homebrew (Optional): Homebrew is a package manager for macOS that simplifies the process of installing software. If you don't have Homebrew installed, you can do so by running the following command in Terminal:

```
/bin/bash -c "$(curl -fsSL
https://raw.githubusercontent.com/Homebrew/install/HEAD/install.sh)"
```

3. Update Homebrew (Optional): After installing Homebrew, it's a good idea to update it to ensure you have the latest version of available packages:

```
brew update
```

4. Install Python with Homebrew: Use Homebrew to install Python by running the following command in Terminal:

```
brew install python
```

5. Verify Installation: After the installation is complete, verify that Python is installed correctly by running:

```
python --version
```

6. Optional: Install pip (Python Package Manager): If pip is not installed automatically, you can install it using the following command:

```
sudo easy install pip
```

Editors

Editors, or Integrated Development Environments (IDEs), are applications that enable users to write, edit, debug, and run programming code. They typically feature user-friendly interfaces with integrated tools, compilers, and debuggers tailored for specific languages. Some editors support multiple languages, while others are designed for a particular language.

Popular editors for Python development include:

- PyCharm
- Visual Studio Code
- Sublime Text
- Notepad++

Additionally, Python comes with its own integrated environment called IDLE. IDLE provides an interactive environment for writing and running Python code, making it particularly useful for practicing coding skills.

Using IDLE

Using IDLE for Python coding is straightforward. Here's how to get started:

1. **Launch IDLE:**
   On Windows, open the Start menu and type "IDLE" to launch the IDLE editor.
   On Linux, open a terminal and type "idle" to launch IDLE.

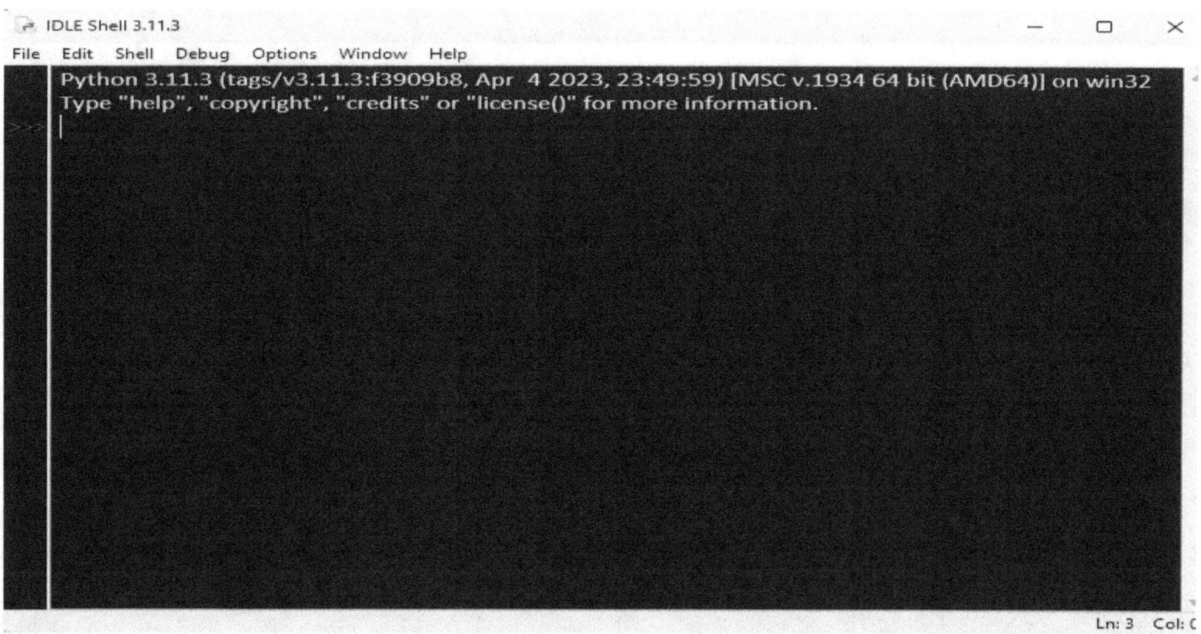

Figure: 2.1

2. Create a New File:
Once IDLE is open, click on the "File" menu and select "New File," or simply press Ctrl + N. This will open a new window where you can start writing your Python code.

3. Write Your Code:
Start writing your Python code in the new file window. You can use all the features of the IDLE editor, such as syntax highlighting and auto-indentation, to make coding easier.

4. Run Your Code:
After writing your code, you can run it by clicking on the "Run" menu and selecting "Run Module," or by pressing F5.
IDLE will execute your code and display the output in the interactive shell window.

Additionally, Python provides other interactive environments like IPython, which offers more advanced features and graphical capabilities for Python coding.

You can also use the native OS shell or command interface for simple Python coding tasks. This approach works the same way across all operating systems, including Windows, Linux, and macOS. Simply open a terminal or command prompt, type *"python"* to enter the Python interactive shell, and start coding directly in the shell environment.

Using the Python Interactive Shell

1. Open the Command Line Interface (CLI):

   - On Windows, type "cmd" into the Windows search bar and press Enter to open the Command Prompt.
   - On Linux or macOS, open a terminal window.

2. Launch the Python Interactive Shell:

   - In the Command Prompt or terminal window, type "python" and press Enter.
   - This command starts the Python interpreter and opens the interactive shell, allowing you to enter Python code and receive immediate feedback.

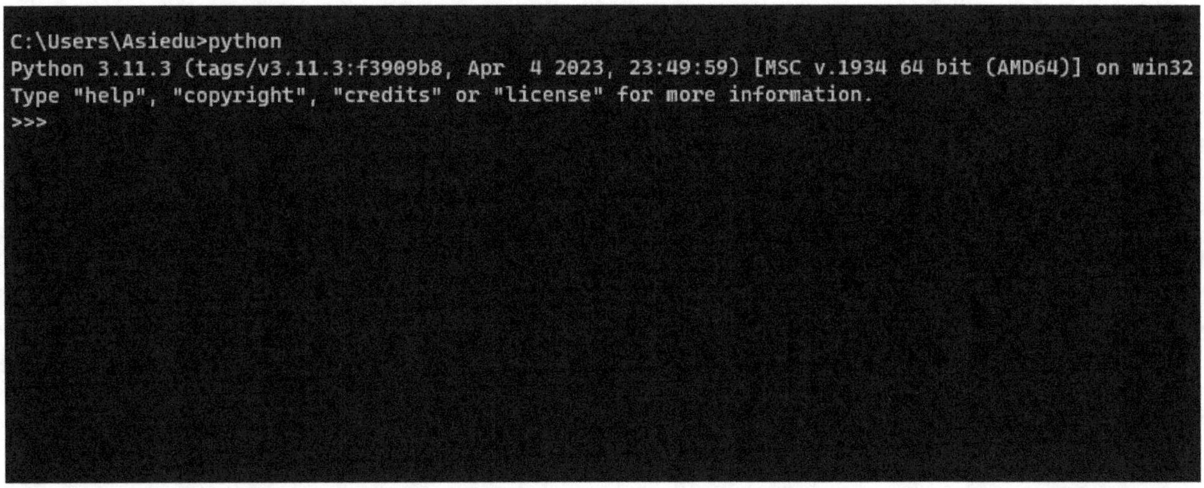

Figure: 2.2

That's it! You're now using the interactive Python shell, where you can experiment with Python code, test small snippets, and explore the language's features in real-time.

Running Python

Running Python code can be accomplished through various methods and integrated development environments (IDEs) like PyCharm, Visual Studio Code, and IDLE. Here's a specific example using Visual Studio Code:

The Visual Studio Code (VS Code)

VS Code is a versatile IDE developed by Microsoft, supporting numerous programming languages such as C, C++, Java, Python, C#, JavaScript, and HTML/CSS. It offers IntelliSense extensions to streamline programming tasks by providing suggestions for classes, functions, variables, and bug detection and correction. Additionally, VS Code is lightweight and features a user-friendly interface with buttons for running and debugging code.

#Windows

1. Download VS Code:
   Visit the Visual Studio Code website or use the following link to download the VS Code executable file: *Visual Studio Code Download*.

2. Run the Installer:
   Once the download is complete, double-click on the downloaded executable file (usually named something like VSCodeSetup.exe) to run the installer.

3. Follow Installation Instructions:
   Follow the on-screen instructions provided by the installer to complete the installation process. You can choose installation options such as adding VS Code to the PATH and creating desktop shortcuts.

#Linux

1. Download VS Code:

   On Linux, you can install Visual Studio Code using your distribution's package manager. For example, on Ubuntu, you can use the following commands in the terminal:

```
$ sudo apt update
$ sudo apt install code
```

#MacOS

1. Download VS Code:
   Visit the Visual Studio Code website or use the following link to download the VS Code for macOS: *Visual Studio Code Download*.
2. Install VS Code:
   Once the download is complete, open the downloaded .dmg file.
   Drag the Visual Studio Code icon to the Applications folder to install VS Code on your macOS system.

After installing Visual Studio Code, you can launch it from the Start menu (Windows), applications menu (macOS), or by typing "code" in the terminal (Linux).

Running Python code in Visual Studio Code

1. Install Python Extension (if not already installed):
   - ✓ Open Visual Studio Code.
   - ✓ Go to the Extensions view by clicking on the square icon on the sidebar or pressing Ctrl + Shift + X.
   - ✓ Search for "Python" or *"Pylance"* in the Extensions view and install the Python extension provided by Microsoft.

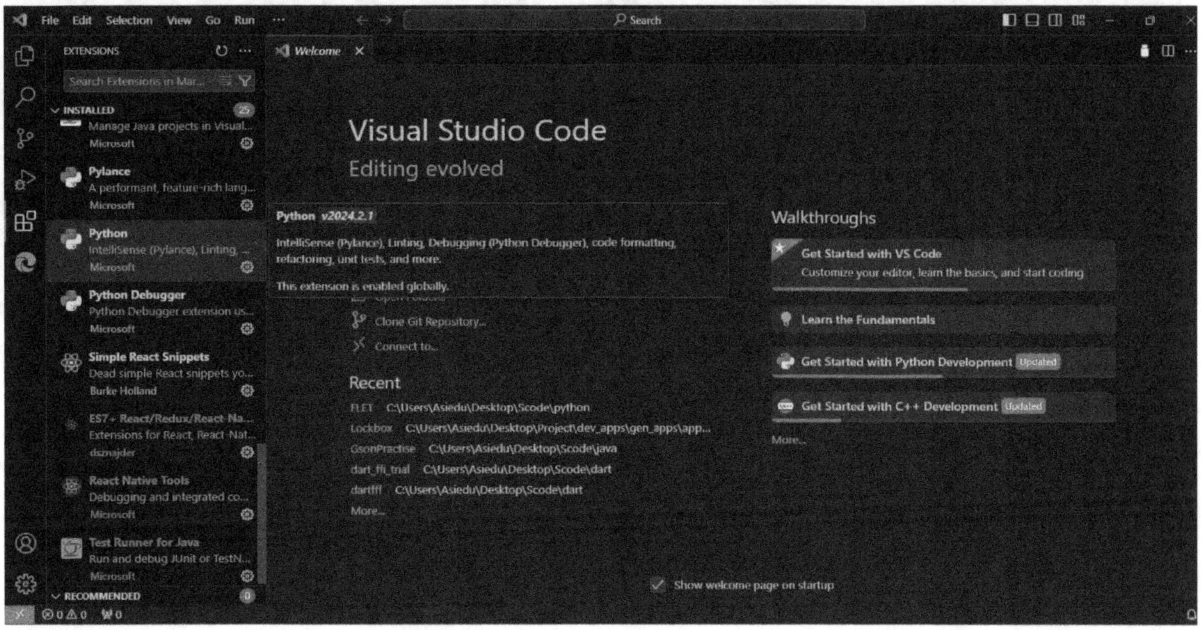

Figure: 2.3

2. Create or Open Python File:

   Create a new Python file or open an existing one in Visual Studio Code.
   - ✓ Click on the **"File"** menu at the top of the VS Code window.
   - ✓ Select **"New File"** to create a new file.
   - ✓ Name Your Python File:
     Type the preferred name of your Python file (e.g., "my_python.py").

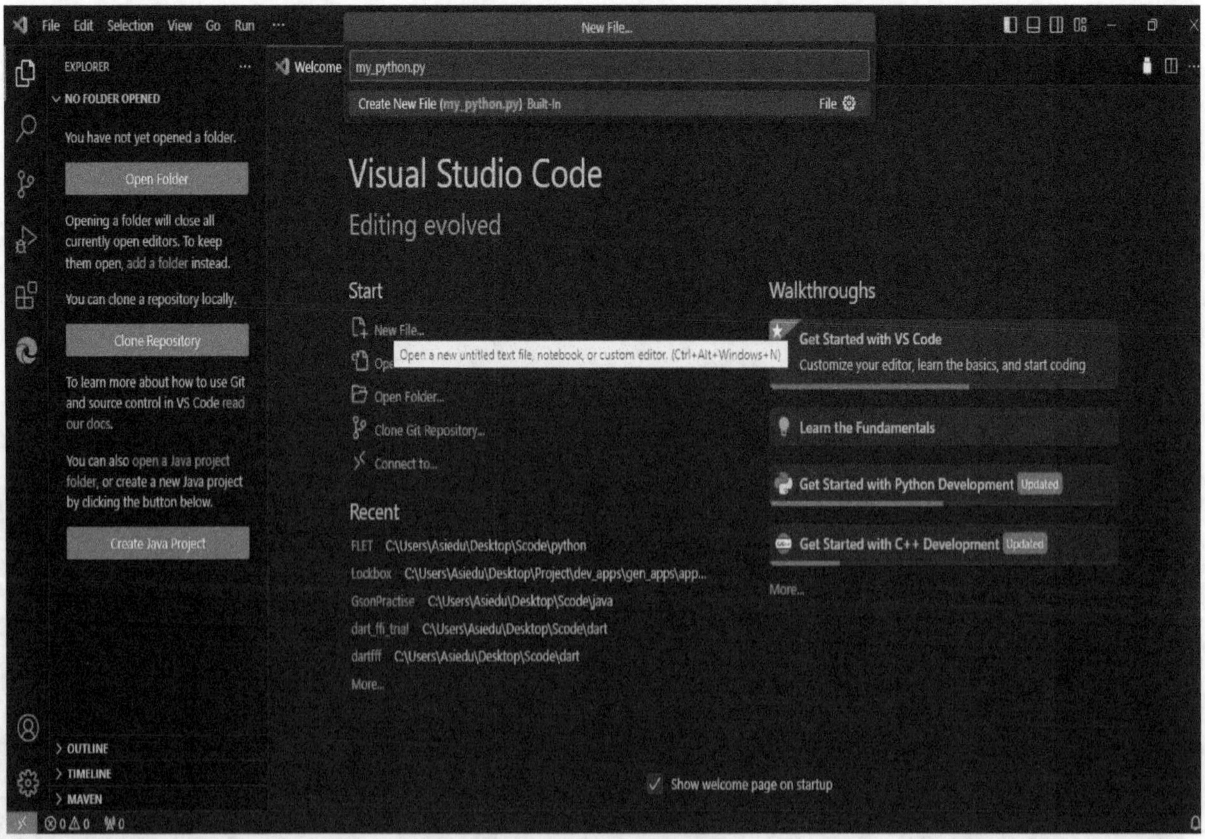

Figure: 2.4

3. Write Python Code:

   Write your Python code in the editor window. VS Code provides syntax highlighting and IntelliSense suggestions to assist you while coding.

Figure: 2.5

4. Run Python Code:

    ✓ To run your Python code, you can use the Run button located in the toolbar at the top of the editor window. Alternatively, you can use the keyboard shortcut Ctrl + F5.

    VS Code will execute your Python code and display the output in the integrated terminal.

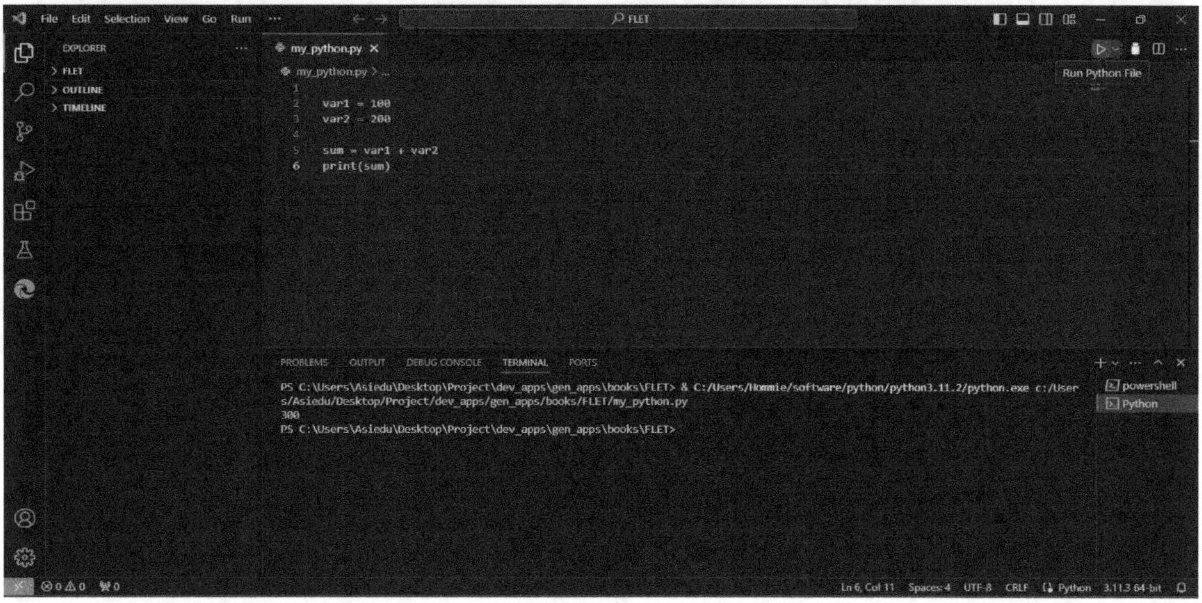

Figure: 2.6

Executing Python from the Command Line

Running Python code from the command line or shell using the python command is a simple and universal approach that works across all operating systems, including Windows, Linux, and macOS.

Here's how you can run Python code from the command line:

Open the Command Line or Terminal:

1. On Windows, open the Command Prompt by searching for *"cmd"* in the Start menu.
2. On Linux or macOS, open the Terminal application.

Navigate to the Directory Containing Your Python File (Optional):

3. Use the **cd** command to navigate to the directory containing your Python file if it's not already there.

Run the Python File:

4. Type **python** followed by the name of your Python file and press the **Enter** key. For example: python my_script.py

```
PS C:\Users\Asiedu\Desktop\Project\dev_apps> python my_python.py
```

View Output (If Any):

If your Python script produces any output, such as printed messages or results, it will be displayed in the terminal after running the script.

This method provides a straightforward way to execute Python code directly from the command line or shell, making it convenient for quick tests or running scripts without the need for an integrated development environment (IDE) or text editor.

Deep

Python files are commonly recognized by their extension. **.py** for regular Python scripts or file and **.pyw** for scripts that run without displaying the console window.

Modules or Libraries

Python modules are collections of code that provide additional functionality to Python programs. These modules are essentially Python files containing classes, functions and objects that can be imported and used in other Python scripts. They help simplify coding tasks by providing pre-defined solutions to common problems, thus saving developers time and effort.

While some modules are included in the Python standard library, many others are developed and maintained by the Python community. These external modules cover a wide range of domains and purposes, catering to diverse needs and preferences. For example, there are modules for web development, data analysis, machine learning, game development, and much more.

The beauty of Python modules lies in their versatility and flexibility. Developers can choose and install only the modules they need for their specific projects, allowing for a lightweight and efficient development process. For example, game developers may focus on installing modules essential for game development, while graphic designers may prefer using image processing libraries or modules to enhance their workflow.

Moreover, the open-source nature of Python encourages collaboration and contribution to module development, ensuring a rich ecosystem of tools and resources for Python programmers worldwide.

Installing Python Modules with Pip

Installing Python modules is straightforward using the pip command, which is included as part of the Python package. Here's how you can install a Python module using pip on the command line or shell of any operating system:

1. Open the Command Line or Terminal:
2. Use the pip Command:

```
pip install module_name
```

Press Enter to execute the command.
For example, to install the NumPy module, you would type:

```
pip install numpy
```

Once the installation is complete, you can start using the module in your Python code. Using the module in your Python code is as simple as using the import keyword followed by the name of the module. For example

</> Python

```
>>> import numpy
>>>
```

This statement imports the specified module into your Python script, allowing you to use its classes, functions, and variables within your code.

Note

Import statement will be covered in more detail in later chapters.

Deep

Bugs, also known as errors, are issues in the code that prevent it from running correctly or producing the expected output. They can occur due to various reasons, such as logic error, semantic error, syntax error and runtime error.

Chapter 3

Variable

After you have studied this chapter, you should be able to:

- Define what a variable is in Python
- Understand the rules for naming variables
- Identify types of variables
- Differentiate between local and global variables
- Understand how to use comments in Python code

Variable

Variable, also known as an identifier, is a term used to describe a letter or word that stores a value. Variables represent data stored in the computer's memory and can consist of any combination of letters, alphabets, or alphanumeric characters.

For example,

```
</> Python
>>> var = 100              #single value assignment
>>>
>>> var1, var2 = 2, 5      #multiple value assignment (var1 = 2, var2 = 5)
>>>
>>> x = y  = "computer"    #multiple value assignment (x = "computer", y = "computer")
```

In the above example:

- var is assigned to 100. Therefore, it holds a value of 100 in the computer memory.
- var1 and var2 are assigned to 2 and 5 respectively.
- x and y are assigned to the same value "computer".

Rules for naming Variables

- Variables are case sensitive.
  example: myvar is not equal to Myvar.

- Variables cannot begin with a number but can be followed by numbers.
  example: myvar25, my63var.

- Variables can begin with underscores.
  example: _myvar

Kinds of Variables

Variables exist in two forms: local and global. Both serve the same purpose of storing values in computer memory, but their functionality is determined by the scope in which they are used.

Local Variables

Local variables are declared **within** a function or block and can only be accessed by members within the same function. They are **not available** outside that block or function.

</> Python

```
global_var = 3

def math:                   #function
    local_var = 2           #local variable
    value = local_var + 5   #using variable
```

For example, the variable local_var is defined inside a function called math, no object outside the math function can access it.

Global Variables

Global variables are declared **outside** any function or block, making them **accessible** to all functions and objects within the program.

</> Python

```
global_var = 3                          #global variable
add = global_var + 10

def math:                               #function
    local_var = 2                       #local variable
    value = local_var + global_var      #using global variable
```

For instance, if a variable global_var is defined globally, it can be used both inside and outside functions. However, **global variables can only be accessed but not modified** from within a function unless explicitly specified using the global or nonlocal keyword.

</> Python

```
city  = "London"

def withoutGlobal():
    city = "New York"

def withGlobal():
    global city
    city = "New York"

withoutGlobal()              #Executing function
print(city)

withGlobal()
print(city)
```

```
#Ouput
London
New York
```

In a scenario where a variable city is modified inside a function withGlobal, the global keyword ensures that the change affects the original global variable, setting its new value to "New York".

Think about it ?

The **nonlocal** keyword works similarly to global, but it is primarily used within nested functions.

But wait... what exactly is a nested function?

Deep

To check if an object is a valid variable name or identifier, use the .isidentifier() method on the string.

```
>>> "100var".isidentifier()
False
>>> "_var".isidentifier()
True
>>>
```

Using None in Python

In most programming languages, especially **C++, Java, JavaScript, and Dart**, variables can be declared without assigning an initial value. These variables are often set to null or left empty, allowing them to be assigned a value later.

However, Python does not allow variables to be declared without assigning a value. Every declared variable must have an initial value. If a value is meant to be defined later, Python provides the special keyword **None**, which represents an empty or uninitialized variable that will be assigned a value in the future.

Example Use Case

</> Python

```python
country = None
city = "New York"

country = "USA"
print(country)
```

```
#Ouput
USA
```

None is commonly used as a placeholder for variables that will receive a value later in the program. It helps indicate that a variable is intentionally left empty rather than undefined.

Think about it ?

Are any of these valid variables?

- xyz
- 45var
- myVar
- _6var1
- #num
- n@um
- --first

Comment

Comments in programming serve as a means to document code, offer explanations, or add notes for better understanding. In Python, comments are not executed; rather, Python identifies them and skips their execution. Comments in Python are denoted by the '#' symbol.

For example:

</> Python

```
>>> num1 = 10  #first number
>>> num2 = 20  #second number
```

Documentation

In Python, apart from using comments (#), you can also use **documentation strings (docstrings)** to document a function, class, or module.

Why use docstrings?
Unlike comments, which are useful for short explanations, **docstrings** are preferred when the text is too long or when you need structured documentation. Writing a comment on every line can become tedious, especially for large blocks of code.

Python uses **triple quotes** (''' ''' or """ """) for docstrings. These docstrings are ignored during program execution but can be accessed using Python's built-in documentation tools, such as help() or .__doc__.

</> Python

```
def Hello():
    """
    This function only returns Helloo
    Wishing you a happy codding
    """
    return "Helloo"

print(Hello.__doc__)
```

```
#Ouput
This function only returns Helloo
Wishing you a happy codding
```

Chapter 4

Reserved Words

After you have studied this chapter, you should be able to:

- Understand what reserved words (keywords) are
- Identify various reserved words in Python
- Use the input() function to receive user input
- Utilize common built-in functions in Python

Reserved Words

Python, like many programming languages, has a set of reserved keywords that serve specific purposes and functions within the language. These keywords are not available for use as variable names or for any other purpose in a Python program. Each reserved word carries a distinct and predefined functionality that is essential for the language's structure and operation.

print	chr	hex	max	super	finally
len	else	range	raise	next	type
set	if	bin	sum	map	or
int	True	try	as	with	global
dict	False	eval	bool	while	local
list	and	not	str	for	catch
object	import	oct	ord	zip	super
exec	del	dir	any	def	return
yield	hash	filter	format	enumerate	delattr
compile	bytearray	bytes	ascii	min	complex
id	local	help	in	open	lambda
input	None	is	nonlocal	assert	class
elif	break	continue	pass	from	case
match	async	await	pow		

Table 4.0: Some keywords used in Python programming

Here are the uses of some keywords

input()

The input() function is used to receive data from the user through a prompt. By default, it takes input as a string, but the input data can be converted to any desired type and assigned to a variable.

Example 1

```python
name = input("What is your name: ")
print(f"Hello {name}")
```

```
#Ouput
>>> What is your name: Alice
....... Hello Alice
```

Example 2

```python
>>> num1 = int( input("first number: "))          #converting input to integer
......  first number: 2
>>> num2 = int( input("second number: "))
......  second number: 3
>>>
>>> total = num1 + num2
>>> total
....... 5
>>>
```

Note

The **int** used above belongs to the integer data type and is used to convert other types to integers. Integers and other data types will be covered in detail in the upcoming chapters.

bin()

The bin returns the binary of an integer or a number.

```python
>>> bin( 8 )
...... '0b1000'
>>>
```

hex()

The hex keyword returns the hexadecimal of an integer or a number.

```
</> Python
>>> hex( 50 )
....... '0x32'
>>>
```

oct()

The oct() function returns the **octal (base-8) representation** of an integer or number.

```
</> Python
>>> oct( 15 )
...... '0o17'
>>>
```

chr()

The chr function accepts an integer and returns its corresponding ASCII character.

```
</> Python
>>> chr( 65 )
...... 'A'
>>> chr( 64 )
...... '@'
```

Index	ASCII	Index	ASCII	Index	ASCII	Index	ASCII
33	!	40	(	49	1	66	B
34	"	42	*	52	4	71	G
35	#	43	+	59	;	93	]
36	$	44	,	60	<	97	a
37	%	46	.	61	=	109	m
38	&	47	/	63	?	165	¥
39	'	48	0	64	@	190	¾

Table 4.1: Some ASCII characters and their corresponding indices

ord()

The ord function accepts an ASCII character in a string and returns its corresponding integer.

```
</> Python
>>> ord( "B" )
...... 66
>>> ord( "%" )
...... 37
```

eval()

The eval() function evaluates expressions in string format and applies mathematical operations to compute the result.

```
</> Python
>>> eval( "5+2*3-1/2" )
...... 10.5
>>> eval( "pow(2,4) -5 + max(10,5)" )
...... 21
```

id()

The id() function returns the **memory address** of a variable.

```
</> Python
>>>var = "computer"
>>> id( var )
...... 2682500645296
```

del()

The del statement deletes a variable or object from memory. Attempting to access a deleted variable will result in an error.

```
</> Python
>>>var = "computer"
>>> del( var )
>>> print(var)
```

```
Traceback (most recent call last):
  File "<python-input-19>", line 1, in <module>
    print(var)
```

Note

Most of the keywords will be covered in detail as you progress through the next chapters.

Chapter 5

Operators

After you have studied this chapter, you should be able to:

- Understand what operators are
- Identify and categorize different types of operators
- Compare and contrast the use of various operators

Operators

Operators are special symbols that appear between two operands (values or variables) and instruct the computer to perform specific operations. These operations can involve mathematical calculations, comparisons, assignments, and logical evaluations.

The various kinds of Python operators include:

- Arithmetic Operators
- Relational Operators
- Assignment Operators
- Logical Operators
- Identity Operators
- Membership Operators
- Bitwise Operators

Arithmetic Operators

Arithmetic operators are used to perform various mathematical functions on numeric data types in programming. They enable you to perform fundamental mathematical operations like addition, subtraction, multiplication, division, and more.

Addition(+)

```
</> Python
>>> x = 5
>>> y = 3
>>> result = x + y
>>> print( result )
...... 8
>>>
```

Subtraction(-)

```
</> Python
>>> x = 10
>>> y = 6
>>> result = x - y
>>> print( result )
...... 4
>>>
```

Multiplication(*)

```
</> Python
>>> num1 = 4
>>> num2 = 2
>>> product = num1 * num2
>>> print( product )
...... 8
>>>
```

Division(/)

```
</> Python
>>> first = 6
>>> second = 2
>>> first / second
...... 3
>>>
```

Modulo(%)

```
</> Python
>>> x = 3
>>> y = 11
>>> y % x
...... 2
>>>
```

Floor division(//)

```
</> Python
>>> x = 9
>>> y = 2
>>> x // y
...... 4
>>>
```

Exponential (**)

```
</> Python
>>> _exp = 2
>>> _num = 4
>>> _num **  _exp
...... 16
>>>
```

Relational Operators

Relational operators, also known as comparison operators, are essential components of conditional statements in Python. They are used to compare two values or operands and determine the relationship between them. Relational operators return a Boolean value, either **'True'** or **'False'**, based on the result of the comparison.

Relational operators are crucial for making decisions in programs. They help answer questions like "Is this value equal to that one?" or "Is this value greater than that one?"

Equal to (==)

```
</> Python
>>> "wheat" == "whaet"   #equal to
......  False
>>> x, y = 100, 100
>>> x == y
.....  True
```

Not equal to (!=)

</> Python

```
>>> "Computer" != "computer"
...... True
>>> x = y = 4
>>> x != y
...... False
```

Less than or equal to (<=)

</> Python

```
>>> 10 <= 20
...... True
>>> m = n = 5
>>> m <= n
...... True
```

Greater than or equal to (>=)

</> Python

```
>>> 10 >= 20
...... False
>>> x, y = 4 , 2
>>> x >= y
...... True
```

Think about it ?

- How is **>** different from **>=**?
- What about **<** and **<=**?

Assignment Operators

Assignment operators serve the primary function of assigning a value on the right side to a variable on the left side. This assignment results in the variable holding the assigned value, thereby making it accessible for subsequent operations or references in your code. In Python, the most commonly used assignment operator is the equals sign (=), which assigns the value on the right side to the variable on the left side. For example:

Equal(=)

</> Python

```
>>> x = 5
>>> name, age = "Alice", 20
>>> y = z = 10
>>>
```

Addition assignment (+=)

The addition assignment operator adds the right operand to the left operand and assigns the result to the left operand or the variable.

</> Python

```
>>> x = 5
>>> x += 2
>>> print( x )
...... 7
```

Subtraction assignment (-=)

The subtraction assignment (-=) operator subtracts the right operand from the left operand and assigns the result to the left operand or the variable.

</> Python

```
>>> m = 3
>>> m -= 2
>>> print( m )
..... 1
```

Multiplication assignment (*=)

The multiplication assignment (*=) operator multiplies the left operand by the right operand and assigns the result to the left operand.

```
</> Python
>>> var = 5
>>> var *= 3
>>> print( var )
...... 15
```

Division assignment (/=)

The division assignment (/=) operator divides the left operand by the right operand and assigns the result to the left operand or the variable. The result is always a float.

```
</> Python
>>> var = 8
>>> var /= 2
>>> print( var )
...... 4.0
```

Floor division assignment (//=)

The floor division assignment (//=) operator performs floor division (truncating the decimal part) and assigns the result to the left operand or the variable.

```
</> Python
>>> n = 17
>>> n //= 4
>>> print( n )
...... 4
```

Modulus assignment (%=)

The modulus assignment (%=) operator calculates the remainder when the left operand is divided by the right operand and assigns the result to the left operand or the variable.

```
</> Python
>>> mod = 12
>>> mod %= 5
>>> print( mod )
...... 2
```

Exponential assignment (**=)

The exponentiation assignment (**=) operator raises the left operand to the power of the right operand and assigns the result to the left operand or variable.

```
</> Python
>>> exp = 4
>>> exp **= 2
>>> print( exp )
...... 16
```

Logical Operators

Logical operators are essential elements in Python used for making logical assumptions and decisions. They operate on Boolean values and return either 'True' or 'False' based on the logical conditions they evaluate. Logical operators are or, and, not. These operators are mostly used in decision making structures.

> **Note**
> Logical operators are mostly used in **if** clauses for making conditional statements or decision-making. This will be studied later under Decision making statements.

or

The **or** operator returns True if at least one of the operands is True; otherwise, it returns False.

```
</> Python
x = 10
if (x < 2 or x > 20):          #False or False = False
   print("Great")
else:
   print("Oouch!")
```

```
#Output
Oouch!
```

and

The **and** operator returns True only if both operands are True; otherwise, it returns False.

```python
var = 4
if (var <= 5 and var % 2 == 0):          #True and True = True
    print("Awesome Python")
else:
    print("Oouch!")
```

```
#Output
Awesome Python
```

not

The **not** operator returns the logical negation of the operand, meaning it converts True to False and False to True.

```python
var = True
if ( not var ):          #not  True = False
    print("Awesome Python")
else:
    print("Oouch!")
```

```
#Output
Oouch!
```

Deep

The if and else statements are conditional statements that control the flow of a program based on conditions. They will be explored in more detail under Decision-Making Statements in later chapters.

Identity Operators

Identity operators in Python are tools used to verify or check whether two variables or objects are stored at the same memory location. They allow you to determine if two variables or objects refer to the same entity in memory, rather than comparing their values. Identity operators are essential for understanding object identity and reference equality. The two identity operators are is and is not.

```
</> Python
>>> m = n = 10
>>> x = 5
>>> m is n
...... True
>>> m is x
...... False
>>> m is not x
...... True
>>>
```

Membership Operators

Membership operators in Python are tools used to check if a specific item is present in a collection of items. These operators are invaluable for determining whether an element belongs to a set, list, tuple, string, or any other iterable. They provide a straightforward way to search for the presence of an item within a container.

```
</> Python
>>> var = "computer"
>>> even = [2, 4, 6, 8]
>>> "com"  in var
...... True
>>> "z"  in var
...... False
>>> 5 not in even
...... True
>>>
```

Chapter 6

Data Types

After you have studied this chapter, you should be able to:

- Understand what data types are in Python
- Differentiate between integers and floating-point numbers
- Use basic math functions in Python
- Work with strings and apply various string methods
- Format strings effectively
- Use lists and perform common list operations

Data Types

Data encompasses raw values that can manifest in various forms, such as numbers, letters, special characters or a blend thereof. Data types serve to classify data based on their attributes and functionalities.

In Python, data types represent instances or objects of specific classes, each characterized by unique traits and behaviors. The Python programming language encompasses approximately eight fundamental data types. The various types of data types in Python include:

- Numbers (Integer and Float)
- String
- List
- Dictionary
- Tuple
- Set
- Boolean
- Bytes

Deep

To check the data type of an object, use the type() function.

```
>>> var = 3
>>> type(var)
...... class <'int'>
>>> mystr = "Computer"
>>> type(mystr)
...... class <'str'>
```

Numbers

Number data types include all real numbers, such as positive and negative integers, decimals, and other numerical values.

Integer

The integer class encompasses all numbers, including negative numbers, without decimal points. Example include, 2, 13, -5, 100, 2000 ......

Deep

The int() function is employed to convert from one type to the integer type

```
>>> num = "5"        #string to integer
>>> int(num)
...... 5
>>> var = 12.58      #float to integer
>>> int(var)
...... 12
```

Float

On the other hand, floats represent the class of all numbers with decimal points. Example include, -6.25, 8.5245, -5.3, 100.6 ......

Deep

To convert from one type to the float type, the float() function is utilized.

```
>>> dec = "8.258"       #string to float
>>> float(dec)
...... 8.258
>>> var = 35            #integer to float
>>> float(var)
...... 35.0
```

The math Module

The **math** module provides a wide range of mathematical functions and constants for performing numerical computations. It includes methods for working with equations, geometry, trigonometry, logarithms, and more. These functions are essential for handling mathematical concepts in Python.

Deep

You can explore more methods of math with the dir() function.

```
>>> import math
>>> dir(math)
...... [............]
```

Commonly Used Functions in the math Module

Function	Description
math.sqrt(x)	Returns the square root of x.
math.pow(x, y)	Returns x raised to the power of y (equivalent to x ** y).
math.exp(x)	Returns e raised to the power of x.
math.log(x)	Returns the natural logarithm (base e) of x.
math.log10(x)	Returns the logarithm of x to base 10.
math.log2(x)	Returns the logarithm of x to base 2.
math.factorial(x)	Returns the factorial of x (x!).
math.gcd(x, y)	Returns the greatest common divisor (GCD) of x and y.
math.lcm(x, y)	Returns the least common multiple (LCM) of x and y.
math.fabs(x)	Returns the absolute value of x.
math.ceil(x)	Rounds x up to the nearest integer.
math.floor(x)	Rounds x down to the nearest integer.
math.trunc(x)	Returns the truncated integer part of x.
math.modf(x)	Splits x into its fractional and integer parts as a tuple.
math.copysign(x, y)	Returns x with the sign of y.
math.fsum(iterable)	Returns the precise sum of an iterable of numbers.
math.isfinite(x)	Checks if x is a finite number.
math.isinf(x)	Checks if x is infinite (+∞ or -∞).
math.isnan(x)	Checks if x is NaN (Not a Number).

pow(x, y)

```
</> Python
import math
>>> pow( 2, 4)
...... 16
>>> math.pow(3, 2)
...... 9.0
```

sqrt(x)

```
</> Python
import math
>>> math.sqrt( 25 )
...... 5.0
```

log10(x)

```
</> Python
import math
>>> math.log10( 10 )
...... 1.0
```

ceil(x)

```
</> Python
import math
>>> math.ceil( 3.845 )
...... 4
```

floor(x)

```
</> Python
import math
>>> math.floor( 5.389 )
..... 6
```

factorial(x)

```
</> Python
import math
>>> math.factorial( 6 )
...... 720
```

Trigonometric Functions

Function	Description
math.sin(x)	Returns the sine of x (in radians).
math.cos(x)	Returns the cosine of x (in radians).
math.tan(x)	Returns the tangent of x (in radians).
math.asin(x)	Returns the arcsine of x (inverse of sine).
math.acos(x)	Returns the arccosine of x (inverse of cosine).
math.atan(x)	Returns the arctangent of x (inverse of tangent).
math.degrees(x)	Converts x from radians to degrees.
math.radians(x)	Converts x from degrees to radians.
math.sinh(x)	Returns the hyperbolic sine of x.
math.cosh(x)	Returns the hyperbolic cosine of x.
math.tanh(x)	Returns the hyperbolic tangent of x.
math.asinh(x)	Returns the inverse hyperbolic sine of x.
math.acosh(x)	Returns the inverse hyperbolic cosine of x.
math.atanh(x)	Returns the inverse hyperbolic tangent of x.

sin(x)

</> Python

```
import math
>>> math.sin( 45 )
...... 0.8509035245341184
```

cos(x)

</> Python

```
import math
>>> math.cos( 90 )
...... -0.4480736161291701
```

tan(x)

</> Python

```
import math
>>> math.tan( 30 )
...... 0.15425144988758405
```

Mathematical Constants

Function	Description
math.pi	Represents the value of π (3.14159...).
math.e	Represents Euler's number (2.71828...), the base of natural logarithms.
math.tau	Represents the constant τ (τ = 2π).
math.inf	Represents positive infinity (+∞).
math.nan	Represents "Not a Number" (NaN).

Special Functions

Function	Description
math.erf(x)	Returns the error function of x.
math.erfc(x)	Returns the complementary error function of x.
math.gamma(x)	Returns the gamma function of x ((x-1)!).
math.lgamma(x)	Returns the natural logarithm of the absolute value of the gamma function of x.

String

A string is a sequence of characters, including alphabets, numbers, or special characters, enclosed within quotes. String can be in a single or double quote.

For example,

</> Python

```
>>> var1 = 'single'
>>> var2 = "double"
>>> var3 = '''triple'''
>>> var4 = """triple"""
```

Deep

The str() method is used to convert other data types to a string.

```
>>> var = 3.45
>>> string_var = str(var)
>>> print(string_var)
..... '3.45'
>>>
```

String indexing

Indexing refers to the position of each character in a string. The index of a string starts from zero and goes up to the length of the string minus one (0 to length-1). The first character or element of a string typically occupies index 0, the next character takes index 1, and so on.

For example, using "computer"

0	1	2	3	4	5	6	7
c	o	m	p	u	t	e	r
-8	-7	-6	-5	-4	-3	-2	-1

```
</> Python
>>> var = "computer"
>>> var[0]
...... 'c'
>>> var[1]
...... 'o'
>>> var[-6]
...... 'm'
>>>
```

Concatenating string

Concatenating strings involves adding two or more separate strings to form one complete string using the plus (+) operator.

For example,

```
</> Python
>>> var1 = "com"
>>> var2 = "puter"
>>> var3 = var1 + var2
>>> print(var3)
...... 'computer'
>>>
```

Slicing a string

String slicing allows you to extract substrings from a string. The syntax for string slicing is **string**[start : end], where *start* indicates where the slicing should begin and *end* indicates where it should end. Both start and end parameters can be omitted, in which case Python will set them to default values (0 for start and the last index of the string for end).

Formulas for String Slicing

string[start: end]	→	Returns a substring starting from the specified start index up to (but not including) the end index.
string[start:]	→	Returns a substring starting from the specified start index to the end of the string.
string[: end]	→	Returns a substring starting from the beginning (index 0) up to (but not including) the specified end index.
string[:]	→	Returns the entire string from index 0 to the last character.

For example,

</> **Python**

```
>>> var = "Hello World"
>>> var[0:5]                #start = 0, end=5
...... 'Hello'
>>> var[6:]                 #start = 6, end= length of string
...... 'World'
>>> var[:3]                 #start = 0, end=3
...... 'Hel'
>>> var[1:5]                #start = 1, end=5
...... 'ello'
>>>
```

String Methods

Deep

To view the various methods available for a string, use the dir() function on a string object.

```
>>> mystring = "Hello World"
>>> dir(mystring)
...... [............]
```

Case Conversion Methods

upper()	Converts all characters in the string to uppercase.
lower()	Converts all characters in the string to lowercase.
capitalize()	Converts the first character of the string to uppercase and the rest to lowercase.
title()	Converts the first character of each word in the string to uppercase.
swapcase()	Swaps uppercase characters to lowercase and vice versa.
casefold()	Converts the string to lowercase, more aggressive than lower(), used for case-insensitive comparisons.

</> Python

```
>>> var = "The brown fox"
>>>
>>> var.upper()
...... 'THE BROWN FOX'
>>>
>>> var.lower()
...... 'the brown fox'
>>>
>>> var.capitalize()
...... 'The brown fox'
>>>
>>> var.title()
...... 'The Brown Fox'
>>>
>>> var.swapcase()
...... 'tHE BROWN FOX'
>>>
>>> var.casefold()
...... 'the brown fox'
>>>
```

Whitespace and Padding Methods

strip()	Removes leading and trailing whitespace.
lstrip()	Removes leading (left-side) whitespace.
rstrip()	Removes trailing (right-side) whitespace.
zfill(width)	Pads the string with zeros (0) on the left to match the given width.
center(width, char)	Centers the string within a given width using the specified character (default is space).
ljust(width, char)	Left-aligns the string within a given width, padding with the specified character.
rjust(width, char)	Right-aligns the string within a given width, padding with the specified character.

</> Python

```
>>> mystring = "   let me have a coffee.   "
>>>
>>> mystring.strip()
...... 'let me have a coffee.'
>>>
>>> mystring.lstrip()
...... 'let me have a coffee   '
>>>
>>> mystring.rstrip()
...... '   let me have a coffee'
>>>
>>> mystring.zfill( 30 )
...... '000000  let me have a coffee  '
>>>
>>> mystring.center(30, '@' )
...... '@@@  let me have a coffee  @@@'
>>>
>>> mystring.ljust(28, '$' )
...... '  let me have a coffee  $$$$'
>>>
>>> mystring.rjust(28, '$' )
...... '$$$$  let me have a coffee  '
```

Searching and Finding Methods

find(substring, start, end)	Returns the index of the first occurrence of substring in the string. Returns -1 if not found.
rfind(substring, start, end)	Similar to find(), but searches from the right.
index(substring, start, end)	Similar to find(), but raises an error if the substring is not found.
rindex(substring, start, end)	Similar to rfind(), but raises an error if the substring is not found.
count(substring, start, end)	Counts the occurrences of substring in the string.

</> Python

```
>>> var = "Programming"
>>>
>>> len( var )                    #returns the length of the string
...... 11
>>>
>>> var[0]                        #returns a character by the index
...... 'P'
>>>
>>> var.find( "o" ,1, 6)
...... 2
>>> var.find( "g" )               #returns the first occurrence of  g
...... 3
>>>
>>> var.rfind( "g" )              #returns the last occurrence of g
...... 10
>>>
>>> var.index( "r" , 1, 6 )       #start from index 1  ( r ) , end at index 5 (a)
...... 1
>>>
>>> var.rindex( "r" , 1, 6 )      #start from index 1  ( r ) , end at index 5 (a)
...... 4
>>>
>>> var.count( "m")
...... 2
>>>
```

Splitting and Joining Methods

split(delimiter, maxsplit)	Splits the string into a list using the specified delimiter. The optional maxsplit limits the number of splits.
rsplit(delimiter, maxsplit)	Similar to split(), but splits from the right.
splitlines(keepends)	Splits the string at line breaks (\n) and returns a list. If keepends=True, line breaks are kept.
partition(separator)	Splits the string into three parts: before separator, separator, and after separator.
rpartition(separator)	Similar to partition(), but searches from the right.
join(iterable)	Joins elements of an iterable (list, tuple) into a string using the calling string as a separator.

```
</> Python
>>> var = "coding @ with @ coffee"
>>>
>>> substring = var.split( )                    #delimiter is the default whitespace
>>> print(substring)
...... ['coding', '@', 'with', '@', 'coffee']
>>>
>>> substring = var.split( "@" )                #delimiter is the "@"
>>> print(substring)
...... ['coding ', ' with ', ' coffee']
>>>
>>> substring = var.split( "@" , 1 )            #delimiter is the "@", maxsplit is 1
>>> print(substring)
...... ['coding ', ' with @ coffee']
```

```
</> Python
>>> var = "Crack Codes-Great Python!"
>>>
>>> substring = var.partition(" ")
>>> print(substring)
...... ('Crack', ' ', 'Codes-Great Python!')
>>>
>>> substring = var.partition("-")
>>> print(substring)
```

```
..... ('Crack Codes', '-', 'Great Python!')
>>>
>>>
>>> var = "Programming"
>>> substring = " - ".join( var )
>>> print(substring)
...... P - r - o - g - r - a - m - m - i - n – g
```

String Modification and Replacement Methods

replace(old, new, count)	Replaces occurrences of old with new. The optional count limits the number of replacements.
removeprefix(char)	Removes the specified leading character or substring from a string.
removesuffix(char)	Removes the specified trailing character or substring from a string.

</> Python

```
>>> newstring = "The big brown cat"
>>>
>>> newstring.replace("cat", "fox")
...... 'The big brown fox'
>>>
>>> substring = "Crack Codes and Coffee ".replace("C", "K", 2)
>>> print(substring)
...... 'Krack Kodes and Coffee'
```

</> Python

```
>>> var = "*programming"
>>>
>>> var.removeprefix("*")
...... 'programming'
>>>
>>> var.removesuffix("ming")
...... '*program'
```

String Checking Methods (True or False)

Method	Description
startswith(prefix, start, end)	Returns True if the string starts with prefix.
endswith(suffix, start, end)	Returns True if the string ends with suffix.
isalpha()	Returns True if the string contains only alphabetic characters (A-Z, a-z).
isdigit()	Returns True if the string contains only digits (0-9).
isalnum()	Returns True if the string contains only alphanumeric characters (letters and numbers).
isspace()	Returns True if the string contains only whitespace characters.
islower()	Returns True if all characters in the string are lowercase.
isupper()	Returns True if all characters in the string are uppercase.
istitle()	Returns True if the string follows title case (each word starts with an uppercase letter).
isnumeric()	Returns True if the string contains only numeric characters, including Unicode numerals.
isdecimal()	Returns True if the string contains only decimal characters.
isidentifier()	Returns True if the string is a valid Python identifier (variable name).
isascii()	Returns True if the string contains only ASCII characters (0-127).

</> Python

```
>>> "computer".startswith("com")
..... True
>>> "computer".endswith("k")
..... False

>>> "coding".isalpha()
..... True
>>> "code250".isalpha()
..... False

>>> "code250".isdigit()
..... False
>>> "250".isnumeric()
..... True
```

```
>>> "code250".isalnum()
..... True

>>> "code250@_#".isalnum()
..... False

>>> "code250@_#".isascii()
..... True

>>> second_char = "I love programming"[1]
>>> second_char.isspace()
..... True

>>> "Programming".isupper()
..... False
>>> "PROGRAMMING".isupper()
..... True

>>> "Programming".islower()
..... False
>>> "programming".islower()
..... True

>>> "Python Programming".istitle()
..... True
>>> "Python programming".istitle()
..... False

>>> "_var".isidentifier()
..... True
>>> "23var".isidentifier()
..... False
```

String Formatting

In Python, inserting variables into a string to make the output dynamic is called **string formatting**. Instead of directly placing a variable inside a string (which would be treated as plain text), Python provides multiple ways to format strings properly.

❌ Wrong formatting

```python
var = 100
print(" Total is var")
```

```
#Output
Total is var
```

Here, var is treated as part of the string instead of a variable.

Python provides three main ways to format strings properly:

1. Using f-strings (f"" notation) – Recommended

Introduced in Python 3.6, **f-strings** allow embedding variables directly into a string using curly brackets { }.

Syntax:

```
f"{variable or expression}"
```

Example 1,

```python
var = 100
print(f" Total is { var }")
```



```
#Output
Total is 100
```

Example 2,

```
</> Python
import math
num = 16
print(f" The final answer  is { math.sqrt( num ) * 2 }")
```

```
#Output
The final answer is 8.0
```

2. Using .format() method

Before f-strings, the .format() method was commonly used. It replaces {} placeholders with values passed inside .format().

Syntax:

```
"{}".format(variable)
"{}{}".format(variable1, variable2)
"{1} {0}".format(variable1, variable2)  # Positional indexing
```

Example 1,

```
</> Python
var = 25
results = "Alice is {} years".format( var )
print( results )
```

```
#Output
'Alice is 25 years'
```

Example 2,

```python
name = "John"
age = 30

profile = "Name: {}, Age: {}".format( name, age )
print( profile )
```

```
#Output
'Name: John, Age: 30'
```

Example 3,

```python
planets = "The fourth planet is {1} and third is {0}".format("earth","mars")
print( planets )
```

```
#Output
The fourth planet is mars and third is earth
```

3. Using % Formatting (Old Method)

Older versions of Python (before 3.6) used % for formatting, similar to C-style formatting. This method is mostly **deprecated** in favor of f-strings and .format().

Example 1

```python
price = 100

print( "Total is $%d" % price )      # %d is for integers
```

```
#Output
Total is $100
```

Escape Characters in Python

In programming, escape characters are special sequences used to format strings by providing short commands that instruct the compiler on how to display text. These commands help in creating new lines, adding tab spaces, inserting special symbols, and more.

Escape characters always begin with a backslash (\), followed by a specific character that represents an action. Below is a list of commonly used escape characters in Python:

Escape Character	Description
\n	Inserts a new line (line break)
\t	Adds a horizontal tab space
\\	Inserts a backslash (\)
\'	Inserts a single quote (') inside a string enclosed in single quotes
\"	Inserts a double quote (") inside a string enclosed in double quotes
\r	Carriage return – moves the cursor to the beginning of the line
\b	Backspace – removes the previous character

\f	Form feed – moves to the next page (used in printing)
\v	Vertical tab – adds a vertical tab space
\000	Represents an octal value (e.g., \101 represents 'A')
\xhh	Represents a hexadecimal value (e.g., \x41 represents 'A')

Table 6.0 : The escape characters

Example, using newline (\n)

</> Python

```
print( "Hello everyone! \nDo you like Python?" )
```

```
#Output
Hello everyone!
Do you like Python?
```

List

A list is a collection of items of the same type or different types, enclosed in square brackets [ ]. Lists perform functions similar to arrays in C, C++, and Java. They can contain other lists, making them a preferred choice for storing large data of different types.

For example,

</> Python

```
>>> even = [2, 4, 6, 8, 10]                                      #list of numbers
>>> items = ["mouse", "keyboard", "microphone"]                  #list of string
>>> mix = [ 5, "mouse", 4.25, ('age', 30), {'name' : "John"}, [2, 4] ]   #list of different types
>>>
```

Note

The first element of a list occupies index **0**, the next at index **1** and so on.
For example, cities = ["London", "New York", "Ontario", "Chicago"]

item	London	New York	Ontario	Chicago
index	0	1	2	3

Accessing Items in a List

Elements of a list can be retrieved by specifying their index within square brackets ([]).
For example,

</> Python

```
>>> cities = ["London", "New York", "Ontario", "Chicago"]
>>> cities[0]
...... 'London'
>>> cities[2]
...... 'Ontario'
>>>
```

Deep

The list() function is used for converting other data types to list.

```
>>> list("programming")
...... ['p', 'r', 'o', 'g', 'r', 'a', 'm', 'm', 'i', 'n', 'g']
>>>
```

Slicing a list

Lists can be divided to obtain sub-lists using slicing notation list[start : end]. The *start* parameter is optional and specifies where the division should begin. If start is not set, Python begins the division from the first element (index 0). Similarly, the *end* parameter is optional. If not specified, Python sets it to the last index of the list.

Formulas for Slicing a List

list[start: end]	→	Returns a sub list starting from the specified start index up to (but not including) the end index.
list[start:]	→	Returns a sub list starting from the specified start index to the end of the list.
list[: end]	→	Returns a sub list starting from the beginning (index 0) up to (but not including) the specified end index.
list[:]	→	Returns the entire list from index 0 to the last character.

For example,

</> Python

```
>>> cities = ["London", "New York", "Ontario", "Chicago"]
>>> cities[1:3]
...... ['New York', 'Ontario']

>>> cities[1:]
...... ['New York', 'Ontario', 'Chicago']

>>> cities[:2]
...... ['London', 'New York']
>>>
```

List Methods

Method	Description
append(item)	Adds an item to the end of the list.
extend(iterable)	Extends the list by appending elements from an iterable (e.g., another list, tuple, or set).
insert(index, item)	Inserts an item at a specified position in the list.
remove(item)	Removes the first occurrence of the specified item from the list.
pop(index=-1)	Removes and returns the item at the given index. If no index is specified, removes the last item.
clear()	Removes all elements from the list, making it empty.
index(item, start, end)	Returns the index of the first occurrence of an item. Raises an error if the item is not found.
count(item)	Returns the number of times an item appears in the list.
sort(key, reverse)	Sorts the list in ascending order by default. You can use reverse=True for descending order and key for custom sorting.
reverse()	Reverses the order of elements in the list.
copy()	Returns a shallow copy of the list.

append(item)

</> Python

```
>>> num = [2, 4]
>>> num.append( 6 )

>>> print(num)
..... [2, 4, 6]

>>> var = ["apple", "berry", "banana"]
>>> var.append( "orange"  )

>>> print(var)
...... ['apple', 'berry', 'banana', 'orange']
```

extend(iterable)

```
</> Python
>>> even = [2, 4]
>>> odd = [5, 7]

>>> even.extend( odd )
>>> print(even)
...... [2, 4, 5, 7]
```

insert(index, item)

```
</> Python
>>> var = [2, 4]

>>> var.insert( 1, 3 )
>>> print(var)
...... [2, 3, 4]
```

remove(item)

```
</> Python
>>> lang = ["English", "French", "Spanish"]

>>> lang.remove( "French" )
>>> lang
..... ['English', 'Spanish']
```

pop(index)

```
</> Python
>>> lang = ["English", "French", "Dutch", "Spanish"]

>>> lang.pop(  )
...... 'Spanish'
>>> lang
...... ['English', 'French', 'Dutch']
```

```
>>> lang.pop(0 )
..... 'English'
>>> lang
...... ['French', 'Dutch']
```

clear( )

```
</> Python
>>> var = [1, 2, 3]

>>> var.clear( )
>>> print(var)
...... [ ]
```

index(item, start, end)

```
</> Python
>>> country = ["USA", "Canada", "Ukraine", "USA", "Rusia"]

>>> country.index( "USA")
..... 0
>>> country.index( "USA", 1)          #start = 1 , end = length of the list
..... 3
```

count(item)

```
</> Python
>>> var = [1, 2, 3, 2, 4]

>>> var.count( 2 )
...... 2
>>> var.count( 4 )
...... 1
```

sort(reverse)

</> Python

```
>>> num = [5, 3, 2, 4, 1]

>>> num.sort( )
>>> num
...... [1, 2, 3, 4, 5]

>>> num.sort( reverse = True )
>>> num
..... [5, 4, 3, 2, 1]

>>> letters = [ 'c', 'a', 'b', 'd' ]
>>> letters.sort( )
>>> letters
...... ['a', 'b', 'c', 'd']
```

reverse( )

</> Python

```
>>> program = ["Python", "Java", "C++"]
>>> program.reverse( )
>>> program
...... ['C++', 'Java', 'Python']
```

copy( )

</> Python

```
>>> my_list = [ 1, 3, 5]
>>> copied = my_list.copy( )
>>> print( copied )
...... [1, 3, 5]
```

Other List Methods

Method	Description
len(list)	Returns the number of elements in the list.
max(list)	Returns the maximum value in the list (if elements are comparable).
min(list)	Returns the minimum value in the list.
sum(list)	Returns the sum of all numerical elements in the list.
list(iterable)	Converts an iterable (e.g., tuple, string, or set) into a list.
sorted(list, key, reverse)	Returns a new sorted list without modifying the original.
any(list)	Returns True if at least one element in the list is truthy, otherwise False.
all(list)	Returns True if all elements in the list are truthy, otherwise False.
enumerate(list, start)	Returns an enumerate object that contains index-value pairs.

len( ), sum( ), min( ) and max()

</> Python

```
>>> var = [ 6, 1, 3]

>>> length = len( var )
>>> print( length )
.....  3

>>> total = sum( var )
>>> print( total )
...... 10

>>> minimum = min( var )
>>> print( minimum )
.....  1

>>> maximum = max( var )
>>> print( maximum )
......  6
```

Using iter() and __iter__() to Iterate Over a List

Iteration is the process of accessing each item in a sequence (such as a list, tuple, set, or dictionary) one at a time.
Python makes iteration simple and flexible, especially when working with lists. In many other programming languages, iterating over arrays (Python's equivalent of lists) is typically done using loops (for, while, and do-while). However, Python provides an alternative approach using the **iter()** function and the **__iter__()** method along with **next()** or **__next__()**.

iter()

</> Python

```
var = [ 2, 4, 6]
items = iter(var)
print( next(items) )
print( next(items) )
print( next(items) )
```

```
#Output
2
4
6
```

- iter**(var)** creates an iterator for the list.
- **next(**items**)** retrieves the next item in the list.
- When there are no more items, calling **next()** again raises a StopIteration error.

__iter__()

</> Python

```
program = ["Java", "Python", "C++"]
items = program.__iter__()
print( next(items) )
print( next(items) )
print( next(items) )
```

```
#Output
Java
Python
C++
```

- **__iter__()** is automatically called when using **iter()**, but it can also be accessed explicitly.
- The result is an iterator that can be used with **next()**.

__next__()

```python
cities = ["New York", "London", "Toronto"]
items = cities.__iter__()
print( items.__next__() )
print( items.__next__() )
print( items.__next__() )
```

```
#Output
New York
London
Toronto
```

Tuple

Tuples are collections of elements of different data types enclosed in parentheses ( ) and separated by commas. The elements of tuples are immutable, meaning they cannot be changed once created, but they can still be accessed.

For example,

```
</> Python
>>> tup1 = (3, 4, 2)                                              #tuple of numbers
>>> tup2 = ("Python", "Java",  "C++")                             #tuple of strings
>>> tup3 = (5, 3.25, ('id', 30), "Texas", {'name' : "Alice"}, [6, 2] )  #tuple of different types
>>>
```

Deep

The tuple() function is used to convert other data types to tuple.

```
>>> var = "code"                #string to tuple
>>> tuple(var)
..... ('c', 'o', 'd', 'e')

>>> var = ["USA", "Spain", "Italy"]    #list to tuple
>>> tuple(var)
..... ('USA', 'Spain', 'Italy')

>>> var = {2, 4, 6, 8}          #set to tuple
>>> tuple(var)
...... (8, 2, 4, 6)
```

Accessing Elements from a Tuple

Tuples, like other iterables such as **strings** and **lists**, allow elements to be accessed using **indexing**. Each element in a tuple is assigned an **index**, starting from **0** for the first element, **1** for the second, and so on. For example,

</> Python

```
>>> planets = ("mercury", "venus", "earth", "mars")
>>> planets[0]
..... 'mercury'

>>> planets[2]
...... 'earth'

>>> profile = ( ("Alice", 25), ("John", 30), ("Bob", 10) )

>>> profile[0]
...... ('Alice', 25)

>>> profile[1][0]
..... 'John'

>>> profile[2][1]
...... 10
```

Tuple Methods

Method	Description
index(item, start, end)	Returns the index of the first occurrence of the specified value. Raises a ValueError if the value is not found.
count(item)	Returns the number of times a specified value appears in the tuple.

index(item, start, end)

</> Python

```
>>> tup = ("apple", "berry", "banana")

>>> tup.index("apple")
..... 0

>>> tup.index("banana")
..... 2
```

count(item)

```
</> Python
>>> var = ( 2, 3, 4, 2 )

>>> var.count( 2 )
..... 2
```

Other Tuple Methods

Method	Description
len(iterable)	Returns the number of elements in the tuple.
sum(iterable)	Returns the sum of all elements in a tuple (works for numeric values).
max(iterable)	Returns the maximum value in a tuple (works if elements are comparable).
min(iterable)	Returns the minimum value in a tuple.
sorted(iterable)	Returns a sorted list of tuple elements.

len(iterable)

```
</> Python
>>> var = ( 5, 3, 4)
>>> len( var )
..... 3
```

sum(iterable)

```
</> Python
>>> var = ( 40, 20, 35 , 10)
>>> sum( var )
...... 105
```

sum(iterable)

```
</> Python
>>> var = ( 4, 6, 2)
>>> sum( var )
...... 12
```

max(iterable)

```
</> Python
>>> var = ( 20, 2, 10)
>>> max( var )
...... 20
```

min(iterable)

```
</> Python
>>> var = ( 20, 2, 10)
>>> min( var )
...... 2
```

sorted(iterable)

```
</> Python
>>> letters = ('d', 'b', 'e', 'a', 'c')
>>> sorted = sorted( letters )
>>> print( sorted )
...... ['a', 'b', 'c', 'd', 'e']
```

Dictionary

A dictionary is a data structure that consists of a collection of **key-value** pair items, separated by commas, and enclosed within curly braces { }. Dictionaries can contain items of various data types. In a key-value pair, one item (the key) is associated with another item (the value), and they are linked by a colon (key : value).

For example,

```
Dictionary_name = { key : value }
```

</> Python

```
>>> dict1 = {'name' : "Alice", 'age' : 20, 'country' : "USA"}
>>> dict2 = {'numbers' : [2, 4],  'languages' : ("Python", "Java") }
>>> dict3 = { 1 : 100,  2 : 200,  3 : 300}
>>>
```

Note

Dictionary keys can be either numbers or strings, whereas values can be any object, including strings, numbers, dictionaries, tuples, sets, and bytes. Dictionary keys are immutable.

Deep

The dict() function is used to convert other data types (tuple) to dictionary.

```
>>> var = ( ("name", "John"), ("ID", 250), ("city", "London") )        #Tuple
>>> dict(var)
...... {'name': 'John', 'ID': 250, 'city': 'London'}
>>>
```

Dictionary Methods

Method	Description
get(key, default)	Returns the value of the key. If the key is not found, returns the specified default value.
items()	Returns a view of all dictionary key-value pairs as tuples.
keys()	Returns a view of all dictionary keys.
values()	Returns a view of all dictionary values.
pop(key, default)	Removes and returns the value for the specified key. If the key is not found, returns the default value.
popitem()	Removes and returns the last inserted key-value pair as a tuple.
update(iterable)	Updates the dictionary with key-value pairs from another dictionary or iterable of key-value pairs.
setdefault(key, default)	Returns the value of the key if present; otherwise, inserts the key with the specified default value.
fromkeys(seq, value)	Creates a new dictionary from a sequence of keys, all having the specified value.
copy()	Returns a shallow copy of the dictionary.
clear()	Removes all key-value pairs from the dictionary.

In a dictionary, values can be accessed using their corresponding keys in two ways:

① Using Square Brackets (dictionary[key])

This method retrieves the value associated with the specified key. However, if the key does not exist in the dictionary, it raises a KeyError.

</> Python

```
>>> program = {1: "Python", 2: "Java",  3: "C++"}
>>> program[1]
...... 'Python'

>>> program[3]
...... 'C++'

>>> profile = {"name": "Alice",  "age": 25}
>>> profile["name"]
..... 'Alice'

>>> profile["age"]
...... 25
```

② Using the get(key) Method

The get() method returns the value associated with the specified key. Unlike square brackets, if the key is not found, it returns None (or a default value if specified), preventing potential errors.

get(key)

```
</> Python
>>> profile = {"name": "Alice",  "age": 25}

>>> profile.get("name")
...... 'Alice'

>>> profile.get("age")
...... 25
```

Updating Dictionary Items

Dictionary values can be updated in two ways:

① Using the square bracket notation (dictionary_name[key] = value)

This method updates the value of an existing key or adds a new key-value pair if the key does not exist.

dictionary_name[key]

```
</> Python
>>> profile = {"name": "Alice",  "age": 25}

>>> profile["name"] = "Bob"
>>> print(profile)
...... {'name': 'Bob', 'age': 25}

>>> profile["country"] = "Italy"
>>> print(profile)
...... {'name': 'Bob', 'age': 25, 'country': 'Italy'}
```

② Using the update() method

This method allows multiple updates at once by passing a dictionary of key-value pairs.

update(iterable)

```python
>>> profile = {"name": "Alice",  "age": 25}

>>> profile.update({"name": "Bob",  "city": "London"})
>>> print(profile)
...... {'name': 'Bob', 'age': 25, 'city': 'London'}
```

setdefault(key, default)

```python
>>> person = {"name": "Bob"}

>>> person.setdefault("name", "Alice")
......  'Bob'
>>> print(person)
...... {'name': 'Bob'}

>>> person.setdefault("college", "Harvard")
......  'Harvard'
>>> print(person)
.....  {'name': 'Bob', 'college': 'Harvard'}
```

copy() and clear()

```python
>>> profile = {"name": "Alice",  "age": 25}

>>> new_dict = profile.copy()
>>> print(new_dict)
...... {'name': 'Alice', 'age': 25}

>>> profile.clear()
>>> print(profile)
...... { }
```

pop(key, default)

```
</> Python
>>> student = {"firstname":"John", "lastname":"Wood", "index":3251, "GPA":3.7}

>>> student.pop("lastname")
...... 'Wood'

>>> print(student)
..... {'firstname': 'John', 'index': 3251, 'GPA': 3.7}
```

popitem()

```
</> Python
>>> student = {"firstname":"John", "lastname":"Wood", "index":3251, "GPA":3.7}

>>> value = student.popitem( )

>>> print(value)
...... ('GPA', 3.7)

>>> print(student)
......{'firstname': 'John', 'lastname': 'Wood', 'index': 3251}
```

items(), keys() and values()

```
</> Python
>>> animals = {'wild':[ 'lion', 'snake' ], 'domestic':[ 'dog', 'cat' ], aquatic': 'Tilapia'}

>>> animals.items( )
..... dict_items([('wild', ['lion', 'snake']), ('domestic', ['dog', 'cat']), ('aquatic', 'Tilapia')])

>>> animals.keys( )
...... dict_keys(['wild', 'domestic', 'aquatic'])

>>> animals.values( )
......dict_values([['lion', 'snake'], ['dog', 'cat'], 'Tilapia'])
```

Set

A set is an unordered collection of unique elements. Sets enclose their members within curly braces { }. Sets can hold members of strings, integers, floats, and tuples, but not dictionaries, lists, or other sets. Sets are commonly used to perform mathematical operations such as intersection, union, or symmetric difference.

For example,

</> Python

```
>>> set1 = {1, 3, 5, 7}

>>> set2 = {"a", "b", "c", "d"}

>>> set3 = {2, 4, 6, "orange", "apple" }
```

Deep

The set() function is used to convert other data types to set.

```
>>> list_var = [2, 3, 5]      #list to set
>>> set(list_var)
...... {2, 3, 5}

>>> string_var = "Hello"   #string to set
>>> set(string_var)
..... {'l', 'H', 'o', 'e'}

>>> tuple_var = (2, 5, 8)   #tuple to set
>>> set(tuple_var)
...... {8, 2, 5}

>>> dictionary_var = {1:'Python', 2:'Java', 3:'C#'}   #dictionary to set
>>> set(dictionary_var)
...... {1, 2, 3}
```

Set Methods

Method	Description
add(item)	Adds an element or item to the set. If the element already exists, it does nothing.
copy()	Returns a shallow copy of the set.
clear()	Removes all elements from the set, making it empty.
difference(*sets)	Returns a new set with elements that are in the original set but not in the given set(s).
difference_update(*sets)	Removes elements from the original set that are present in the given set(s). Modifies the original set.
discard(item)	Removes the specified item from the set if it exists. Does nothing if the element is not found.
remove(item)	Removes the specified item from the set. Raises a KeyError if the element is not found.
pop()	Removes and returns a random element from the set. Raises a KeyError if the set is empty.
intersection(*sets)	Returns a new set containing elements common to the original set and all given set(s).
intersection_update(*sets)	Modifies the original set to keep only elements also found in all given set(s).
isdisjoint(set)	Returns True if the set has no elements in common with other set, otherwise returns False.
issubset(set)	Returns True if all elements of the set are in other set, otherwise returns False.
issuperset(set)	Returns True if the set contains all elements of other set, otherwise returns False.
union(*set)	Returns a new set containing all unique elements from the original set and given set(s).
update(*sets)	Adds elements from given set(s) to the original set. Modifies the original set.
symmetric_difference(set)	Returns a new set with elements that are in either the set or other set, but not both.
symmetric_difference_update(set)	Modifies the original set to include only elements unique to either set.

add()

</> Python

```
>>> even = {2, 4, 6}
>>> even.add(8)
```

```
>>> print(even)
..... {8, 2, 4, 6}
>>>
```

update(*set)

```
>>> set1 = {2, 4}
>>> set2 = {1, 3}
>>> set1.update(set2)
>>> print(set1)
..... {1, 2, 3, 4}

>>> rainbow = {"blue","purple", "white"}
>>> primary, secondary = {"red", "green"}, {"yellow","orange"}
>>> rainbow.update(primary, secondary)
>>> rainbow
...... {'red', 'blue', 'white', 'orange', 'purple', 'green', 'yellow'}
```

copy()

```
>>> even = {2, 4, 6}
>>> copied = even.copy()
>>> print(copied)
...... {2, 4, 6}
>>>
```

discard(item)

```
>>> even = {1, 4, 8}
>>> even.discard( 4 )
>>> print(even)
...... {8, 1}
>>>
```

remove(item)

```
</> Python
>>> num = {3, 6, 9}
>>> num.remove( 3 )
>>> print(num)
...... {9, 6}
>>>
```

pop( )

```
</> Python
>>> num = {3, 6, 9}
>>> num.pop( )
...... 9
>>> print(num)
...... {3, 6}
>>>
```

clear( )

```
</> Python
>>> var = {'a', 'b', 'c', 'd'}
>>> var.clear( )
>>> print(var)
...... set()
>>>
```

difference(*set)

```
</> Python
>>> U = {1, 2, 3, 4, 5, 6, 7, 8, 9, 10}
>>> even = {2, 4, 6, 8, 10}
>>> difference = U.difference(even )
>>> print(difference)
...... {1, 3, 5, 7, 9}
>>>
```

difference_update(*set)

```
</> Python
>>> U = {1, 2, 3, 4, 5, 6, 7, 8, 9, 10}
>>> even = {2, 6, 10}
>>> odd = {3, 5, 9}
>>> U.difference_update(even, odd )
>>> print( U )
...... {1, 4, 7, 8}
>>>
```

intersection(*set)

```
</> Python
>>> setA = {1, 4, 6, 8}
>>> setB = {2, 3, 4, 5}
>>> setC = setA.intersection( setB )
>>> print( setC )
...... {4}
>>>
```

intersection_update(*set)

```
</> Python
>>> setA = {3, 6, 9, 12}
>>> setB = {2, 6, 10, 12}
>>> setA.intersection_update( setB )
>>> print( setA )
...... {12, 6}
>>>
```

symmetric_difference(*set)

```
</> Python
>>> setA = {3, 6, 9, 12}
>>> setB = {2, 6, 10, 12}
```

```
>>> result = setA.symmetric_difference( setB )
>>> print( result )
...... {2, 3, 9, 10}
>>>
```

union(*set)

```
</> Python
>>> even = {2, 4, 6}
>>> odd = {1, 3, 5}
>>> U = even.union( odd )
>>> print( U )
..... {1, 2, 3, 4, 5, 6}
>>>
```

isdisjoint(set)

```
</> Python
>>> even = {2, 4, 6}
>>> odd = {1, 3, 5}
>>> even.isdisjoint( odd )
...... True
>>>
```

issuperset(set)

```
</> Python
>>> U = {1, 2, 3, 4, 5, 6, 7, 8, 9, 10}
>>> even = {2, 4, 6, 8, 10}
>>> U.issuperset( even )
..... True
>>>
```

issubset(set)

</> Python

```
>>> U = {1, 2, 3, 4, 5, 6, 7, 8, 9, 10}
>>> odd = {1, 3, 5, 7, 9}
>>> U.issubset( odd )
...... False
>>>
>>> odd.issubset( U )
...... True
```

Think about it ?

What is the difference between **symmetric_difference(set)** and **symmetric_difference_update(set)**?

Note

***set** has been used as a parameter in most of the examples above. The * denotes that the method must take at least one set as an argument.

Other Set Methods

Method	Description
len(iterable)	Returns the number of elements in the set.
sum(iterable)	Returns the sum of all elements in a set (works for numeric values).
max(iterable)	Returns the maximum value in a set (works if elements are comparable).
min(iterable)	Returns the minimum value in a set.
sorted(iterable)	Returns a sorted list of set elements.
in	Checks if an element exists in a set (item in set).
not in	Checks if an element is not a member of the set.

len(set)

```
</> Python
>>> var = {2, 3, 5, 7}
>>> len( var )
..... 4
```

sum(set)

```
</> Python
>>> var = {5, 10, 15}
>>> sum( var )
...... 30
```

min(set) and max(set)

```
</> Python
>>> var = {2, 6, 3, 4}
>>> min( var )
...... 2
>>> max( var )
...... 6
```

sorted(set)

```
</> Python
>>> var = {2, 1, 4, 5, 3}
>>> sorted =  sorted( var )
>>> print( sorted )
...... [1, 2, 3, 4, 5]
```

in and not in

```
</> Python
>>> var = {2, 4, 5, 6}
>>>3 in var
...... False
>>> 8 not in var
...... True
```

Chapter 7

Decision Making Statements

After you have studied this chapter, you should be able to:

- Understand the purpose of decision-making statements
- Identify different types of conditional statements in Python
- Construct nested conditional statements for complex logic

Decision Making Statements

Decision making is crucial in programming, especially when you want your program to execute only when a certain condition is true or false. These statements, known as conditional statements, are based on a Boolean value (True or False). There are three different kinds of conditional statements:

① if Statement:

This is a simple conditional statement that executes a program or instructions if a condition is true or false

</> Python

```
if condition:
  #code
```

For example,

A program to print "Hello World!" when an input number is greater than or equal to 10.

</> Python

```
var = int(input("type any number: "))  #convert input to integer

if var >= 10:
  print("Hello World!")
```

```
#Output
type any number: 20
Hello World!
```

② if – else Statement:

The if-else conditional statement provides two options for program execution. If the given condition is true, the program executes the statements in the if block; otherwise, if the condition is false, the statements within the else block execute.

</> Python

```
if condition:
  #code
else :
  #code
```

For example:

A program to print *"Great Python"*, if a variable is greater than 5, otherwise print *"Awesome Python"*.

</> Python

```
var = int(input("type any number: "))  #convert input to integer

if  var > 5:
    print("Great Python!")
else:
    print("Awesome Python!")
```

```
#Output
type any number: 8
Great Python!
```

Example 2,

A program that asks the user to input their age. If the age is below 18, it prints *'You are underage, sorry you cannot vote'*. Otherwise, it prints *'You can vote'*.

```python
age = int(input("How old are you?: "))

if   age <  18:
    print("You are underage,\nSorry, you cannot vote")
else:
    print("You can vote")
```

```
#Output
How old are you?: 16
You are underage,
Sorry, you cannot vote
```

③ if – elif – else Statement:

This conditional statement is necessary for multiple decision making

```python
if condition1:
   #code

elif condition2:
   #code

elif condition3:
   #code
.......
.......
else :
   #code
```

For example:

A program to print *"great Python!"*, if a variable is equal to 5. If it is greater than 5, print *"awesome Python"*; otherwise print *'good Python'*.

</> Python

```
var = 3
if   var == 5:
    print("Great Python")

elif var < 5:
    print("Awesome Python")

else :
    print("Good Python")
```

```
#Output
Awesome Python
```

Example 2

A program that asks the user to input their scores in Accounting, Mathematics, and English. It then calculates the average marks and assigns a grade as follows: *'Failed'* if the average is below 40, *'Pass'* if the average is between 40 and 59, and *'Excellent'* if the average is 60 or above.

</> Python

```
english = float(input("English: "))
accounting = float(input("Accounting: "))
math = float(input("Math: "))

total = english + accounting + math
average = total/3

if average < 40:
   print(f"Average: {average} -> Failed!")

elif average >= 40 and average <= 59:
```

```
    print(f"Average: {average} -> Passed")

else:
    print(f"Average: {average} -> Excellent")
```

```
#Output
English: 48
Accounting: 67
Math: 52
Average: 55.666666666666664 -> Passed
```

Nested Conditional Statements

In programming or real-world scenarios, there are instances where an if condition, when true, may require another if condition to be checked. In this situation, an if statement is placed inside another if statement. A nested if statement is, therefore, a structure where conditions are evaluated within other conditions, creating complex decision-making logic.

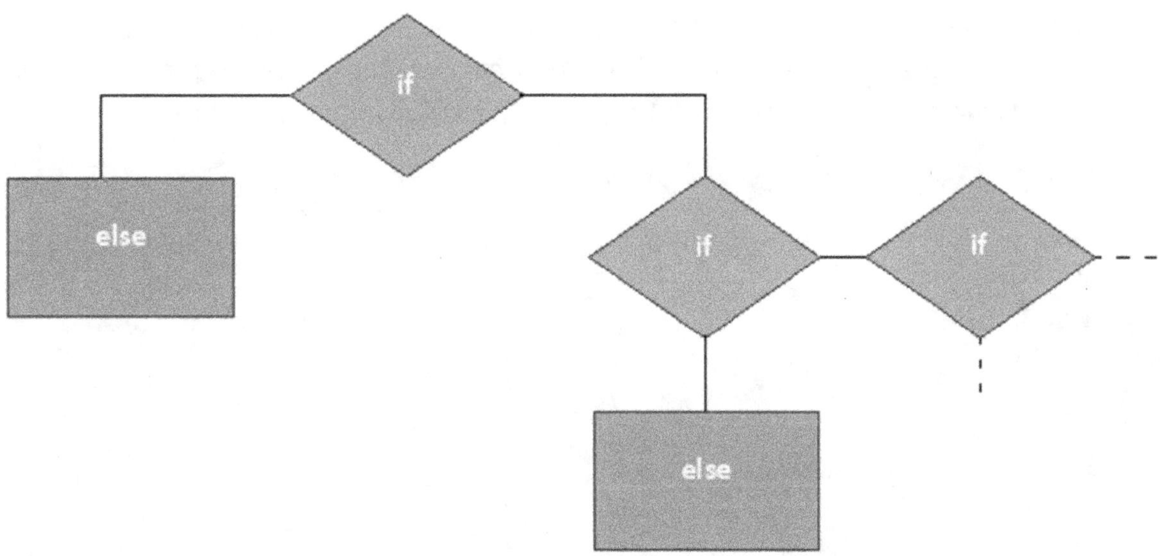

Example 1,

A program that checks if a variable is in a list of numbers. If the number is found, it determines whether it is even or odd and prints *'The number is even'* for even numbers *and 'The number is odd'* for odd numbers. Otherwise, it prints *'The number cannot be found.'*

</> **Python**

```python
data = [2, 3, 5, 8, 10]
var = 5

if var in  data :
   if var % 2 == 0 :
      print("The number is even")
   else:
      print("The number is odd ")

else:
   print("The number cannot be found")
```

```
#Output
The number is odd
```

Example 2

A program that asks the user to input their gender ('male' or 'female') and age. If the person is male and their age is above 25, print *'You are a mature man'*; otherwise, print '*You are a young man*'. If the person is female, print *'You are a beautiful woman'*.

</> **Python**

```python
gender = input("Gender: ")
age = int(input("Age: "))

if gender.lower() == "male" :
   if age > 25 :
      print("You are a mature man")
   else:
      print("You are a young man")
```

```
else:
    print("You are a beautiful woman")
```

```
#Output
Gender: male
Age: 30
You are a mature man
```

Chapter 8

Loops

After you have studied this chapter, you should be able to:

- Understand the importance of loops in programming
- Identify different types of loops in Python
- Use the range() function effectively
- Apply break and continue statements within loops
- Generate and work with iterables

Loops

A loop is a control structure that enables the repetitive execution of a statement or a group of statements. Loops are built around **conditions**, **steps**, and **statements**. They continue executing as long as the condition remains true. There are two main types of loop structures in Python: for loops and while loops.

Needed for Loops:

Automate repetitive tasks
Loops are ideal for automating tasks that need to be repeated multiple times, saving time and effort.

Handle large amounts of data
Loops are efficient for processing items in a list, dictionary, or any other data structure.

Improving code readability
Reduces redundancy by eliminating the need for repeated statements.

Iterate over sequences
You can use loops to go through sequences like strings, lists, or ranges without manually indexing each item.

Perform calculations or updates
Loops can be used to continuously calculate or update variables until a specific condition is met.

Reduce human error
By automating repetitive tasks, loops minimize the chances of mistakes.

The for loop

The for loop is a control structure that allows the repetitive execution of statements in a top-to-bottom approach. It is used to iterate over elements of sequential data types such as lists, strings, or tuples.

Syntax:

```
for item in iterable:
    #code
```

Note

Iterable is an object capable of returning its members one at a time. It can be traversed or looped over using **for** loops. Examples include list, tuple, string, dictionary and set.

For example,

</> Python

```python
var = "code"

for i in var:
   print(i)
```

```
#Output
c
o
d
e
```

Example2,

A program that calculates the sum of a list of numbers by iterating through the list and adding each item.

</> Python

```
num = [ 1, 2, 3, 4]
total = 0

for i in num:
    total = total + i
    print(total)
```

```
#Output
1
3
6
10
```

Note

- Indentation is crucial in **for** and **while** loops.
- Every **for** or **while** statement must end with a colon (:).

Range

Loop structures execute code based on user-given instructions, specifying where to begin, end, and the steps. These instructions can be easily implemented using the **range()** function.

The range(start, end, step) function is used to specify the range of values and steps a control structure must follow to execute the program. The *start* parameter is optional and denotes where to begin the loop. It is set to **0** by default. The *end* parameter must always be specified and denotes the integer to end the loop. The *step* is also an optional parameter that specifies the interval of execution. It is set to 1 by default.

For example,

range(end)

```python
for i in range( 4 ):     #end = 4
    print( i )
.....
```

```
#Output
0
1
2
3
```

range(start, end)

```python
for i in range( 2, 6 ):     #start = 2 , end = 4
    print( i )
.....
```

```
#Output
2
3
4
5
```

range(start, end, step)

```
</> Python
for  i in range( 0, 10, 2 ):      #start = 0 , end = 10, step = 2
        print( i )
.....
```

```
#Output
0
2
4
6
8
```

The while loop

The while loop is another control structure used to iterate or repeatedly execute a set of statements based on a true condition. The loop terminates when the condition is no longer true.

Syntax

```
while condition:
      #code
```

For example,

```
</> Python
i = 0                    #initial value set to 0
while i < 4:             #repeat iteration until i >= 4  (condition becomes false or no longer true)
....      i = i + 1      #increment i by one in each iteration
....      print( i )
```

```
#Output
1
2
3
4
```

Deep

To create an infinite loop, set the condition to always be True and terminate with Ctrl + C.
Infinite loop:

```
while True:
    print("Hello World!")
.....

#output
Hello World!
Hello World!
Hello World!
....
....
```

Think about it ?

Did the loop run forever using the True condition? How true is that? Infinite loops can gradually consume system resources, degrading performance. You can interrupt the iteration using Ctrl + C.

The break statement

The break statement is a Python keyword used mostly in loop structures to halt or terminate execution prematurely once a given condition is true.

For example,

```
</> Python
for  i in range( 1, 5 ):
     if  i == 3:           #terminate loop once i = 3
        break
      print( i )
.....
```

```
#Output
1
2
```

Example 2,

A program that continuously accepts numbers and computes their sum. The program should terminate when the input is "=" and then display the final result.

```
</> Python
total = 0

while True:
     num = input("type number: ")

     if num == "=":
          print(f"total = {total}")
          break
     else:
          total = total + float(num)
```

```
#Output
type number: 2
type number: 5
type number: =
total = 7
```

The continue statement

The continue statement is also a Python keyword implemented in loops to skip a step or iteration when a particular condition is true.

For example,

</> Python

```
for i in range( 1, 5 ):
    if i == 3:          #skip step 3
        continue
    print( i )
.....
```

```
#Output
1
2
4
```

Example 2,
A program that prints all odd numbers from 1 to 10. If a number is even, the program should skip it.

</> Python

```
i = 0

while i < 10:
    i = i +1
    if i % 2 == 0:
        continue
    print(f"{i} is odd number")
```

```
#Output
1 is odd number
3 is odd number
5 is odd number
7 is odd number
9 is odd number
```

Data Generation

Data and programs are the core components of any application or software, making them essential resources in programming. Programs process data to perform tasks, and data can either be provided by users or generated by the system. Manually generating large datasets can be tedious, but programs can automate this process by generating data in structured or unstructured patterns.

In Python, loops, particularly **for loops**, are ideal for generating data efficiently.

List comprehension

Generating a list of squared numbers from 0 to 9

</> Python

```
data = [ item**2  for item  in range(10) ]
print(data)
```

```
#Output
[0, 1, 4, 9, 16, 25, 36, 49, 64, 81]
```

Generating a list of odd numbers from 0 to 15

</> Python

```
data = [ item  for item  in range(15)  if item%2 != 0]
print(data)
```

```
#Output
[1, 3, 5, 7, 9, 11, 13]
```

Generating a matrix (list of lists) filled with random numbers

```python
import random
data = [ [ random.randrange(10)  for _  in range(3)]  for _ in range(5)]
print(data)
```

```
#Output
[[2, 2, 8], [0, 4, 9], [5, 2, 4], [0, 2, 6], [0, 0, 1]]
```

Set comprehension

Generating a set of factorial numbers from 1 to 6

```python
import math
data = { math.factorial( x )  for x  in range(1, 7) }
print(data)
```

```
#Output
{1, 2, 6, 24, 120, 720}
```

Think about it ?

1. Can you generate a set of even numbers from 1 to 20?
2. Generate a set of prime numbers from 0 to 20.

Dictionary comprehension

Generating a dictionary of numbers and their cubes (1 to 5)

```
</> Python

data = { x: x**3  for x  in range(1, 6) }
print(data)
```

```
#Output
{1: 1, 2: 8, 3: 27, 4: 64, 5: 125}
```

Generator expression

Generating a tuple of numbers multiplied by 3

```
</> Python

data = tuple( x*3   for x  in range(10) )
print(data)
```

```
#Output
(0, 3, 6, 9, 12, 15, 18, 21, 24, 27)
```

Chapter 9

Function

After you have studied this chapter, you should be able to:

- Understand the concept of functions
- Recognize the importance of functions in programming
- Differentiate between types of functions
- Define and execute functions in Python
- Pass arguments to functions
- Create functions with unlimited arguments using *args
- Use the pass keyword appropriately
- Understand and use lambda (anonymous) functions
- Utilize lambda functions with map() and filter()
- Understand basic threading in Python for concurrent programming

Function

A function is a block of organized and related statements used to perform a specific task. It can contain variables, loops, decision-making statements, other functions, statements, and objects that can be used repeatedly in different parts of a program. Functions are also referred to as methods, procedures, subprograms, routines, or subroutines.

Importance of Functions:

- Enhanced Readability and Comprehensibility:

Functions improve the readability and comprehensibility of a program by breaking it down into smaller, logical units. Each function performs a specific task, making the code easier to understand.

- Efficiency through Minimization of Repetitions:

Functions help minimize repetitions in code by encapsulating repetitive tasks into reusable blocks. This reduces the amount of code duplication and makes the program more efficient to maintain.

- Breaking Complex Programs into Smaller Segments:

Functions allow complex programs to be broken down into smaller and more manageable segments. Each function focuses on a specific aspect of the program's functionality, making it easier to develop and debug.

- Improved Time Efficiency:

By organizing code into functions, developers can optimize performance and improve time efficiency. Functions enable code reuse, which reduces development time and effort, leading to faster and more efficient programming.

Types of Functions:

There are two types of functions in the Python programming language: Built-in Functions and User-defined Functions.

Built-in Functions:

Built-in functions are provided by the Python language and are readily available to be used in programs. They serve various purposes and are commonly used for tasks such as mathematical operations, data conversion, string manipulation, and more.

Examples include: sum(), eval(), hex(), bin(), oct(), chr(), ord(), dir(), del(), max(), min() and len()

Example of using built-in functions

```
</> Python
>>> var = [2, 4, 6]
>>> total = sum( var )
>>> print( total )
...... 12
>>>
```

User-defined Functions:

User-defined functions are functions created by the user according to Python syntax. These functions allow developers to encapsulate specific tasks or operations into reusable blocks of code, enhancing code modularity and reusability.

Syntax

```
def function_name(param):
    #statement

    return  #statement
```

✏ The def Keyword:
The def keyword is used to define a function in Python. It is the keyword used to create a function.

✏ Function Name:
The function name is the identifier given to the function. It can start with either a capital or lowercase letter and can include underscores, but it cannot start with a number.

✏ Parameters:
Parameters, also known as arguments, are optional and used to pass data or values to the function. They are specified within the parentheses following the function name.

✏ Colon:
A colon (:) marks the end of the function header, indicating the start of the function block or body.

✏ Statement(s):
Every function block or body contains at least one statement, which defines the actual logic or purpose of the function. These statements are executed when the function is called.

✏ The return Statement:
The return keyword is optional and is used if the function is defined to return or produce a value. If the function is designed to return no value, there is no need to use the return statement.

Example 1: A function to print "Hello World!"

</> Python

```
def hello( ):
    print( "Hello World!" )
```

Example 2: A function to accept two numbers and return their sum

</> Python

```
def total( x, y ):
    result = x + y

    return result
```

Calling Functions

Calling a function simply means executing the function. Function calls can be made through the Python prompt, within another function, or within a program.

① Executing a function call directly in the interpreter.

```
</> Python
>>> def greetings():
.......     print( "Hi\nGoodmorning" )
.......
>>> greetings()     #calling the greetings function
...... Hi
       Goodmorning
>>>
```

② Executing a function within a program.

```
</> Python
def myFun():
    var = 200
    return var

value = myFun( )                 #calling the myFun function
print( value )
```

```
#Output
200
```

③ Invoking a function from within another function.

```
</> Python
def myFunc():
    num = 10
    return num
```

```
def price():
    myfun = myFunc()          #calling the myFunc  function within price()
    return  myfun + 5

value =  price()              #calling the price function
print( value )
```

```
#Output
15
```

Argument Functions

Functions in Python can be designed to perform tasks automatically using variables and other objects without requiring user interaction. These types of functions do not take any parameters and are called **argumentless functions**.

On the other hand, some functions require input data to operate, either from the user or another function. These inputs, known as **parameters** or **arguments**, can include numbers, strings, lists, dictionaries, or even other functions. The function processes these parameters during execution.

Unlike some other programming languages, Python does not require specifying the data type of parameters. Instead, Python determines the type dynamically based on the value assigned to them.

Syntax

```
def myFun(x, y):
    pass
```

Example,

</> Python

```
def average( x, y, z):
    total = x + y + z
    avg = total/3

    return avg


result =  average( 6, 8, 10)    #x=6,  y= 8, z= 10
print( result )
```

```
#Output
8.0
```

Optional Arguments

Some functions are designed to accept parameters, but they can still function without them. These parameters are called **optional arguments** because they are not required for the function to execute successfully.

If a parameter is not optional, it must always be provided when calling the function; otherwise, an error will occur. To make a parameter optional, you assign it a **default value**. If the argument is not supplied, the function will use the default value instead.

Syntax

```
def myFun( x= 0, z=None):
    pass
```

In this example, x has a default value of 0, and z is set to None, making them optional parameters. If no value is passed for x or z, their default values will be used.

Note

When defining a function with both required and optional parameters, the required parameters must always come first, followed by the optional parameters.
This ensures that Python correctly assigns values to the parameters when the function is called.

```
def  myFun(x, y=5):          ☑ Correct
      print( x, y)


def  myFun(x=0,  y):         ✕ Wrong
      print( x, y)
```

If optional parameters are placed before required ones, Python will not know how to correctly assign values, leading to a syntax error.

Executing Argument Functions

When calling or executing functions with arguments, values can be passed in two ways:

1. **Positional Arguments** – Values are supplied in the same order as the function parameters.
2. **Keyword Arguments** – Parameters are explicitly assigned values using their names, allowing flexibility in the order.

</> Python

```
def products( x, y):
    results = x * y
    return results


value1 =  products( 10, 2 )          #positional argument (x=10,  y= 2)
value2 =  products( y= 2,  x= 10 )   #keyword arguments
```

```
print( value1 )
print( value2 )
```

```
#Output
20
20
```

Unlimited Arguments

In programming, there are situations where a function needs to accept a large or **unknown number of arguments**. Defining each argument separately is not practical, especially when the number of inputs varies.

To handle this efficiently, Python allows using * **(asterisk) notation** before a parameter. This collects all passed arguments into a **tuple**, enabling the function to accept multiple values without explicitly defining them.

Key Points:

- The * notation allows a function to accept an unlimited number of arguments.
- The collected arguments are stored as a **tuple**, which can be accessed using indexing.
- Arguments must be passed separated by commas inside the function call.

Syntax

```
def myFun( *args):

    pass
```

Example,
A program to sum all passed arguments

```python
def total( *args ):
    result = 0
    for item in args:                    #iterating through the args (contains the arguments)
        result = result + item

    return result


value =  total( 2, 5, 10, 3, 4 )        #calling the total function with multiple arguments
print( value )
```

```
#Output
24
```

Understanding the pass Keyword

The pass keyword, as used in the function block above, is not limited to functions alone—it can also be used in other code structures such as loops and conditional statements.

It serves as a **placeholder** when a function, loop, or block of code is defined but does not yet contain any statements. This is useful when writing code that will be implemented later, preventing syntax errors that would occur if the block were left empty.

A function or block cannot be left empty without using pass, as Python requires at least one statement inside it.

```python
def total( ):
    pass

def greetings():
    return "Hello, Friend!"
```

Lambda Function

Python functions are normally defined with the **def** keyword, but there is another way to create functions without using the def keyword and a function name. This can be achieved using Python Lambda functions.

Syntax

```
>>> variable = lambda arguments : expression
```

- **Variable:** This is the variable that will store the lambda function.
- **Argument:** These are the input values provided to the lambda function.
- **Expression:** This is the logic that defines the function.

Example 1 : Lambda function to add two numbers.

</> Python

```
>>> add = lambda x , y : x + y
>>> add( 2, 5)
...... 7
>>>
```

Example 2 : Lambda function to return the square of a number.

</> Python

```
>>> square = lambda x  : x ** 2
>>> square( 4 )
...... 16
>>>
```

Example 3 : Lambda function to check if a number is even.

</> Python

```
>>> even = lambda x  : x % 2 == 0
>>> even( 6 )
...... True
>>>
```

Using map() and filter() with Lambda Functions

Lambda functions can be used to create new iterables by transforming or filtering elements from an existing iterable. This is achieved using the **map()** and **filter()** functions.

map() Function

The map() function applies a given function to each element of an iterable and returns a new iterable with the modified values.

Syntax

```
new_iterable = type(map(lambda argument: expression, iterable))
```

Example 1,

```python
numbers = [1, 2, 3, 4]
squared = list(map(lambda x: x**2, numbers))
print(squared)
```

```
#Output
[1, 4, 9, 16]
```

Examples 2,

```python
import math

numbers = [3, 4, 5, 6]
factorial = set(map(lambda x: math.factorial(x), numbers))
print(factorial)
```

```
#Output
{6, 24, 120, 720}
```

filter() Function

The filter() function is used to select elements from an iterable based on a given condition. It returns a new iterable containing only elements that satisfy the condition.

Syntax

```
new_iterable = type(filter(lambda argument: condition, iterable))
```

Example 1,

</> Python

```python
numbers = [1, 2, 3, 4, 5, 6]
evens = list(filter(lambda x: x%2 == 0, numbers))
print(evens)
```

```
#Output
[2, 4, 6]
```

Examples 2,

</> Python

```python
numbers = [2, 3, 4, 5, 6, 7, 8, 9]
multiple_three = tuple(filter(lambda x: x%3==0, numbers))
print(multiple_three)
```

```
#Output
(3, 6, 9)
```

Multiprocessing

Multiprocessing refers to the execution of multiple functions or processes simultaneously. In programming, functions are typically executed sequentially in a linear manner, following a first-come, first-served basis. This means that the function called first is executed before any subsequent functions. Execution progresses from the top of the program to the bottom, and any function waiting to execute must remain idle until the currently running function completes. This happens because execution occurs within the system's single thread by default.

Drawbacks of Sequential Execution:

- It is inefficient for tasks that require real-time processing or produce crucial results needed for subsequent operations.
- It slows down performance, especially when dealing with CPU-intensive tasks.
- It prevents full utilization of multi-core processors, as only a single core is used at a time.
- Functions that take longer to execute can block the execution of other functions, causing delays.

</> Python

```python
import time

def first():
    time.sleep(5)            #delay execution for 5 seconds
    print("First Function")

def second():
    print("Second Function")

first()      #calling the first() function
second()     #calling the second() function
```

```
#Output
First Function
Second Function
```

In the example above, **second()** runs only after **first()** has finished executing. This demonstrates a performance issue, as subsequent functions must wait for the previous ones to complete, leading to potential delays and inefficiencies.

To overcome these limitations, functions or processes can be executed concurrently on different threads, allowing multiple tasks to run simultaneously. This is made possible using threading for lightweight concurrent execution and **multiprocessing** for parallel execution across multiple CPU cores.

Threading

Threading allows multiple functions or processes to execute simultaneously without waiting for the completion of another process before starting. This improves performance by enabling parallel execution. In Python, the **threading** module provides various methods for managing and working with threads.

Threading Methods

Function	Description
Thread()	Creates a thread
active_count()	Returns the currently executing thread object.
current_thread()	Returns a list of all active Thread objects.
enumerate()	Returns a list of all active Thread objects.
excepthook()	Used to handle uncaught exceptions in threads.
get_ident()	Returns the thread identifier (a unique integer for each thread).
get_native_id()	Returns the native (OS-level) thread identifier.
getprofile()	Retrieves the profiling function for the current thread.
gettrace()	Returns the trace function for the current thread.
local()	Creates thread-local data storage. Each thread maintains its own separate copy.
main_thread()	Returns the main thread object.
setprofile()	Used to set a profiling function for threads.
settrace()	Sets a trace function for debugging threads.
stack_size()	Returns the stack size used when creating new threads.

Thread(target, name, args, kwargs, daemon, group)

target	→	Specifies the function that the thread will execute when started. If None, no function runs, and the thread does nothing.
name	→	A string representing the thread's name. If None, a default name like "Thread-1", "Thread-2", etc., is assigned.
args	→	A tuple containing arguments to pass to the target function. If the function requires multiple arguments, they must be passed as a tuple.
kwargs	→	A dictionary containing keyword arguments (key=value pairs) for the target function.
daemon	→	Determines whether the thread is a **daemon thread** (runs in the background and stops when the main program exits). If None, it inherits the main thread's daemon status.
group	→	Reserved for future implementation. Always set to None.

</> Python

```
import time
import threading


def first():
    time.sleep(5)
    print("First Function")

def second():
    print("Second Function")

def third(x, y):
    print(x + y)


#creating threads

thread1 = threading.Thread( target = first)
thread2 = threading.Thread( target = second, name = "second_thread" )
thread3 = threading.Thread( target = third, args = (10, 20), daemon= True )
```

Thread Object Methods

start()	Starts the execution of the thread.
daemon	A boolean attribute that determines whether a thread is a daemon thread. Daemon threads run in the background and automatically terminate when the main program exits.
name()	Retrieves or sets the thread's name.
indent	Returns the thread's unique identifier (assigned by Python).
is_alive()	Returns True if the thread is still running, False otherwise.
join()	Waits for the thread to finish execution before continuing.
native_id()	Returns the OS-assigned native thread ID.
run()	Defines the code that runs when the thread starts. Typically, you override this method when creating a custom thread class.

Example1

</> Python

```python
import time
import threading

def worker1():
    time.sleep(5)
    print("First Function")

def worker2(x, y):
    value = x + y
    print(f"Sum: { value  }" )


#creating threads

thread1 = threading.Thread( target = worker1)
thread2 = threading.Thread( target = worker2, args = (10, 20) )

#running the threads
thread1.start()
thread2.start()
```



```
#Output
Sum: 30
First Function
```

Example2

```
</> Python
import threading
import time

def worker():
    time.sleep(2)
    print("Thread is running")


#creating thread
thread = threading.Thread( target = worker)

thread.daemon = True
thread.start()


#wait until thread finish executing
thread.join()

name = thread.name
status = thread.is_alive()


print(f"Name: {name}")
print(f"Status: {status}")
```

```
#Output
Thread is running
Name: Thread-1 (worker)
Status: False
```

active_count()

```
</> Python
import threading
import time

def worker():
    time.sleep(2)
    print("Thread is running")


threading.Thread( target = worker).start()
print(threading.active_count())
```

```
#Output
2
Thread is running
```

current_thread()

```
</> Python

threading.Thread( target = worker).start()
print(threading.current_thread())
```

```
#Output
<_MainThread(MainThread, started 17988)>
Thread is running
```

stack_size()

```
</> Python

threading.Thread( target = worker).start()
print(threading.stack_size())
```

```
#Output
0
Thread is running
```

Chapter 10

Class and Object

After you have studied this chapter, you should be able to:

- Understand the concepts of classes and objects
- Differentiate between attributes and methods
- Access class methods and attributes
- Use the __init__() constructor method
- Pass arguments to class constructors
- Instantiate and use classes in programs
- Create reusable Python modules and libraries

Class and Object

Python is a **multi-paradigm language**, but it is primarily **object-oriented** (OOP), meaning **everything in Python is an object**. Objects in Python can include fundamental data types such as integers, floats, strings, lists, dictionaries, functions, and even modules.

Classes and Objects

A **class** is a blueprint or template for creating objects. It is a user-defined data type, similar to built-in types like list, dict, str, float, and int.
An **object** is a specific instance of a class. When a class is defined, no memory is allocated until an object is created. Objects store data and behavior defined by their class.

Attributes and Methods

Classes contain two main components:

1. **Attributes (Instance Variables)** - These are variables that hold data specific to each object.
2. **Methods** - These are functions defined inside a class that operate on the object's attributes and define its behavior.

Example:

</> Python

```python
class MyClass:                    #class name
    num = 10                      #class attribute (variable)
    name = "Bob"

    def greetings():              #class method (function)
        value =  "Hello World!"
        return value
```

Key Points

- **Classes** define the structure and behavior of objects.
- **Objects** are created from classes and hold specific data and functionality.
- **Methods** (functions inside classes) define the behavior of objects.
- **Instance variables** store object-specific data.

Deep

Similar to functions, class names can contain both letters and numbers. However, they must begin with a letter if they include both. Class names can start with either an uppercase or lowercase letter, but by convention, Python follows PascalCase (e.g., MyClass, StudentRecord).

Creating Object

Objects are created by assigning a class to a variable. The variable then becomes an instance (or object) of the class. This means the object inherits the class's attributes and methods, allowing it to access and manipulate them independently.

Syntax

```
class MyClass:
      num = 10

      def greetings(self):
          return "Helloo"
```

```
object = MyClass()      #instantiating the class
```

Accessing Methods and Attributes of a Class

Methods and attributes of a class can be accessed using the instance or object of the class.

Syntax

```
var = object.variable              #eg: object.num
method = myobject.function()   #eg: object.greetings
```

Example 1

```python
class StudentRecords:

    school = "Harvard"
    school_ID = 5879

    def student(input):
        data = {'name':"George Wood", 'age': 25, 'index':3056, 'course':"Computer Science"}

        value = data.get(input)
        return value


#creating object of the class StudentRecords
obj = StudentRecords()

#Accessing attributes
sch = obj.school

#Accessing method
name = obj.student("name")
age = obj.student("age")
course = obj.student("course")

print(f"School: {sch}")
print(f"Name: {name}")
print(f"Age: {age}")
print(f"Course: {course}")
```

```
#Output
School: Harvard
Name: George Wood
Age: 25
Course: Computer Science
```

Example 2,

```python
import math

class Calculation:

    greetings = "Hello\nThis is a calculation class. Just crack the numbers!...."

    def sum( *input ):
        value = 0
        for i in input:
            value = value + i
        return value

    def factorial( input ):
        value = math.factorial( input )
        return value


#creating object of the class Calculation

cal = Calculation()
greet = cal.greetings
total = cal.sum(10, 20, 5)
factor = cal.factorial( 6 )

print(f"Greetings: {greet}")
print(f"Total: {total}")
print(f"Factorial: {factor}")
```

```
#Output
Greetings: Hello
This is a calculation class. Just crack the numbers!.....
Total: 35
Factorial: 720
```

The __init__ Method

In Python, the __init__() method serves as a **constructor**, used to initialize objects, variables, and methods within a class. When an instance of a class is created, the __init__() method is automatically executed.

This approach is similar to other programming languages like C, C++, Dart, and Java, which use a main() function to initiate execution. However, unlike main(), __init__() is specific to object instantiation.

Accessing Class Attributes in Methods

By default, methods cannot directly access attributes declared at the class level. To ensure that attributes are accessible across methods and instances, they must be assigned using the self keyword inside __init__().

Understanding self

- The self keyword represents the instance of the class, allowing access to attributes and methods within the class.
- Attributes prefixed with self become instance attributes, meaning they can be accessed and modified by any method within the class.
- Attributes without self are considered **class attributes** (shared across all instances) or private attributes if prefixed with double underscores (__).

Public and Private Attributes

- **Public attributes:** Declared using self.attribute_name, making them accessible within and outside the class.
- **Private attributes:** Defined with double underscores (__attribute_name), restricting access from outside the class.

Public and Private Methods

- **Public methods:** Defined with self as the first parameter (e.g., def my_method(self):).
- **Private methods:** Prefixed with double underscores (e.g., def __my_method(self):), making them inaccessible outside the class

For example,

```python
class Geometry:

    def __init__(self):
        self.pi = 3.14

    def area_circle(self , radius ):
        area =  pow(radius, 2) * self.pi
        return area

    def area_square( self , size ):
        area = size *size
        return area

    def area_rectangle( self , width, height ):
        area = width * height
        return area


geo = Geometry()
pi = geo.pi
circle = geo.area_circle( 7 )
square = geo.area_square( 12 )
rec = geo.area_rectangle( 4, 6 )


print(f"pi = {pi}")
print(f"Area of a circle : {circle}")
print(f"Area of a square: {square}")
print(f"Area of a rectangle: {rec}")
```

```
#Output
pi = 3.14
Area of a circle : 153.86
Area of a square: 144
Area of a rectangle: 24
```

Deep

In Python, instantiating a class with or without the __init__() constructor behaves differently.

1. Without __init__()

When a class does not have an __init__() method, an instance can be created simply by referencing the class name:

```
class MyClass:
        pass

#Instantiating
object = MyClass
```

2. With __init__()

When a class has an __init__() constructor, it must be instantiated with parentheses:

```
class MyClass:
        def __init__(self):
                print("instance")

#Instantiating
object = MyClass()
```

Argument Class

In Python, arguments can be passed to a class in the same way they are passed to functions. These arguments are processed by the __init__() constructor, allowing the class to initialize instance attributes that can be used by methods and objects.

The __init__() method takes self as its first parameter, followed by any additional arguments:

```
def __init__(self, arg1, arg2, ....):
    self.arg1 = arg1
    self.arg2 = arg2
```

The arguments are assigned to instance attributes using self, making them accessible within the class.

These arguments must be provided when instantiating the class:

```
obj = MyClass(value1, value2)
```

For example,

```python
class Statistic:

    def __init__(self, scores):
        self.scores = scores
        self.average = self.average()

        print(f"average: { self.average }")

    def average(self ):
        total = sum(self.scores)
        length = len(self.scores)

        print(f"total: { total }")
        avg = total/length
        return avg



data = [65, 30, 84, 72]
stat = Statistic( data )
```

```
#Output
total: 251
average: 62.75
```

Running a Class

In Python, a class can be used in different ways within a program. Generally, classes are instantiated by creating objects, but in some cases, they can be executed without explicitly creating an object.

① Instantiating a Class

Normally, to use a class, you create an instance (object) of it:

```python
class Greet:
        print("Hello,\nGood day Buddy")

# Creating an object and calling a method
obj = Greet()
```

```
#Output
Hello,
Good day Buddy
```

② Running a Class Without Instantiation

In Python, a class can contain class-level methods that can be called without creating an object.

```python
class Greet:
        print("Hello,\nGood day Buddy")

# Calling the method without an instance
Greet()
```

```
#Output
Hello,
Good day Buddy
```

③ Using if __name__ == "__main__":

This approach ensures that the class runs only when the script is executed directly, and not when imported as a module.

```python
class Greet:
    print("Hello,\nGood day Buddy")

if __name__ == "__main__":
    obj = Greet
```

```
#Output
Hello,
Good day Buddy
```

Creating a Module (Library) from a Class

In Python, modules are reusable code files that contain classes, functions, and variables. These modules can be imported into other programs using the import statement, allowing developers to reuse functionality without rewriting code. Python comes with several built-in modules, which are stored in the installation directory. However, developers can also create custom modules and save them in the working directory for reuse.

Using modules enhances **code reusability, modularity, maintainability, and debugging efficiency**, ultimately improving programming speed and reducing errors.

Steps to Create a Module from a Class

1. **Create a new Python file** and name it your_file.py. Save it in the working directory.
2. **Define a class** inside the file and implement its methods and attributes.
3. **Open another Python file** where you want to use the module.
4. **Import the module** using one of the following methods:

Method 1: Importing the Entire Module

```
import module

obj = module.class_name()
```

Example,

#myprogram.py

```python
import sample

add  = sample.MyMath.addition(6, 2)
avg  = sample.MyMath.average([4, 2, 8])

name  = sample.MyProfile.name
edu  = sample.MyProfile.education()

course  = edu.get("course")

print( add )
print( avg )
print( name )
print( course )
```

```
#Output
8
4.666666666666667
George Wood
Computer Science
```

#sample.py

```python
class MyMath:

    def addition(x, y):
        return x + y

    def average(input):
        total = sum(input)
        length = len(input)
        return total/length

class MyProfile:

    name = "George Wood"

    def education():
        map = {'college':"Cambridge",
        'year':2,
        'course':"Computer Science"}

        return map
```

Method 2: Importing the Class Directly

```
from module import class_name

obj = class_name()
```

Example,

#myprogram.py

```python
from sample import MyMath, MyProfile

add  = MyMath.addition(10, 5 )
avg  =  MyMath.average([3, 5, 2])

name  =  MyProfile.name
edu  = MyProfile.education()

college  = edu.get("college")


print( add )
print( avg )
print( name )
print( college )
```

```
#Output
15
3.3333333333333335
George Wood
Cambridge
```

#sample.py

```python
class MyMath:

    def addition(x, y):
        return x + y

    def average(input):
        total = sum(input)
        length = len(input)
        return total/length

class MyProfile:

    name = "George Wood"

    def education():
        map = {'college':"Cambridge",
        'year':2,
        'course':"Computer Science"}

        return map
```

Chapter 11

Random,Calendar and Datetime

After you have studied this chapter, you should be able to:

- Understand the purpose of the random module
- Use key methods in the random module
- Create a simple guessing game using random
- Utilize the calendar module and its methods
- Understand the datetime module and its usage
- Format and manipulate dates and times

Random Module

The random module is one of Python's most widely used libraries, particularly in areas such as game development, simulations, cryptography, and statistical modeling. It allows for the generation of random numbers and the selection of elements in a non-linear or unsequential manner.

Random Methods

Function	Description
random.random()	Returns a random floating-point number between 0.0 and 1.0.
random.choice(iterable)	Randomly selects a single element from a sequence (list, tuple, string, etc.).
random.choices(iterable)	Returns a list of k randomly selected elements from a sequence, with optional weights for probability control.
random.randint(a, b)	Returns a random integer between a and b (both inclusive).
random.randrange(start, end)	Returns a random integer within a range, similar to range().
random.shuffle(iterable)	Randomly rearranges the elements of a mutable sequence.
random.uniform(a, b)	Returns a random float in the range [a, b].
random.triangular(low,high, mode)	Returns a random float from a Triangular distribution.
random.sample(population, k)	Returns a unique list of k elements randomly selected from the population.
random.seed()	Initializes the random number generator with a seed to produce repeatable results.
random.randbytes(n)	Returns a bytes object with n random bytes.
random.getstate()	Returns the current internal state of the random number generator.
random.setstate(state)	Restores the random number generator state to a previously saved state.
random.betavariate(alpha,beta)	Returns a random float from a Beta distribution with parameters alpha and beta.
random.binomialvariate(n, p)	Returns a random number based on a Binomial distribution, where n is the number of trials and p is the probability of success in each trial.
random.expovariate(lambda)	Returns a random number from an Exponential distribution with a given lambda (λ), which determines the rate of decay.
random.gammavariate(alpha,beta)	Returns a random number based on a Gamma distribution with shape alpha and scale beta.

random.gauss(mu, sigma)	Generates a random number from a Gaussian (Normal) distribution with mean mu and standard deviation sigma.
random.getrandbits(k)	Returns a random integer represented by k random bits.
random.lognormvariate(mu,sigma)	Generates a number from a Log-normal distribution, where mu and sigma determine the shape.
random.normalvariate(mu,sigma)	Returns a random number based on a Normal (Gaussian) distribution.
random.paretovariate(alpha)	Generates a random number following a Pareto distribution with a shape parameter alpha.
random.vonmisesvariate(mu,kappa)	Generates a random number from a Von Mises distribution (used in circular data analysis).
random.weibullvariate(alpha,beta)	Returns a random number based on a Weibull distribution, which is commonly used in reliability engineering.

random()

</> Python

```
import random

>>> random.random()
..... 0.43203036719075705
>>> random.random()
..... 0.44621094293757324
```

randint(a, b)

</> Python

```
import random

>>> random.randint( 2, 6 )
...... 3
>>> random.randint( 2, 6 )
...... 5
>>> random.randint( 10, 20 )
...... 12
>>> random.randint( 10, 20 )
...... 18
```

randrange(start, stop, step)

```
</> Python
import random
>>> random.randrange( 5 )              # start = 0, end = 5
...... 4
>>> random.randrange( 100, 200 )        # start = 100, end = 200
...... 120
>>> random.randrange( 2, 10, 3 )        # start = 2, end = 10, steps = 3
....... 8
```

choice(iterable)

```
</> Python
import random

>>> fruits = ["apple", "berry", "orange", "grape"]

>>> random.choice( fruits )
...... 'grape'
>>> random.choice( fruits )
...... 'orange'

>>> even = [2, 4, 6, 8, 10]
>>> random.choice( even )
...... 6
```

choices(iterable)

```
</> Python
import random

>>> fruits = ["apple", "berry", "orange", "grape"]

>>> random.choices( fruits )
...... ['berry']
```

gauss(mu, sigma)

```
</> Python
import random
>>> random.gauss( )
...... -0.01385969404444731
```

sample(iterable, k)

```
</> Python
import random

>>> fruits = ["apple","berry","orange", "grape"]

>>> random.sample( fruits, 2 )
..... ['orange', 'apple']

>>> random.sample( fruits, 3 )
...... ['berry', 'apple', 'grape']
```

uniform(a, b)

```
</> Python
import random

>>> random.uniform( 2, 10 )
...... 9.291435998100061

>>> random.uniform( 2, 10 )
......  7.6744910036199325
```

Deep

The Guess Game

The Guess Game is an interactive game where the user inputs a number within a specified range. If the entered number matches the randomly generated number by the program, the user wins. Otherwise, they must continue guessing until they find the correct number. However, the game can be terminated at any time by entering a non-digit character.

```
def getRandomNumber():
    value = random.randint(0, 10)
    return value

while True:
  getInput = input("Guess a number 0-10:  ")

  if getInput.isalpha():
    print("Input is not a number\nGame Over")
    break
  else:
    value = getRandomNumber()
    if value == int(getInput):
      print("You've won!\nCongratulations")
      break
    else:
      print("Wrong!\nGuess again")
```

```
#Output
Guess a number 0-10:  5
Wrong!
Guess again

Guess a number 0-10:  3
Wrong!
Guess again

Guess a number 0-10:  8
You've won!
Congratulations
```

Calendar Module

The **calendar** module is essential for working with dates and time in a system. It allows you to display the calendar for any given year, past or future. Additionally, it provides various methods for checking leap years, retrieving the number of days in a month, and working with months and weekdays.

Calendar Methods

Function	Description
calendar.calendar()	The main module used for handling date-related functionalities.
calendar.datetime()	A separate module in Python that works with date and time objects.
calendar.day_abbr()	A list of abbreviated weekday names (e.g., ['Mon', 'Tue', 'Wed', ...]).
calendar.day_name()	A list of full weekday names (e.g., ['Monday', 'Tuesday', ...]).
calendar.different_locale	Returns the current setting for the first day of the week (default is Monday).
calendar.firstweekday()	Sets the first day of the week (e.g., setfirstweekday(calendar.SUNDAY)).
calendar.format(formatstring)	Used for formatting calendar outputs.
calendar.formatstring	A string pattern used for formatting calendar output.
calendar.global_enum	Internal attribute related to global enumeration.
calendar.isleap(year)	Checks if a given year is a leap year (returns True or False).
calendar.leapdays(y1, y2)	Returns the number of leap years between two years (exclusive).
calendar.main()	Runs a demo of the calendar module when executed as a script.
calendar.mdays	A list where the index represents a month (1-12), and the value is the number of days in that month.
calendar.month(year, month)	Returns a string representation of a month's calendar.
calendar.month_abbr	A list of abbreviated month names (e.g., ['', 'Jan', 'Feb', 'Mar', ...]).
calendar.month_name	month_name: A list of full month names (e.g., ['', 'January', 'February', ...]).
calendar.monthcalendar(yr, m)	Returns a list of weeks for the specified month. Each week is a list of seven integers, where 0 represents days outside the month.

calendar.monthrange(year, month)	Returns a tuple (start_day, num_days), where start_day is the weekday index of the first day of the month, and num_days is the total number of days in that month.
calendar.prcal(year,w, l, c)	Prints a formatted calendar for a full year.
calendar.prmonth(yr, m, w, l)	Prints a formatted calendar for a single month.
calendar.prweek(week,w,l)	Prints a formatted representation of a single week.
calendar.repeat(year, count)	Repeats the year's calendar count times.
calendar.setfirstweekday(weekday)	Sets the first day of the week (e.g., setfirstweekday(calendar.SUNDAY)).
calendar.timegm(tuple)	Converts a time tuple (like one returned by time.gmtime()) into a Unix timestamp (seconds since epoch).
calendar.week(yr, week, firstweek)	Returns a list of (year, month, day) tuples for each day in a given week number.
calendar.weekday(year, month,day)	Returns the weekday index for a given date (Monday = 0, Sunday = 6).
weekheader	Returns a header string with abbreviated weekday names up to n characters per name.

calendar(theyear = int, w = int , l=int, c=int, m=int)

</> Python

```
import calendar

cal = calendar.calendar(theyear=2025)
print(cal)
```

#Output

```
                                  2025

      January                   February                   March                     April
Mo Tu We Th Fr Sa Su      Mo Tu We Th Fr Sa Su      Mo Tu We Th Fr Sa Su      Mo Tu We Th Fr Sa Su
       1  2  3  4  5                      1  2                      1  2          1  2  3  4  5  6
 6  7  8  9 10 11 12       3  4  5  6  7  8  9       3  4  5  6  7  8  9       7  8  9 10 11 12 13
13 14 15 16 17 18 19      10 11 12 13 14 15 16      10 11 12 13 14 15 16      14 15 16 17 18 19 20
20 21 22 23 24 25 26      17 18 19 20 21 22 23      17 18 19 20 21 22 23      21 22 23 24 25 26 27
27 28 29 30 31            24 25 26 27 28            24 25 26 27 28 29 30      28 29 30
                                                    31
```

....

isleap(year)

```
</> Python
import calendar

>>> calendar.isleap( 2024)
..... True
>>> calendar.isleap( 2025)
...... False
```

leapdays(y1, y2)

```
</> Python
import calendar

>>> calendar.leapdays( 2014, 2025)
...... 3
```

month(month, year)

```
</> Python
import calendar

>>> calendar.month(  2025, 1)
.....
   January 2025
Mo Tu We Th Fr Sa Su
       1  2  3  4  5
 6  7  8  9 10 11 12
13 14 15 16 17 18 19
20 21 22 23 24 25 26
27 28 29 30 31
```

leapdays(y1, y2)

```
</> Python
import calendar

>>> calendar.leapdays( 2014, 2025)
...... 3
```

monthrange(year, month)

```
</> Python
import calendar

>>> calendar.monthrange( 2025, 2)
...... (calendar.SATURDAY, 28)
```

prmonth(year, month, w, l)

```
</> Python
import calendar

>>> calendar.prmonth( 2025, 4)

......
     April 2025
Mo Tu We Th Fr Sa Su
    1  2  3  4  5  6
 7  8  9 10 11 12 13
14 15 16 17 18 19 20
21 22 23 24 25 26 27
28 29 30
```

Datetime Module

The datetime module in Python is used to work with **dates and times** based on the system's current settings. It provides several methods for handling months, years, time zones, and formatting date-time values.

Datetime Methods

Function	Description
astimezone	Converts the given datetime object to the specified time zone (tz). It is useful for handling time zones when working with global applications.
combine(date, time)	Combines a date object and a time object into a single datetime object.
ctime	Returns a string representation of the date-time in a human-readable format.
date	Extracts and returns the date portion from a datetime object.
day	Returns the day of the month as an integer (1-31).
dst	Returns the daylight saving time (DST) offset for time zones that observe DST.
fold	Used when dealing with ambiguous times in time zones that observe DST transitions.
fromisocalendar(yr,wk,d)	Converts an ISO calendar (year, week number, weekday) into a datetime object.
fromisoformat	Converts an ISO 8601 formatted string into a datetime object.
fromordinal(ordinal)	Converts a Gregorian ordinal (days since 01-01-0001) into a date object.
fromtimestamp	Converts a timestamp (seconds since epoch) into a datetime object.
hour	Returns the hour of the day (0-23).
isocalendar	Returns a tuple representing the year, week number, and weekday.
isoformat	Returns an ISO 8601 formatted string of the datetime object.
isoweekday	Returns the weekday as an integer (1=Monday, 7=Sunday).
max, min	datetime.max → The maximum representable date-time (9999-12-31 23:59:59.999999). datetime.min → The minimum representable date-time (0001-01-01 00:00:00).
microsecond	Returns the microsecond component of the datetime object (0-999999).
minute	Returns the minute of the hour (0-59).

month	Returns the month of the year (1-12).
now	Returns the current local date-time. If a time zone (tz) is provided, it returns the date-time in that time zone.
replace	Returns a new datetime object with modified values.
resolution	Returns the smallest time unit (datetime can measure microseconds).
second	Returns the second component (0-59).
strftime(format)	Converts a datetime object into a formatted string.
strptime(string, format)	Parses a string and converts it into a datetime object based on the given format.
time()	Extracts the time portion from a datetime object.
timestamp()	Returns the timestamp (seconds since epoch) for a datetime object.
timetuple()	Returns a time.struct_time object representing the date-time.
timetz()	Extracts the time and time zone from a datetime object.
today()	Returns the current local date.
toordinal()	Converts the datetime object to a Gregorian ordinal (days since 01-01-0001).
tzinfo()	Returns information about the time zone of the datetime object.
tzname()	Returns information about the time zone of the datetime object.
utcfromtimestamp()	Converts a timestamp into a UTC datetime object.
utcnow()	Returns the current UTC date-time.
utcoffset()	Returns the time zone offset from UTC.
utctimetuple()	Converts a datetime object to a UTC time.struct_time.
weekday()	Returns the day of the week (0=Monday, 6=Sunday).
year	Returns the year as integer

now( )

</> Python

```
from datetime import datetime

>>> datetime.now()
...... datetime.datetime(2025, 3, 31, 15, 13, 4, 726455)    #current date and time
```

day , month, weekday() and year

```python
from datetime import datetime

>>> datetime.now()
...... datetime.datetime(2025, 3, 31, 15, 13, 4, 726455)    #year, month, day, hour, min, sec

>>> datetime.now().day
...... 31

>>> datetime.now().month
...... 3                                  #March

>>> datetime.now().weekday()
...... 0                                  #March

>>> datetime.now().year
...... 2025
```

hour, minute, second and microsecond

```python
from datetime import datetime

>>> date = datetime.now()
>>> print(date)
...... datetime.datetime(2025, 3, 31, 15, 13, 4, 726455)    #year, month, day, hour, min, sec

>>> datetime.now().hour
...... 15

>>> datetime.now().minute
...... 13

>>> datetime.now().second
...... 4

>>> datetime.now().microsecond
...... 726455
```

today()

```python
from datetime import datetime

>>> today = datetime.today()
>>> print(today)
...... datetime.datetime(2025, 3, 31, 15, 41, 58, 492555)    #year, month, day, hour, min, sec
```

time()

```python
from datetime import datetime

>>> time = datetime.now().time()
>>> print(time)
...... datetime.time(15, 43, 45, 989477)    #hour, minute, second,  microsecond
```

strftime(format)

Format	Description	Example
%Y	Four-digit year	2025
%y	Two-digit year	25 (for 2025)
%m	Month	01 to 12
%B	Full month name	March
%b / %h	Abbreviated month name	Mar
%d	Day of the month	01 to 31
%j	Day of the year	001 to 366
%H	Hour (24 hour format)	00 to 23
%I	Hour (12 hour format)	01 to 12
%p	AM/PM notation	AM or PM
%M	Minutes	00 to 59
%S	Seconds	00 to 59
%f	Microseconds	000000 to 999999

%z	UTC offset	+0000, -0400
%Z	Timezone name	UTC, EST, IST
%A	Full weekday name	Monday
%a	Abbreviated weekday name	Mon
%w	Weekday as a number (Sun =0, Mon =1)	0 to 6
%W	Week number of the year (Monday start)	00 to 53
%U	Week number of the year (Sunday start)	00 to 53
%c	Full date and time representation	Sat Mar 31 14:30:45 2025
%x	Date representation	03/31/2025
%X	Time representation	14:3045

Table 11.0: Datetime string format

</> Python

```
from datetime import datetime

>>> today = datetime.now()
>>> print(today)
...... datetime.datetime(2025, 3, 31, 20, 54, 35, 345904)

>>> today.strftime("%d - %m - %Y")        #date
...... '31 - 03 - 2025'

>>> today.strftime("%d  %B, %Y")          #date
...... '31 March, 2025'

>>> today.strftime("%d  %B, %Y  %H: %M:%S ")      #date and time
...... '31 March, 2025  21:01:26'

>>> today.strftime("%c ")                          #date and time
...... 'Mon Mar 31 21:01:26 2025'
```

Chapter 12

The OS and SYS Module

After you have studied this chapter, you should be able to:

- Understand the importance of the os module
- Work with files and directories programmatically
- Retrieve basic system information
- Explore the sys module and its capabilities
- Use sys.argv to handle command-line arguments

OS (Operating System) Module

The OS module is a crucial library in Python programming as it provides direct access to the underlying operating system. It allows users to create, rename, manage system resources, and retrieve system information. Its functionalities are broadly categorized into the following groups:

File and Directory Management
Handling file creation, deletion, and renaming.

Process Management
Managing system processes and execution.

System Information Retrieval
Fetching system details such as OS type, environment variables, and user information.

Path and Directory Navigation
Working with file paths, directories, and symbolic links.

Permissions and Security
Managing file access permissions and inheritance.

OS Methods

① File and Directory Management

Function	Description
mkdir	Creates a directory.
makedirs	Creates a directory along with any necessary parent directories.
rmdir	Removes an empty directory.
removedirs	Removes multiple nested directories.
rename	Renames a file or directory.
renames	Renames a file, creating any needed intermediate directories.
replace	Replaces a file or directory.
remove	Deletes a file.
unlink	Alias for remove(), used to delete a file.

listdir	Lists files and directories in a specified path.
scandir	Returns an iterator for directory entries.
walk	Generates file names in a directory tree.

mkdir(path)

```
</> Python
import os
>>> os.mkdir("mydir")
>>> os.mkdir("music")
>>> os.listdir()          #listing all the directories
...... ['music', 'mydir']
```

makedirs(path)

```
</> Python
import os
>>> os.makedirs("media/music/reggae")
```

rename(src, dst)

```
</> Python
import os
>>> os.listdir()
...... ['mydir', 'music']
>>> os.rename("mydir", "document")     #rename mydir to document
>>> os.listdir()
...... ['document', 'music']
```

renames(old , new)

```
</> Python
import os
>>> os.renames("media/music/reggae", "media/song/cools")
```

remove(path) and unlink(path)

```python
>>> os.remove("document")
>>> os.unlink("mydir")
```

replace(src, dst)

```python
>>> os.replace("document",  "doc")
>>>
```

scandir( )

```python
import os
>>> files  = os.scandir( )
>>> for items in files:
......       print( items )
......
...... <DirEntry 'music'>
       <DirEntry 'mydir'>
       <DirEntry 'pictures'>
```

walk(path, topdown)

```python
import os
>>> for dirs in os.walk("Media"):
......       print( dirs )
......
...... ('Media\\Music', ['Reggae'], [])
       ('Media\\Music\\Reggae', [], [])
       ('Media\\Pictures', ['Nature'], [])
       ('Media\\Pictures\\Nature', [], [])
```

② Process Management

Function	Description
abort	Immediately terminates the process.
kill	Sends a signal to terminate a process by its PID.
waitpid	Waits for a child process to terminate.
system	Executes a command in the system shell.
spawnl, spawnle, spawnv, spawnve	Starts a new process.
execl, execle, execlp, execlpe, execv, execve, execvp, execvpe	Replaces the current process with a new one.
popen	Opens a pipe to a command.

system(cmd)

</> Python

```
import os

>>> results = os.system("python --version")
>>> print(results)
...... Python 3.13.0

>>> ip_address = os.system("ipconfig/all")
>>> print(ip_address)
...... Windows IP Configuration
       Host Name . . . . . . . . . . . . : AsieduPC
       Primary Dns Suffix  . . . . . . . :
       Node Type . . . . . . . . . . . . : Mixed
       IP Routing Enabled. . . . . . . . : No
       WINS Proxy Enabled. . . . . . . . : No

       Ethernet adapter Ethernet:
```

Note

os.system() requires native OS commands, which are specific to the operating system platform. The examples above use Windows OS commands, which differ from those used in Linux or macOS.

getpid( ) and kill(pid)

```
</> Python
import os

>>> results = os.getpid( )
>>> print(results)
...... 12568                #current process ID

>>> os.kill( pid=12568 )   #terminating process with pid:12568
>>>
```

spawnl, spawnle, spawnv, and spanwve( )

```
</> Python
import os

# Launching Notepad (Windows example)
>>> os.spawnl(os.P_NOWAIT, "C:\\Windows\\System32\\notepad.exe", "notepad.exe")
```

③ System Information

Function	Description
getcwd	Returns the current working directory.
getcwdb	Returns the current working directory as bytes.
getpid	Returns the process ID of the current process.
getppid	Returns the parent process ID.
getlogin	Returns the username of the logged-in user.
uname_result	Retrieves system-related information like OS name and version.
environ	Returns environment variables.
getenv	Fetches the value of an environment variable.
putenv	Sets an environment variable.
unsetenv	Removes an environment variable.

getcwd( )

```
</> Python
>>> import os
>>> os.getcwd()
...... 'D:\\Project\\Python\\mydir'
```

getpid( )

```
</> Python
>>> import os
>>> os.getpid()
...... 12568
```

getlogin( )

```
</> Python
>>> import os
>>> os.getlogin()
...... "John"
```

getenv(key)

```
</> Python
>>> import os
>>> os.getenv("JAVA_HOME" )
...... 'C:\\Program Files\\Java\\jdk-21'
```

putenv(name, value)

```
</> Python
>>> import os
>>> os.putenv("JAVA_HOME", "C:\\Program
Files\\Java\\jdk-21")
```

environ

```
</> Python
>>> os.environ
...... environ({'ALLUSERSPROFILE':
'C:\\ProgramData', 'APPDATA':
'C:\\Users\\Asiedu\\AppData\\Roaming',
'CHOCOLATEYINSTALL':
'C:\\ProgramData\\chocolatey' })
```

④ Path and Direction Navigation

Function	Description
chdir	Changes the current working directory.
curdir	Represents the current directory (".").
pardir	Represents the parent directory ("..").
altsep	Alternate path separator.
pathsep	Separator used for file paths in PATH environment variable.
sep	The OS-specific file path separator (/ for Linux, \ for Windows).
extsep	Extension separator (.).

chdir(path)

```
</> Python
>>> import os
>>> os.chdir("D:\\Project\\Python" )
>>> os.getcwd()
...... 'D:\\Project\\Python'
```

pathsep

```
</> Python
>>> import os
>>> os.pathsep
...... ';'
```

sep

```
</> Python
>>> import os
>>> os.sep
...... '\\'        #Windows
```

extsep

```
</> Python
>>> import os
>>> os.extsep
...... '.'
```

⑤ Permissions and Security

Function	Description
chmod	Changes the permissions of a file.
lchmod	Changes the permissions of a symbolic link.
fchmod	Changes file permissions using a file descriptor.
access	Checks user permissions for a file or directory.
umask	Sets the file mode creation mask.

⑥ System Utilities

Function	Description
open	Opens a file descriptor.
close	Closes a file descriptor.
dup, dup2	Duplicates file descriptors.
fsync	Flushes file data to disk.
truncate	Truncates a file to a given size.
read	Reads data from a file descriptor.
write	Writes data to a file descriptor.

lseek	Moves the file pointer to a specific position.
cpu_count	Returns the number of CPU cores available.
get_terminal_size	Returns the terminal window size.
isatty	Checks if a file descriptor refers to a terminal.
urandom	Generates secure random bytes.
linesep	Returns the OS-specific line separator (\n for Linux/macOS, \r\n for Windows).
error	Contains error-related exception classes.
strerror	Returns error message strings based on error codes.

cpu_count( )

</> Python

```
import os

>>> os.cpu_count()
...... 4
```

get_terminal_size( )

</> Python

```
import os

>>> os.get_terminal_size()
...... os.terminal_size(columns=66, lines=11)
```

SYS Module

The **sys** module is a powerful utility in Python used to interact with and retrieve abstract information about the system. It provides insights into the operating system, Python runtime environment, and interpreter settings. This module is widely used for handling system-level functionalities, command-line arguments, runtime configuration, and process management.

Key Functionalities of the sys Module

The sys module's functionality can be broadly categorized into the following areas:

✎ **System & Environment Information**
Retrieve system-related details like OS, version, and execution environment.

✎ **Python Runtime Configuration**
Access interpreter settings, execution parameters, and runtime limits.

✎ **Memory & Performance Management**
Optimize memory allocation and manage recursion limits.

✎ **Input/Output Handling**
Redirect standard input, output, and error streams.

✎ **Module & Path Management**
Modify the Python module search path and interact with the import system.

SYS Methods

① System & Environment Information

Function	Description
argv	Retrieves command-line arguments passed to the script.
executable	Returns the path of the Python interpreter binary.
platform	Returns the name of the operating system.
winver	Retrieves the Windows version (Windows only).
getwindowsversion	Returns version information about Windows OS (Windows only).
hexversion	Returns Python's version as a hexadecimal number.
version	Returns the Python version.
version_info	Provides version details as a tuple.

copyright	Displays Python's copyright information.
dllhandle	Returns the DLL handle of the Python process (Windows).
orig_argv	Retrieves the original command-line arguments.
flags	Displays command-line flags passed to the interpreter.
prefix	Returns the installation directory of Python.
base_prefix	Similar to base_exec_prefix, returns the base directory.
base_exec_prefix	Gets the base directory of the Python installation.
platlibdir	Retrieves the directory for platform-specific libraries.

sys.argv

The sys.argv module provides a way to access command-line arguments within a Python script. These arguments are stored as a list, where the first element (sys.argv[0]) is typically the script's filename, and the subsequent elements are the arguments passed via the command line, separated by whitespace.

The following demonstrates how to retrieve command-line arguments:

#sample.py

```python
import sys
def addition():
    x = sys.argv[1]          #first argument
    y = sys.argv[2]          #second argument

    add = float(x) + float(y)  #converting argument to float
    return add

#calling the function
result = addition()
print(result)
```

```
PS D:\Project\Development\Python> python  sample.py  20  10
30.0
```

executable

```
</> Python
>>> import sys
>>> sys.executable
...... 'C:\\Python313\\python.exe'
```

platform

```
</> Python
>>> import sys
>>> sys.platform
...... 'win32'
```

version

```
</> Python
>>> import sys
>>> sys.version
...... '3.13.0 (tags/v3.13.0:60403a5, Oct  7
2024, 09:38:07) [MSC v.1941 64 bit (AMD64)]'
```

platlibdir

```
</> Python
>>> import sys
>>> sys.platlibdir
...... 'DLLs'
```

② Python Runtime Configuration

Function	Description
dont_write_bytecode	Prevents Python from generating .pyc files.
pycache_prefix	Specifies the location for storing .pyc files.
meta_path	Lists meta path finders used for importing modules.
path	Lists directories where Python looks for modules.
path_hooks	Contains hooks for path-based module importers.
path_importer_cache	Caches module importers.
modules	Displays all currently loaded modules.
stdlib_module_names	Lists standard library module names.
builtin_module_names	Lists all built-in modules compiled into Python.
implementation	Provides details about the Python implementation (e.g., CPython, PyPy).
exec_prefix	Retrieves the path of platform-specific libraries.
warnoptions	Lists warning options set by the interpreter.

path

```python
import sys

>>> sys.path
...... ['', 'C:\\Python313\\python313.zip', 'C:\\Python313\\DLLs', 'C:\\Python313\\Lib',
'C:\\Python313', 'C:\\Python313\\Lib\\site-packages']
```

modules

```python
import sys

>>> sys.modules
{'sys': <module 'sys' (built-in)>, 'builtins': <module 'builtins' (built-in)>, '_frozen_importlib':
<module '_frozen_importlib' (frozen)>, '_imp': <module '_imp' (built-in)>, '_thread':
'calendar': <module 'calendar' from 'C:\\Python313\\Lib\\calendar.py'>}
```

③ Memory and Performance Management

Function	Description
getsizeof()	Returns the memory size of an object in bytes.
getallocatedblocks()	Returns the number of allocated memory blocks.
getrefcount()	Returns the reference count of an object.
getprofile()	Retrieves the profiling function set by sys.setprofile().
setprofile()	Sets a profiling function for debugging.
gettrace()	Returns the trace function set for debugging.
settrace()	Sets a debugging trace function.
getrecursionlimit()	Gets the maximum recursion depth.
setrecursionlimit	Sets the maximum recursion depth.
get_int_max_str_digits()	Returns the maximum number of digits allowed in an integer.
set_int_max_str_digits()	Sets the maximum allowed digits in an integer.
setswitchinterval()	Configures the thread switch interval.
getswitchinterval()	Gets the interval for thread switching.
maxsize	Retrieves the maximum size of a Python object.

maxunicode	Returns the largest Unicode code point supported.
int_info	Returns system-specific integer properties.
float_info	Returns system-specific float precision and limits.
float_repr_style	Indicates how floating-point numbers are represented.
hash_info	Provides details about Python's hash function.

④ Input/Output Handling

Function	Description
stdin	Standard input stream.
stdout	Standard output stream.
stderr	Standard error output stream.
displayhook	Controls how output is displayed in interactive mode.
excepthook	Holds the last exception object.
unraisablehook	Handles unraisable exceptions.

⑤ Process, Debugging, Module, Execution and Exception Handling

Function	Description
exit()	Terminates the program with an optional exit status.
exc_info()	Retrieves information about the last exception.
exception	Holds the last exception object.
breakpointhook()	Defines the behavior when calling breakpoint().
audit()	Reports security-sensitive operations to the auditing system.
addaudithook()	Adds an auditing hook for security checks.
monitoring	Provides monitoring hooks for the interpreter.
activate_stack_trampoline()	Activates stack trampolining for optimization.
deactivate_stack_trampoline()	Deactivates stack trampolining.
is_stack_trampoline_active()	Checks if stack trampolining is enabled.
call_tracing()	Runs a function with tracing enabled for debugging.
is_finalizing()	Checks if Python is in the process of shutting down.
thread_info	Retrieves threading implementation details.

byteorder	Indicates the byte order (endianness) of the system.
getfilesystemencoding()	Returns the encoding used for file system operations.
getfilesystemencodeerrors()	Retrieves the error handling strategy for filesystem encoding.
getunicodeinternedsize()	Returns the memory usage of interned Unicode strings.

Chapter 13

Pathlib and Glob

After you have studied this chapter, you should be able to:

- Understand the benefits of using the pathlib module
- Use pathlib classes and methods for file system operations
- Read from and write to files using pathlib
- Search for files and directories effectively
- Utilize glob.glob() for advanced file search operations
- Perform file input/output operations with ease

Pathlib Module

Programming across multiple operating systems (Windows, Linux, macOS) presents challenges, especially when working with file paths. Each OS follows different path conventions, which can lead to compatibility issues. Python provides a unified way to handle file paths seamlessly across different operating systems using the pathlib module.

With pathlib, a file path written for Windows can work on Linux without modification, reducing the likelihood of path-related errors. However, pathlib is not just for handling paths—it also allows you to search for files, create directories, check file existence, rename, replace files, and even read or write text and bytes efficiently.

Pathlib Classes

Class	Description
Path	Represents a file system path and provides methods for working with files and directories.
PosixPath	A subclass of Path used for Unix-like operating systems (Linux/macOS).
WindowsPath	A subclass of Path designed for Windows paths.
PurePath	A version of Path that handles paths in a platform-independent manner but doesn't interact with the file system.
PurePosixPath	A subclass of PurePath that represents Unix-style paths.
PureWindowsPath	A subclass of PurePath that represents Windows-style paths.

Path Methods

① Path Representation and Properties

Method	Description
absolute()	Returns the absolute path of the file/directory.
anchor	Returns the root part of the path (C:\ on Windows, / on Unix).
drive	Returns the drive letter (Windows) or an empty string (Linux).
home()	Returns the home directory of the current user.
root	Returns the root of the path (e.g., / on Unix, C:\ on Windows).
name	Returns the filename or last part of the path.

stem	Returns the filename without the extension.
suffix	Returns the file extension (e.g., .txt).
suffixes	Returns all file extensions if there are multiple (eg., .tar.gz).
parents	Returns a sequence of parent directories.
parent	Returns the immediate parent directory.
parts	Returns a tuple representing different components of the path.

home()

```
</> Python
>>> import pathlib
>>> path = pathlib.Path.home()
>>> print( path )
...... C:\Users\Asiedu
```

root

```
</> Python
>>> import pathlib
>>>pathlib.Path("D:\\dev\\myfile.py").root
...... \
>>>
```

name

```
</> Python
>>> import pathlib
>>> pathlib.Path("D:\\dev\\myfile.py").name
...... myfile.py
>>>
```

stem

```
</> Python
>>> import pathlib
>>> pathlib.Path("D:\\dev\\book.docx").stem
...... book
>>>
```

suffix

```
</> Python
>>> import pathlib
>>> pathlib.Path("D:\\dev\\book.docx").suffix
...... '.docx'
>>>
```

suffixes

```
</> Python
>>> import pathlib
>>> pathlib.Path("ebooks.tar.gz").suffixes
...... ['.tar', '.gz']
>>>
```

parts

```
</> Python
>>> import pathlib
>>> pathlib.Path("D:\\dev\\book.docx").parts
...... ('D:\\', 'dev', 'book.docx')
>>>
```

parent

```
</> Python
>>> import pathlib
>>> pathlib.Path("D:\\dev\\myfile.py").parents[0]
...... 'D:\\dev'
>>>
```

② File and Directory Operations

Method	Description
mkdir(parents, exist_ok)	Creates a new directory.
rmdir()	Removes an empty directory.
unlink(missing_ok)	Deletes a file.
rename(target)	Renames the file or directory to a new location.
replace(target)	Renames a file or directory, overwriting if necessary.
touch(mode, exist_ok)	Creates an empty file or updates its timestamp.
symlink_to(target)	Creates a symbolic link to the target file/directory.
hardlink_to(target)	Creates a hard link to the target file.

mkdir(mode, parents, exist_ok)

</> Python

```
>>> import pathlib
>>> pathlib.Path("Desktop\\NewDoc").mkdir()
>>>
```

rmdir()

</> Python

```
>>> import pathlib
>>>pathlib.Path("D:\\dev\\Doc").rmdir()
>>>
```

unlink(missing_ok)

</> Python

```
>>> import pathlib
>>> pathlib.Path("newfile.docx").unlink()
>>>
```

rename(target)

</> Python

```
>>> import pathlib as plib
>>> plib.Path("book.txt").rename("mybook.txt")
>>>
```

replace(target)

</> Python

```
>>> import pathlib as plib
>>> plib.Path("book.txt").replace("ebook.py")
>>>
```

touch()

</> Python

```
>>> import pathlib
>>> pathlib.Path("newbook.docx").touch()
>>>
```

③ File and Directory Status

Method	Description
exists()	Returns True if the path exists.
is_absolute()	Returns True if the path is absolute.
is_relative_to(other)	Returns True if the path is relative to other.
is_reserved()	Returns True if the path is reserved (Windows only).
is_dir()	Returns True if the path is a directory.
is_file()	Returns True if the path is a file.
is_symlink()	Returns True if the path is a symbolic link.
is_mount()	Returns True if the path is a mount point.
is_fifo()	Returns True if the path is a FIFO (named pipe).
is_socket()	Returns True if the path is a socket.
is_junction()	Returns True if the path is a junction (Windows only).

exists()

</> Python

```
>>> import pathlib
>>> pathlib.Path("D:\\dev\\Doc ").exists()
..... True
>>>
```

is_absolute()

</> Python

```
>>> import pathlib as plib
>>> plib.Path("D:\\dev\\Doc ").is_absolute()
..... True
```

is_file()

</> Python

```
>>> import pathlib
>>> pathlib.Path("Ebook.docx ").is_file()
..... True

>>> pathlib.Path("MyDoc ").is_file()
..... False
```

is_dir()

</> Python

```
>>> import pathlib
>>> pathlib.Path("D:\\dev\\Doc").is_dir()
..... True

>>> pathlib.Path("D:\\dev\\myfile.txt ").is_dir()
..... False
```

④ File and Directory Searching

Method	Description
glob(pattern)	Finds all files matching the pattern (e.g., "*.txt").
rglob(pattern)	Recursively searches for files matching the pattern.
match(pattern)	Checks if the path matches a given pattern ("*.txt").
walk()	Iterates through the directory tree.
iterdir()	Iterates over files and directories in the current directory.

glob(pattern, case_sensitive)

case_sensitive → If True, the search will distinguish between uppercase and lowercase letters.

</> Python

```
import pathlib
files = pathlib.Path("D:\\Project").glob("*docx")

for items in files:
    print(items)
```

```
#Output
D:\Project\Employee.docx
D:\Project\Student.docx
D:\Project\template.docx
D:\Project\Letter.docx
D:\Project\sample.docx
```

Deep

"*" → Lists all files in the specified path.
"*end" → Lists all files that end with "end" in the path.
"begin*" → Lists all files that start with "begin" in the path.
"begin*end" → Lists all files that start with "begin" and end with "end" in the path.

glob.glob()

The glob.glob() function works similarly to Path.glob(), both being used to search for files that match a specified pattern.

Key Difference

- glob.glob(pattern, path) → The path is passed as a parameter to the glob function.
- Path(path).glob(pattern) → The path is specified inside the Path class before calling glob().

Example ,

</> Python

```python
import glob
files = glob.glob(pathname= "*mp3", root_dir=".")

for items in files:
    print(items)
```

```
#Output
westlife.mp3
demo.mp3
crack_records.mp3
```

Other glob Methods

Method	Description
iglob(pattern, recursive)	Works like glob() but returns an iterator instead of a list, which is more memory-efficient.
escape(pathname)	Escapes special characters (*, ?, []) in a given pathname so they are treated as literal characters instead of wildcards.
fnmatch(filename, pattern)	Checks if a filename matches a given pattern, considering case sensitivity based on the OS.
fnmatchcase(filename, pattern)	Similar to fnmatch(), but case-sensitive regardless of the OS.
has_magic(pattern)	Returns True if the pattern contains wildcard characters (*, ?, [ ]).

glob0(dirname, basename)	Helper function that performs non-recursive matching within a directory.
glob1(dirname, pattern)	Similar to glob0(), but specifically for non-recursive wildcard expansion in a directory.
translate(pattern)	Converts a glob pattern into a regular expression (re) pattern for use in filtering.
contextlib	Used for context management (e.g., safely handling file access).
functools	Provides higher-order functions like caching and function composition.
itertools	Supports efficient looping constructs and iteration utilities.
operator	Provides efficient operations for function-based comparisons.
os	Used to interact with the filesystem (e.g., listing directories).
re	Used for translating wildcard patterns into regex for pattern matching.
stat	Retrieves file status and metadata.
sys	Provides access to system-specific parameters.
magic_check(pattern)	Validates if the given pattern contains wildcard characters.
magic_check_bytes(pattern)	Similar to magic_check(), but works on byte strings instead of text.

walk( )

</> **Python**

```python
import pathlib

files = pathlib.Path("D:\\Project\\Python").walk()

for items in files:
    print(items)
```

```
#Output
(WindowsPath('D:/Project /Python'), ['mydir', '__pycache__'], ['chapter.jpg', 'chapter.xcf',
'justpython.py', 'mumvoce.mp3', 'Python.docx', , 'pytonTemp.docx', 'template.docx',
'~$Python.docx', '~$tonTemp.docx', '~WRL0106.tmp'])
(WindowsPath('D:/Project/ Python/mydir'), ['doc', 'Document', 'media', 'music', 'MyDir',
'pictures'], [])
```

iterdir( )

```
</> Python
import pathlib

files = pathlib.Path("C:\\Users\\PC\\Desktop").iterdir()


for items in files:
    print(items)
```

```
#Output
C:\Users\PC\Desktop\Adobe InDesign 2020.lnk
C:\Users\PC\Desktop\cook.txt
C:\Users\PC\Desktop\Documents.lnk
C:\Users\PC\Desktop\Excel.lnk
C:\Users\PC\Desktop\Facebook.lnk
C:\Users\PC\Desktop\Gmail.lnk
C:\Users\PC\Desktop\Pizza on the Grill Recipe.lnk
```

⑤ File Reading and Writing

Method	Description
open(mode, encoding)	Opens the file for reading or writing.
read_bytes()	Reads the file as bytes.
read_text(encoding)	Reads the file as a string.
write_bytes(data)	Writes bytes to the file.
write_text(data,encoding)	Writes a string to the file.

open( )

```
import pathlib

text= pathlib.Path("sample.txt").open()

for line in text.readlines():
    print(line)
```

```
#Output
Python coding is awesome
Just give me a coffee
```

Deep

The use of Pathlib for reading and writing files is explored in more detail in the next chapter on File Handling and Byte Operations.

⑦ Path Modification and Construction

Method	Description
as_posix()	Returns a POSIX-style (Unix-like) string representation of the path.
as_uri()	Converts the path into a file URI (file:///C:/Users/...).
expanduser()	Expands ~ to the user's home directory.
joinpath(*other)	Joins multiple path components (p.joinpath("subdir", "file.txt")).
relative_to(*other)	Returns a relative path based on the given base path.
resolve()	Returns the absolute path, resolving any symbolic links.
with_name(new_name)	Returns a new path with the same directory but a different filename.
with_stem(new_stem)	Returns a new path with the same directory but a different filename without changing the extension.
with_suffix(new_suffix)	Returns a new path with the same directory but a different file extension.

joinpath(path)

```
</> Python
>>> import pathlib
>>> path = pathlib.Path("Document").joinpath("Data" , "MyData.docx" )
>>> print(path)
...... Document\Data\MyData.docx

>>> path = pathlib.Path.home().joinpath("video.mp4" )
>>> print(path)
...... C:\Users\Asiedu\video.mp4
```

as_posix( )

```
</> Python
>>> import pathlib

>>> path = pathlib.Path.home()
>>> print(path)
...... C:\Users\Asiedu

>>> posix_path = pathlib.Path.home().as_posix()
>>> print(posix_path)
...... C:/Users/Asiedu
```

as_uri( )

```
</> Python
>>> import pathlib
>>> path = pathlib.Path("C:\\media\\music\\westlife.mp3").as_uri()
>>> print(path)
...... file:///C:/media/music/westlife.mp3
```


with_name(filename)

```
</> Python
>>> import pathlib
>>> path = pathlib.Path("Document\\Books\\redbook.pdf").with_name("greenbook.pdf")
>>> print(path)
...... Document\Books\greenbook.pdf
```

with_suffix(suffix)

```
</> Python
>>> import pathlib
>>> path = pathlib.Path("Books\\mybook.pdf").with_suffix(".docx")
>>> print(path)
...... Books\mybook.docx
```

⑧ File Metadata and Permissions

Method	Description
chmod(mode)	Changes the file's permissions.
lchmod(mode)	Changes the file's permissions but doesn't follow symbolic links.
owner()	Returns the owner of the file.
group()	Returns the group owner of the file.
stat()	Returns file metadata (size, creation date, etc.).
lstat()	Like stat(), but doesn't follow symbolic links.
samefile(other_path)	Returns True if both paths point to the same file.

Chapter 14

Handling Errors and Exceptions

After you have studied this chapter, you should be able to:

- Understand the need for error handling in programming
- Identify the types of errors in Python
- Recognize common syntax errors and their causes
- Handle runtime exceptions using try-except blocks and related constructs

Handling Errors and Exceptions

Programming inherently involves errors or *bugs*. Writing code requires applying human logic while adhering to the programming language's structure, syntax, and semantic rules. However, mistakes in logic, incorrect syntax, or unforeseen runtime conditions can lead to errors or exceptions.

Errors in a program are commonly referred to as *bugs*. Regardless of a programmer's experience, encountering bugs is inevitable, making error handling an essential part of software development. Errors can cause programs to behave unexpectedly, produce incorrect results, or fail to run entirely.

Python is an interpreted language, meaning it executes code line by line. When an error occurs, execution stops immediately, preventing further code from running. To ensure smooth execution and prevent abrupt program crashes, error handling is crucial.

Reasons for Handling Errors in Programming

✎ **To prevent program crashes:** Proper error handling ensures that a single error does not cause the entire program to terminate unexpectedly.

✎ **To allow a program to continue running despite encountering an error:** Handling exceptions gracefully allows a program to recover from errors and continue execution.

✎ **To display user-friendly error messages:** Instead of showing cryptic system-generated messages, developers can provide clear error messages to guide users on what went wrong.

✎ **To use errors as conditions for executing alternative tasks:** Some exceptions may indicate an expected situation that can be handled by executing a fallback solution.

✎ **To log errors for debugging and future reference:** Logging errors helps developers identify issues and improve the software over time.

✎ **To enhance security:** Some unhandled errors can expose sensitive information or allow attackers to exploit vulnerabilities in the software.

✎ **To improve software reliability and maintainability:** Well-structured error handling ensures that software remains stable and easy to maintain in the long run.

Errors in Python Programming

In Python, errors can arise due to several factors. They may be caused by logic mistakes, syntax violations, structural misconfigurations, incorrect data handling, incompatible data types, or missing dependencies.

Python errors are broadly categorized into two main types:

1. **Syntax Errors**
2. **Runtime Errors**

Syntax Errors

Every programming language follows a strict set of structural rules for using **variables, objects, functions, keywords, operators, punctuation, and mnemonics**. When these elements are not used correctly, or the required syntax is not followed, Python raises a *syntax error*. Syntax errors occur during the parsing stage and prevent the program from running.

Common Causes of Syntax Errors:

Incorrect indentation – Python enforces indentation to structure code blocks properly.

</> Python

```
def myFunc():
print("Hello World!")    #incorrect indentation
```

```
#Output
IndentationError: expected an indented block after function definition on line 2
```

Missing colons (:) – Required for defining functions, loops, and conditionals.

</> Python

```
def myFunc()                #missing colons
    print("Hello World!")
```

```
#Output
SyntaxError: expected ':'
```

Empty code blocks without the pass keyword – Python does not allow empty function or loop bodies.

</> Python

```
def myFunc():                    #empty block

def hello():
    print("Hello World!")
```

```
#Output
IndentationError: expected an indented block after function definition on line 3
```

Misspelled keywords or function names – Example: writing prnt() instead of print().

</> Python

```
prnt("Hello World!")    #wrong spelling of print
```

```
#Output
NameError: name 'prnt' is not defined. Did you mean: 'print'?
```

Mismatched parentheses, brackets, or braces – Example: print("Hello World" (missing closing parenthesis).

</> Python

```
print("Hello World!"    #no closing parentheses
```

```
#Output
SyntaxError: '(' was never closed?
```

Incorrect use of assignment (=) instead of comparison (==) – Example: if x = 5: instead of if x == 5:.

</> Python

```
var = 5
if var = 5:              #incorrect  use of assignment (==)
```

```
print("Hello World!"
```

```
#Output
SyntaxError: invalid syntax. Maybe you meant '==' or ':=' instead of '='?
```

Unclosed string literals - Example:

</> Python

```
var = "Python    #unclosed string
```

```
#Output
SyntaxError: unterminated string literal (detected at line 2)
```

Using reserved words as variable names - Example: def = 10 (since def is a keyword).

</> Python

```
def = 10            #def is a keyword
```

```
#Output
SyntaxError: invalid syntax
```

Runtime Exception

Runtime errors occur during the execution of a program rather than during compilation or syntax checking. These errors are not caused by violations of the language's syntax or structure but rather by **logical mistakes, incorrect operations, invalid data handling, or unexpected conditions**. Unlike syntax errors, which prevent the program from running, runtime errors appear while the program is running and may cause it to crash or behave unexpectedly.

Common Causes of Runtime Errors:

Runtime exception	Description
ZeroDivisionError	Occurs when a number is divided by zero
KeyError	Attempting to access a dictionary key that does not exist.
NameError	Trying to use a variable that has not been declared.
IndexError	Attempting to access a list, tuple, or string index that does not exist.
TypeError	Performing operation on incompatible types. For example, trying to add a string and an integer.
IndentationError	Wrong indentation in program
FloatingPointError	Operations on floating point fail
ImportError	Imported module is not found
AssertionError	Assertion statements fail
FileNotFoundError	Trying to open a non-existent file
AttributeError	An invalid attribute reference or assignment is attempted
RecursionError	When recursion exceeds the system limit.
UnicodeError	An encoding or decoding operation fails
EOFError	The input() function reaches the end-of-file condition

Table 12.0: Some runtime exceptions in Python

Handling Errors and Exceptions

Errors and exceptions can be addressed in a program during debugging, allowing developers to correct them before deployment. However, some errors may only occur under specific conditions, such as user input errors, file access issues, or network failures. These types of errors are unpredictable and can arise during the production stage of an application. To prevent a program from crashing and to ensure it continues running smoothly, **error handling** is necessary.

Python provides **two main ways** to handle errors and exceptions:

1. **try-except Block** - Used to catch and handle specific errors, preventing the program from crashing when an exception occurs.
2. **try-finally** or **try-except-finally Block** - Ensures that certain cleanup operations (e.g., closing files or releasing resources) are executed, regardless of whether an exception occurs.

try-except

In this approach, the code that is likely to raise an exception is placed inside the try block. If an exception occurs, the except block is executed to handle the error. However, if no exception occurs, the statements inside the except block will not run.

Syntax

```
try:
    #statement or code

except ErrorType:
    #statement or code
```

Note

The **ErrorType** is optional and can be any of the runtime errors listed above. It allows the execution of specific statements when multiple statements are likely to raise different types of errors. However, the program will still handle errors properly even without specifying an ErrorType.

Example 1, the following code demonstrates handling a ZeroDivisionError:

#Handled exception

```python
try:
    result = 200 / 0

except ZeroDivisionError:
    print("Error: Number was divided by zero")
```

```
#Output
Error: Number was divided by zero
```

#Unhandled exception

```python
result = 200 / 0
```

```
#Output
    result = 200 / 0
          ~~~~^~~
ZeroDivisionError: division by zero
```

Example 2, the following code demonstrates handling a TypeError:

#Handled exception

```python
def whenError():
    print("Program has bugs")

try:
    var = 10 + "20"
except:
    whenError():
```

```
#Output
Program has bugs
```

#Unhandled exception

```python
var = 10 +  "20"
```

```
#Output
    var = 10 + "20"
          ~~~^~~~
TypeError: unsupported operand type(s) for
+: 'int' and 'str'
```

try-finally

The try-finally approach is useful in situations where certain statements or functions must execute regardless of whether an error occurs.

- The code that might raise an error is placed inside the try block.
- The except block is optional and can be used to handle specific exceptions.
- The finally block always executes, whether an error occurs or not. The finally block is mainly used for **cleanup operations**, such as closing files, releasing resources, or disconnecting from databases.

Syntax

```
try:
    #statement or code

finally:
    #statement or code
```

```
try:
    #statement or code

except ErrorType:
    #statement or code

finally:
    #statement or code
```

Example 1, the following code demonstrates handling NameError

</> Python

```python
try:
   result = var + 20                    #variable is not defined
finally:
   print("Execution completed")
```

```
#Output
Execution completed
result = var + 20
         ^^^
NameError: name 'var' is not defined. Did you mean: 'vars'?
```

Example 2, the following code demonstrates handling IndexError

</> Python

```
try:
    var = [1, 2, 3]
    item = var[ 10 ]            #index is out of range
except:
    print("IndexError: exception  has occurred")

finally:
    print("Execution completed")
```

```
#Output
IndexError: exception  has occurred
Execution completed
```

Deep

Errors

These are issues that arise due to incorrect code structure, syntax, or system limitations, making the program unable to execute.

Exceptions

These occur during the execution of a program when an unexpected condition is encountered, such as dividing by zero or accessing an invalid index.

Chapter 15

File Handling and Byte Operations

After you have studied this chapter, you should be able to:

- Understand what a file is in computing
- Perform various file operations
- Open and work with files in Python
- Use different file opening modes (e.g., read, write, append, binary)
- Read data from files using multiple techniques
- Write and read binary files
- Append data to existing files
- Access and manipulate file attributes

File Handling

A **file** is a collection of data stored on a computer that can be accessed and manipulated by programs. Files can contain various types of data, including:

- **Text-based content** (e.g., .txt, .csv, .json, .xml, .docx)
- **Binary data** (e.g., images: .jpg, .png, videos: .mp4, .avi, audio: .mp3, .wav)
- **Executable files** (.exe, .bin, .sh)
- **Compressed archives** (.zip, .tar, .rar)
- **Database files** (.sqlite, .db)

In Python, before accessing or modifying a file, it must first be opened. Python provides built-in support for file handling, allowing files to be read, written, modified, and even converted between different formats.

File Operations

Python offers several methods for handling files, including:

- Opening a file
- Reading a file
- Writing to a file
- Appending data to a file (a mode)
- Accessing file attributes
- Closing a file

① Opening Files

Python is a flexible language that provides multiple ways to open a file. However, in this book, we will explore two of the most commonly used methods.

1. Using open()

The open() function is the standard way to open files in Python. It allows you to specify various parameters, including the file path, mode, encoding, and more.

Syntax

```
file = open("path/to/file", "w")
```

or using the **with** statement (which ensures the file is properly closed after use):

```
with open("path/to/file", "w") as file:
    pass    #file operations go here
```

The open() Parameters

```
open(file, mode="r", buffering=-1, encoding=None, newline=None, errors=None)
```

Parameters:

file	→	The path to the file (can be a string or Path object).
mode	→	Specifies how the file should be opened. (See the table below for available modes.)

buffering → Controls buffering: 0 for no buffering (binary mode), 1 for line buffering (text mode), >1 for a custom buffer size, and -1 (default) lets Python decide.

encoding → Specifies the encoding (e.g., "utf-8", "ascii"). Only applicable in text mode.

newline → Determines how newlines are handled (None, '\n', '\r', '\r\n'). Useful when working with different operating systems

errors → Defines how errors in encoding/decoding are handled (e.g., "strict", "ignore", "replace").

closefd → If True (default), the file descriptor is closed when the file is closed. Should be False only when working with file descriptors instead of file paths.

File Modes

Mode	Description
'r'	Read mode (default). Fails if the file does not exist.
'w'	Write mode. Overwrites the file if it exists; creates a new file if it doesn't.
'a'	Append mode. Adds new content to the end of the file. Creates the file if it doesn't exist.
'x'	Exclusive creation mode. Fails if the file already exists.
'rb', 'wb'	Binary mode (e.g., for images, videos, and executables). 'rb' for reading bytes and 'wb' for writing bytes.
'rt', 'wt'	Text mode (default). 'rt' for reading and 'wt' for writing the txt
'+'	Read and write mode (e.g., 'r+', 'w+', 'a+', 'rb+', 'wb+').

2. Using pathlib.Path.open()

Another way to open files is through the pathlib library, which provides a more object-oriented approach to file handling. This method offers the same parameters as open(), but allows working with file paths more intuitively.

Syntax

```
import pathlib
file = pathlib.Path("path/to/file").open()
```

Deep

The pathlib module has been discussed in more detail in Chapter 13: Pathlib and Glob.

② Reading and Writing Files

After opening a file using either the built-in **open()** function or the **pathlib** module, the file can be read from or written to.

Reading Files

① Using open()

Syntax

```
file = open("path/to/file")
file.read()             # Reads the entire content
file.readline()         # Reads a single line
file.readlines()        # Reads all lines into a list
```

Example 1

```python
file  = open("myfile.txt")
text = file.read()
print( text)
file.close()
```

```
#Output
Python coding is awesome
Just give me a coffee
```

Example 2

```python
with open("myfile.txt") as f:
    text = f.readlines()
    print( text)
```

```
#Output
['Python coding is awesome\n', 'Just give me a coffee']
```

Note

The **close()** function is used to manually close a file after it has been opened. However, when a file is opened using the with statement, it is automatically closed once the block is exited. It's always good practice to close a file after use to ensure that system resources are properly released.

② Using pathlib.Path.open()

Syntax

```
from pathlib import Path

path = Path('path/to/file').open()
path.read()                    # Reads the entire content
path.readline()                # Reads a single line
path.readlines()               # Reads all lines into a list
```

Example 1

```python
from pathlib import Path

path = Path('sample.txt').open()
text = path.read()
print(text)
```

```
#Output
Hello,
Hope you're having fine with files?
```

Example 2

```python
from pathlib import Path

path = Path('sample.txt').open()
text = path.readline()
print(text)
```

```
#Output
Hello,
```


③ Using pathlib shortcuts

Syntax

```
from pathlib import Path

text = Path('path/to/file').read_text()          # Reads as text
byte = Path('path/to/file').read_bytes()         # Reads as bytes
```

Example

</> Python

```python
from pathlib import Path

text = Path('mytext.txt').read_text()
print(text)
```

```
#Output
Python coding is awesome
Just give me a coffee
```

Reading Binary Files

Example

</> Python

```python
from pathlib import Path

bytes = Path('image.jpg').read_bytes()
```

Writing to Files

① Using open()

Syntax

```
file = open("path/to/file", "w" )
file.write( data )
file.writelines( data )
```

Example

```
</> Python
file = open("newfile.txt", "w" )

file.write("Hello,\nIt's fun working with files" )

file.writelines( ["Awesome coding,\n", "Happy Pythonizing"] )

file.close()
```

Writing Binary Files

Example, Reading from an Image file and writing to a new image file.

```
</> Python
file = open("image.jpg", "rb" )
bytes = file.read()
file.close()

image = open("newImage.png", "wb")
image.write( bytes )
image.close()
```

② Using pathlib.Path.open()

Syntax

```
from pathlib import Path

path = Path('path/to/file').open( mode = 'w' )
path.write( data )
path.readlines( )
```

Example

```python
path = Path('newfile.txt').open( mode = 'w' )
path.write("Hello, World\n" )
path.writelines( ["Hello\n",  "File handling is interesting\n", "Happy Pythonizing"] )
path.close()
```

Writing Binary Files

Example, Reading from an audio file and writing a new audio file

```python
path = Path('music.mp3').open( mode = 'rb' )
bytes = path.read( )
path.close()


music = Path('mymusic.ogg').open( mode = 'wb' )
music.write(bytes)
music.close()
```

③ Using pathlib shortcuts

Syntax

```
from pathlib import Path

Path('path/to/file').write_text( text )
Path('path/to/file').write_bytes( data )
```

Example

```python
from pathlib import Path

text = 'Hello World'
Path('newFile.txt').write_text( text )
```

Writing Binary Files

```python
from pathlib import Path

bytes = Path('image.jpg').read_bytes()
Path('newImage.png').write_bytes( bytes )
Path('bytefile.exe').write_bytes( b"writing to bytes")
```

③ Appending Data to a File

Appending data to a file means adding new content to an existing file without overwriting its original content—typically used with text files. This is done using the write methods in append mode ('a').

Example 1

</> Python

```python
with open("myfile.txt", "a") as file:
    file.write("\nThis line is added  to the file")
```

Example 2

</> Python

```python
with open("myfile.txt", "a") as file:
    file.write("\nThis line is added  to the file")

with open("myfile.txt", "a") as file:
    text = file.read( )
    print(text )
```

```
#Output
Hello World
This line is added to the file
```

④ Accessing File Attributes

File attributes provide metadata and useful information about a file object. Once a file is opened, you can access several of its attributes to learn about the file's name, mode, encoding, and more.

Attribute	Description
file.name	Returns the name of the file.
file.mode	Returns the mode used to open the file ('r', 'w', 'a', etc.).
file.closed	Returns True if the file is closed; otherwise, False.
file.encoding	Returns the encoding used (for text files only).
file.fileno()	Returns the file descriptor (an integer) used by the operating system.
file.readable()	Returns True if the file was opened in a readable mode.
file.writable()	Returns True if the file was opened in a writable mode.
file.seekable()	Returns True if the file supports random access (seeking).
file.tell()	Returns the current position of the file pointer (in bytes).
file.seek(ofset)	Moves the file pointer to a specified position.

</> Python

```
file = open("sample.txt")
print( file.name )
print( file.mode)
print( file.closed )
print( file.encoding )
print( file.readable )
```

```
#Output
sample.txt
r
False
cp1252
<built-in method readable of _io.TextIOWrapper object at 0x000002E74C507920>
```


Chapter 16

HTTP Requests

After you have studied this chapter, you should be able to:

- Understand the features and capabilities of the requests library
- Identify and use common HTTP request methods (GET, POST, PUT, DELETE, etc.)
- Make HTTP requests using the GET method
- Download files via GET requests
- Upload files using the POST method
- Use additional methods like PATH, PUT, and DELETE in real-world scenarios

HTTP Requests

Python's **requests** library is one of the most popular and user-friendly tools for making HTTP requests. It allows your Python program to interact with web services, download content from the internet, submit data via forms, communicate with APIs, and more.

Key Features:

- Supports all HTTP methods (GET, POST, PUT, DELETE, etc.)
- Easy access to response content in various formats
- Handles cookies, headers, sessions, and authentication
- Works well with JSON APIs
- Simplifies error handling and redirects

Installation

Installation can be done using the **pip install** command in the terminal or command line interface.

```
$ pip install requests
```

Common Requests Methods

Method	Description
get()	Retrieve information from the server
post()	Submit data to the server
put()	Replace existing data on the server
patch()	Partially update data
delete()	Remove data from the server
head()	Return headers without the body

options()	Returns server-supported methods
auth()	Contains support for HTTP Basic/Digest Auth.
cookies	Manage and inspect HTTP cookies.
ssl	Internal SSL utilities.
session	Manage cookies and connections across multiple requests:

GET() Requests

The get() method is used to make an HTTP request to a web server. It returns a response, which can be either successful (positive) or unsuccessful (negative). A negative response typically results from an HTTP error (such as 404 or 500), while a positive response contains data from the server.

The response can be accessed in various formats, such as:

- .text – returns the response body as a string
- .json() – returns the response in JSON format (if applicable)
- .content – returns the response as raw bytes
- .status_code – provides the HTTP status code of the response

Parameters

url	→	The URL you are making a GET request to.
params	→	(dict or bytes) — Appends query string to the URL.
headers	→	(dict) — Custom headers like user-agent, auth token, etc.
cookies	→	(dict or CookieJar) — Send cookies with the request.
auth	→	(tuple) — For basic authentication: ('username', 'password').
timeout	→	(float or tuple) — How long to wait for a response. Prevents hanging.
allow_redirects	→	(bool) — Whether to follow redirects (default is True).
proxies	→	(dict) — Use a proxy server for the request.
stream	→	(bool) — If True, doesn't download the response immediately.
verify	→	(bool or str) — SSL certificate verification. Set to False to ignore SSL (not recommended).
cert	→	(str or tuple) — Client-side SSL certs, if required.

Example 1

```python
import requests
response = requests.get(url= "https://google.com/")
print( response.url )
print( response.json() )
print( response.status_code )
```

```
#Output
https://www.google.com/
<bound method Response.json of <Response [200]>>
200
```

Example 2

```python
import requests

url = "https://google.com/"
params = {"search": "python"}
headers = {"User-Agent": "MyApp"}
cookies = {"session": "123abc"}

response = requests.get(
                url= url,
                params = params,
                headers = headers,
                cookies = cookies,
                timeout = 5,
                allow_redirects = True
                )
print( response.text )
```

```
#Output
<!doctype html><html itemscope="" itemtype="http://schema.org/WebPage" lang="en-GH"><head><meta content="text/html; charset=UTF-8" http-equiv="Content-Type"><meta content="/images/googleg/1x/googleg_standard_color_128dp.png"
})();</script> ..............</body></html>
```

Deep

Common HTTP Status Codes

Code	Meaning	Code	Meaning
200	OK	400	Bad Request
201	Created	401	Unauthorized
204	No Content	403	Forbidden
301	Moved Permanently	404	Not Found
304	Not Modified	500	Internal Server Error

Downloading a File

</> Python

```python
import requests

response = requests.get(url= "https://example.com/image.png")

with open("downloadedImage.jpg", "wb") as file:
    file.write( response.content )
```

POST() Requests

The post() method is commonly used to send data to a server, typically through a form or an API. Unlike get(), which is used for retrieving data, post() is designed for submitting data (e.g., creating a new resource).

Although post() can also return a response, it is not primarily used for retrieving content like get(). The returned response can still be accessed using .text, .json(), or .status_code just like with get().

Parameters

url	→	(str) The endpoint you're sending the request to.
data	→	(dict, bytes, or file-like) Data to send in the body (form-encoded).
headers	→	(dict) — Custom headers like user-agent, auth token, etc.
json	→	(dict) A JSON payload to send (sets Content-Type: application/json).
cookies	→	(dict or CookieJar) — Send cookies with the request.
auth	→	(tuple) — For basic authentication: ('username', 'password').
timeout	→	(float or tuple) — How long to wait for a response. Prevents hanging.
files	→	(dict) Used for file upload. Format: {'file': open('filename', 'rb')}.
allow_redirects	→	(bool) — Whether to follow redirects (default is True).
proxies	→	(dict) To route the request through a proxy.
stream	→	(bool) — If True, doesn't download the response immediately.
verify	→	(bool or str) SSL cert verification. Set to False to skip (not recommended).
cert	→	(str or tuple) — Client-side SSL certs, if required.

Example 1, Sending Form Data

```python
import requests

payload = {'username': 'user', 'password': 'pass'}
response = requests.post('https://httpbin.org/post', data=payload)
print(response.text)
```

Example 2, Sending JSON Data

```python
import requests

json_data = {'id': 101, 'name': 'John'}
response = requests.post('https://httpbin.org/post', json= json_data)
print(response.json())
```

Uploading a File

Example 3

```python
import requests

file = open('myImage.jpg', 'rb')

data = {'file': file }
response = requests.post('https://httpbin.org/post', files = data)
print(response.text)
```

PUT() Requests

- Replaces the entire resource with new data.
- Often used when you know the **full structure** of the resource.

Example

```python
import requests

url = "https://api.example.com/user/123"
data = {"name": "Alice", "email": "alice@example.com"}
response = requests.put(url = url, json = data)
print(response.status_code)
```

PATCH() Requests

- Updates **only part** of the resource.
- Useful when you want to **change one or two fields**.

Example

```python
import requests
url = "https://api.example.com/user/123"
data = {"email": "newemail@example.com"}
response = requests.patch(url = url, json = data)
print(response.status_code)
```

DELETE() Requests

- Deletes the specified resource from the server.
- Usually doesn't require a body.

Example

</> Python

```
import requests

url = "https://api.example.com/user/123"
response = requests.delete( url )
print(response.status_code)
```

Note

PUT, PATCH, and DELETE methods accept the same arguments as POST and GET, such as **headers**, **params**, **data**, **json**, **auth**, and **timeout**. The difference lies in the type of action each method performs on the server.

Chapter 17

JSON and PICKLE

(Serializing and Deserializing Data)

After you have studied this chapter, you should be able to:

- Understand the concept of serialization
- Define deserialization and its role in data storage
- Recognize the importance of JSON for data exchange
- Serialize data into JSON format
- Deserialize JSON back into Python objects
- Write data to a file using Pickle
- Read and load data from Pickle files

JSON

The json module in Python plays a crucial role in **data exchange**, especially between systems or applications. It allows for:

- **Encoding (serialization)**: Converting Python objects into JSON-formatted strings.
- **Decoding (deserialization)**: Converting JSON-formatted strings back into Python objects.

JSON is commonly used when:

- Receiving data from web servers (APIs).
- Communicating with applications written in other languages (e.g., JavaScript, Java, PHP).
- Storing lightweight configuration files or settings.
- Persisting structured data in a human-readable format.

Deep

JSON data is structured as key-value pairs, much like Python dictionaries.
{ key : value }

Why Use JSON?

- Supports structured data like objects, arrays, numbers, strings, booleans, and null.
- Easy to read and write for both humans and machines.
- Lightweight format with small size — great for transmitting over the web.
- Language-independent but supported in almost every programming language.
- Fast parsing and generation.
- Ideal for RESTful APIs.
- Easily integrates with HTTP requests and responses.

Common JSON Methods

Method	Description
json.dump()	Serialize Python object and write to file
json.dumps()	Serialize Python object to JSON string
json.load()	Deserialize JSON content from a file
json.loads()	Deserialize JSON string to Python object

Encoding (Serialization)

dump() **and** dumps()

Common Parameters

Parameter	Type	Description	Example
obj	Any	The Python object to serialize (e.g., dict, list). Required.	json.dumps({"name": "John"})
fp	File object	File-like object with a .write() method where the output is written. Used only in json.dump().	json.dump(data, open("file.json", "w"))
skipkeys	bool	If True, skips non-string dictionary keys instead of raising a TypeError.	skipkeys=True
ensure_ascii	bool	If True, escapes non-ASCII characters using \uXXXX sequences.	ensure_ascii=False
check_circular	bool	If False, disables circular reference checks. Defaults to True.	check_circular=True
allow_nan	bool	If True, allows NaN, Infinity, and -Infinity. Defaults to True.	allow_nan=True
cls	Class	A custom JSONEncoder subclass for custom serialization.	cls=CustomEncoder
indent	int or str	When None, output is compact; an int provides spacing; a str (like "\t") allows custom indent characters.	indent=4 , indent="\t"
separators	tuple	Controls how items are separated: (item_separator, key_separator). Defaults to (', ', ': ').	separators=(',', ':')
default	Function	A function called for objects that can't be serialized by default.	default=str
sort_keys	bool	If True, the output will be sorted by dictionary keys.	sort_keys=True

json.dump( )

```python
import json

data = {
    "firstname" : "George",
    "lastname" : "Wood",
    "country" :  "Canada",
    "age" : 25,
    "id" : 68392
}

with open("data.json", "w") as file:
    json.dump(data, file)
```

- The code above saves a file named data.json that contains JSON-formatted data.
- JSON files use the .json file extension

Deep

Reading and writing files with open() were covered in the previous chapter under File Handling and Byte Operations.

Example 2

```python
import json

profile = {"name" : "Bob", "email" : "bob@gmail.com", "profession" :  "Data Scientist"}

fileObj = open("profile.json", "w")

json.dump( profile, fileObj)
```

json.dumps(obj)

```python
import json

student = {
   "name" : "John",
    "college" :  "Harvard",
    "year" : 2,
    "course" : "Computer Science"
}

#serialize string to JSON
jsonString =  json.dumps(student)

print( jsonString )
```

```
#Output
{"name": "John", "college": "Harvard", "year": 2, "course": "Computer Science"}
```

Key Points about json.dumps():

- json.dumps() takes a Python object (commonly a dictionary) as a required argument.
- It serializes (encodes) the object into a JSON-formatted string.
- The resulting JSON string can then be sent over a network, written to a file, or passed to other systems or languages.
- It ensures the data is converted into a text format that complies with the JSON standard.
- Supports optional parameters such as:
    - **indent** – to pretty-print the output with indentation.
    - **separators** – to control item and key-value separators.
    - **sort_keys** – to sort dictionary keys in the output.

📌 It is the inverse of json.loads(), which is used to decode JSON strings back into Python objects.

📌 It cannot serialize all Python objects (e.g., sets, bytes, or custom objects) unless you provide a default serializer function.

Decoding (Deserialization)

load() and loads()

Common Parameters

Parameter	Type	Description	Example
fp	File object	A file-like object containing a JSON document.	json.load(open("data.json"))
s	str	JSON string to decode.	json.loads('{"name": "Alice"}')
cls	Class	Custom JSONDecoder subclass.	cls=MyDecoder
object_hook	function	Custom function to convert dicts into custom objects.	object_hook=my_converter
parse_float	function	Custom function to parse float values (e.g., to use Decimal).	parse_float=Decimal
parse_int	function	Custom function to parse integer values.	parse_int=lambda x: int(x) * 2
parse_constant	function	Handles constants like NaN, Infinity, and -Infinity.	parse_constant=my_handler
object_pairs_hook	function	Similar to object_hook but called with a list of key-value pairs.	object_pairs_hook=OrderedDict
strict	bool	If False, allows control characters in strings. Defaults to True.	strict = False

json.load( )

Example 1

```
</> Python
import json

file =  open("data.json")

#deserialize JSON String
json_string = json.load( file)
print( json_string )
```

```
#Output
{'firstname': 'Alice', 'lastname': 'Wood', 'country': 'Canada', 'age': 25, 'id': 68392}
```

Example 2

```
</> Python
import json

#deserialize JSON String
with open("profile.json") as file:
    json_string = json.load( file )

print( json_string )
```

```
#Output
{'name': 'Bob', 'email': 'bob@gmail.com', 'profession': 'Data Scientist'}
```

json.loads( )

```
</> Python
import json

json_string = '{"name": "box", "color": "red", "size": 10 }'
decoded = json.loads( json_string )
print( decoded )
```

```
#Output
{'name': 'box', 'color': 'red', 'size': 10}
```

Key Points about json.loads() and json.load()

- json.loads() decodes (deserializes) a JSON **string** into a Python object.
- json.load() loads and decodes a JSON **file** (or file-like object) into a Python object.
- The decoded JSON content is returned as native Python types like dict, list, str, int, float, bool, or None.
- The json.load() method is typically used when working with .json files stored on disk.
- json.loads() is best used when you have JSON data in **string format** (e.g., from an API or text stream).
- Both support optional arguments like object_hook, parse_float, cls, etc., for customizing decoding behavior.
- You can use object_hook or object_pairs_hook to convert JSON dictionaries into custom Python objects (e.g., namedtuples, classes, etc.).
- strict=False (optional) allows invalid escape characters in the input (e.g., unescaped control characters).
- If the JSON data is malformed, a json.JSONDecodeError will be raised — you should wrap calls in try...except.

Pickle

The pickle module in Python is used for serializing and deserializing Python objects. While it serves a similar purpose to the json module in that both can save and load data, pickle is specific to Python and can handle a much wider range of Python objects, not just dictionaries or key-value pairs.

Unlike JSON (which is a text-based format readable across many programming languages), pickle saves data in a binary format. This makes it more powerful for internal use in Python applications, but also less portable.

Key Features of pickle

✏ Allows you to serialize (pickle) and deserialize (unpickle) complex Python objects (e.g., classes, functions, sets, custom objects).

✏ Offers fast and efficient storage and retrieval of Python objects.

✏ Supports almost all Python data types, including those that JSON cannot handle like tuples, sets, and class instances.

✏ Stores data in a **.pkl** or **.pickle** binary file format.

✏ It is Python-specific — data pickled in Python can't be easily read in other languages.

Common Pickle Methods

Method	Description
pickle.dump()	Serializes (pickles) a Python object and writes it to a binary file.
pickle.dumps()	Serializes a Python object and returns it as a byte string.
pickle.load()	Reads a pickled object from a binary file and deserializes it.
pickle.loads()	Deserializes a pickled object from a byte string.
pickle.pickler	A class used to create a custom pickle writer with more control.
pickle.unpickler	A class used to create a custom pickle reader for deserialization.

Writing to a Pickle File (Serializing)

pickle.dump() and pickle.dumps()

Common Parameters

Parameter	Description
obj	The Python object you want to serialize (convert to binary format).
file	A file-like object opened in binary write mode (wb) where the data will be written.
protocol	(Optional) The protocol version to use. 0–5. By default, it uses the highest supported protocol.
fix_imports	If True (default), makes Python 2-to-3 compatible pickles (mainly useful when writing Python 3 pickles that should be readable in Python 2).
buffer_callback	(Optional) For out-of-band buffers (used in advanced scenarios with protocol 5+). Typically not needed unless working with binary data efficiently.

pickle.dump( )

</> Python

```python
import pickle

profile = {
    "name" : "Winifred",
    "profile_id": 205,
    "birthday": "10th April, 1998",
    "email": "wini@gmail.com",
    "favorite" : ["nature", "music", "programming"]
}

with open("profile.pickle", "wb") as file:
    pickle.dump(profile, file)
```

pickle.dumps( )

```python
import pickle

profile = {
    "name" : "Winifred",
    "profile_id": 205,
    "birthday": "10th April, 1998",
    "email": "wini@gmail.com",
    "favorite" : ["nature", "music", "programming"]
}

byte_data = pickle.dumps(profile)
```

Reading from a Pickle File (Deserializing)

pickle.load() and pickle.loads()

Common Parameters

Parameter	Description
file	A file-like object opened in **binary read mode (rb)** containing pickled data.
data	A **bytes-like object** containing pickled data (e.g., from a file, network, etc.)
fix_imports	For Python 2 compatibility. When True, attempts to map old module names to new ones.
encoding	Only used if the pickled data is from Python 2. Common options: 'ASCII', 'latin1', 'bytes'.
errors	Error handling for decoding non-ASCII bytes. Same as in standard text decoding.
buffers	Optional. Sequence of out-of-band buffers if the object uses pickle.PickleBuffer. Used for efficient memory handling in complex objects.

pickle.load( )

</> Python

```
import pickle

file = open("profile.pickle", "rb")
data = pickle.load(file)
name = data.get('name')
birthday = data.get('birthday')
email = data.get('email')
favorites = data.get('favorite')

print(name)
print(birthday)
print(email)
print(favorites)
```

```
#Output
Winifred
10th April, 1998
wini@gmail.com
['nature', 'music', 'programming']
```

</> **Note**

The profile.pickle file was created using pickle.dump(). To view its contents, refer to the explanation of pickle.dump().

pickle.loads( )

```python
import pickle
from pathlib import Path

filebytes = Path('profile.pickle').read_bytes()

data = pickle.loads(filebytes)

name = data.get('name')
id = data.get('profile_id')
birthday = data.get('birthday')
email = data.get('email')
favorites = data.get('favorite')


print(name)
print(id)
print(birthday)
print(email)
print(favorites)
```

```
#Output
Winifred
205
10th April, 1998
wini@gmail.com
['nature', 'music', 'programming']
```

Chapter 18

SQLite3

After you have studied this chapter, you should be able to:

- Understand what SQLite3 is and its role in database management
- Create and connect to a database file
- Create and use cursors for executing SQL commands
- Perform basic queries on the database
- Create new tables and alter existing ones
- Add records to a database
- Update and delete records from a table
- Fetch and display data from the database
- Understand and use common SQL commands

SQLite3

Data is a crucial part of any software application. It often works hand in hand with the logic of a program, which makes it essential to store data persistently for continued use and reference. This process goes beyond just saving data—it involves organizing it in a structured manner and managing it efficiently. This is where database systems come into play.

Almost every application that processes or stores data utilizes a Database Management System (DBMS)—either built into the app or connected externally. In Python, several database modules are available to work with both client-server databases and standalone (embedded) databases.

Examples of Python-compatible database modules include:

- sqlite3 (built-in, embedded)
- mysql-connector-python (for MySQL)
- psycopg2 (for PostgreSQL)
- sqlalchemy (ORM that supports multiple DBMS)
- pyodbc (for Microsoft SQL Server and others)

Some database modules require external server software (e.g., MySQL, PostgreSQL), while others like sqlite3 work without any additional dependencies.

What is SQLite3?

sqlite3 is a lightweight, embedded database engine included in the Python Standard Library. It doesn't require a separate server or installation. Data is stored in a local file with the **.db** or **.sqlite** extension, making it an ideal choice for desktop, mobile, or embedded applications where ease of use and simplicity are a priority.

Key Featured of SQLite3?

- No installation required (bundled with Python)
- Cross-platform compatibility
- Lightweight and fast for small to medium datasets
- Great for prototyping and local storage
- SQL-compliant with support for standard SQL syntax

- Integrated with Python via the sqlite3 module
- Data persistence between program executions
- File-based storage (no need for a server)

Deep

Before using a database, it's important to design your data model or structure in advance. This helps ensure efficient data storage and retrieval. See the sample model below for reference.

User

id (Primary Key)	name	followers

Profile

id	likes	comment

SQLite3 Methods

Methods	Description
sqlite3.connect(database)	Connects to a SQLite database file. Creates the file if it doesn't exist.
connection.cursor()	Returns a Cursor object used to execute SQL commands.
cursor.execute(sql, params)	Executes a single SQL statement. Can use placeholders for parameters.
cursor.executemany(sql, seq)	Executes the same SQL statement for a sequence of parameters.
cursor.executescript(script)	Executes multiple SQL statements at once separated by semicolons.
cursor.fetchone()	Fetches the next row of a query result set. Returns a single tuple or None.
cursor.fetchall()	Fetches all (remaining) rows of a query result. Returns a list of tuples.
cursor.fetchmany(size)	Fetches the next set of rows (up to size) from a query result.
connection.commit()	Saves (commits) all changes made in the current transaction.
connection.rollback()	Rolls back the current transaction.
cursor.close()	Closes the cursor object.
connection.close()	Closes the connection to the database.

sqlite3.connect(':memory:')	Creates a temporary in-memory database instead of a file.
sqlite3.Row	A row factory that enables name-based access to columns (like a dictionary).
sqlite3.version	Returns the version of the sqlite3 module.
sqlite3.sqlite_version	Returns the version of the SQLite engine itself.

Creating and Connecting to a SQLite Database File

Before data can be stored or accessed, it must first be saved in a database file. This file acts as the data source for your application. Losing the database file means losing the stored data, so it's crucial to keep it in a secure location—ideally within your application folder or a protected storage path.

Syntax

```
import sqlite3

object = sqlite3.connect("path/to/db_file")
```

Example,

```python
import sqlite3

conn = sqlite3.connect("my_database.db")
```

Key Points

- The above code creates a new SQLite database file if it doesn't already exist.
- If the specified file already exists, the code connects to the existing database.
- The my_database.db file stores the database in a binary format, including tables, records, and other objects.

Creating a Cursor

Once you've successfully connected to a database file, the next step is to create a **cursor**. A cursor is used to execute SQL commands and interact with the database—such as inserting, retrieving, updating, and deleting records

Syntax

```
object = sqlObject.cursor()
```

Example,

</> Python

```python
import sqlite3

conn = sqlite3.connect("datafile.db")
cursor = conn.cursor()
```

Key Points

- A cursor is an object created from the database connection.
- It acts as a control structure that allows you to execute SQL commands and fetch data from the result set.
- A cursor should be closed (optional but recommended) when no longer needed, using cursor.close().
- You can create multiple cursors from the same connection if needed.

Deep

After making changes to a table or records in the database, it's important to save those changes and properly close the database connection. This is done using connection.commit() to save the changes and connection.close() to close the connection to the database.

Querying in SQLite3

To interact with a SQLite3 database, you must write SQL (Structured Query Language) statements. These statements instruct the database on how to store, update, retrieve, or delete data. They function much like keywords in Python—predefined commands that SQLite understands and executes.

Syntax

```
cursorObject.execute("sql statement", param)
or
cursorObject.executemany("sql statement", [param] )
or
cursorObject.executescript( script )
```

Creating a Table

A database table is similar to a grid consisting of rows and columns. Before data can be stored, a table must be created with a unique name and structured columns, each having its own data type.

Syntax

```
CREATE TABLE IF NOT EXISTS table_name (
   column_name1 DATATYPE PRIMARY KEY,
   column_name2 DATATYPE,
   column_name3 DATATYPE NOT NULL
);
```

Key Points

- IF NOT EXISTS is optional but helps prevent errors if the table already exists.
- table_name can be in any case format—uppercase, lowercase, camelCase, or Capitalized.
- The column definitions must be enclosed within parentheses ().
- column_name can be any valid string identifier. It should describe the type of data the column will hold.
- Data types in SQLite3 include:
    - **INTEGER** → Whole numbers
    - **TEXT** → Strings of any length
    - **VARCHAR(n)** → Strings with a maximum length n
    - **REAL** → Floating-point numbers
    - **BLOB** → Binary Large Objects (e.g., images, audio, files)
    - **BOOLEAN** → True/False (stored as 0/1 internally)
    - **DATE** → Date values
    - **DATETIME** → Date and time values
- PRIMARY KEY is optional but helps uniquely identify each record.
- **NOT NULL** means that a column must contain a value and cannot be left empty.
- Each column definition ends with a comma, except the last one.

Example: Creating a Student Table

</> Python

```
import sqlite3

conn = sqlite3.connect("datafile.db")
cursor = conn.cursor()

cursor.execute('''
        CREATE TABLE IF NOT EXISTS student (
            id INTEGER PRIMARY KEY,
            firstname VARCHAR(100),
            lastname VARCHAR(100),
            year INTEGER NOT NULL,
            department VARCHAR(100),
            course VARCHAR(100)
        );
    ''')
```

Altering Tables

As your application grows, you might need to make changes to your database structure—such as adding new columns, renaming existing ones, or changing column data types. SQLite provides the **ALTER TABLE** command to make such modifications without recreating the entire table.

Syntax

```
#--Add a new column
ALTER TABLE table_name ADD COLUMN column_name DATA_TYPE;

#--Rename an existing table
ALTER TABLE old_table_name RENAME TO new_table_name;

#--Rename a column (SQLite 3.25.0+)
ALTER TABLE table_name RENAME COLUMN old_column_name TO new_column_name;
```

Key Points

- ALTER TABLE is used to modify the structure of an existing table.
- You can add columns, rename tables, and rename columns.
- You cannot drop a column directly in SQLite.
- When adding a column, it must have a default value or allow NULL unless values are provided for existing rows.
- Column types must be valid SQLite data types (e.g., TEXT, INTEGER, REAL, BLOB, NUMERIC).

🚀 Deep

DROP TABLE table_name;
Effect: Deletes the entire table including its structure and data.

Example 1, Add a new column

```python
import sqlite3

conn = sqlite3.connect("datafile.db")
cursor = conn.cursor()

cursor.execute(" ALTER TABLE student ADD COLUMN email  TEXT ")
```

📌 This adds a new column called **email** to the student table.

Example 2, Rename a table

```python
import sqlite3

conn = sqlite3.connect("datafile.db")
cursor = conn.cursor()

cursor.execute(" ALTER TABLE student RENAME TO student_profile ")
```

📌 This renames the **student** table to **student_profile**.

Example 3, Rename a column

```python
import sqlite3

conn = sqlite3.connect("datafile.db")
cursor = conn.cursor()

cursor.execute(" ALTER TABLE student RENAME COLUMN lastname  TO  surname ")
```

📌 This changes the column name **lastname** to **surname**.

Adding Records to a Database

After creating the table(s), you can begin inserting records. The **INSERT INTO** statement specifies the target table and the corresponding columns where values should be stored. Each value must match the data type and order of the specified columns. If a value is not provided for a column, NULL is automatically inserted—unless the column has a NOT NULL constraint.

Syntax

```
INSERT INTO table_name (column1, column2, ...) VALUES (value1, value2, ...);
```

Using Parameters(recommended)

```
cursor.execute("INSERT INTO table_name (column1, column2) VALUES (?, ?)", (value1, value2))
```

Example,

```python
import sqlite3

conn = sqlite3.connect("datafile.db")
cursor = conn.cursor()
cursor.execute(
'''INSERT INTO student (id, firstname, lastname, year, department, course)
VALUES (?, ?, ?, ?, ?, ?)''',
 (205, "Alice", "Wood", 3, "Computing", "Computer Science" )
)

cursor.execute(
'''INSERT INTO student (id, firstname, lastname, year, department, course)
VALUES (?, ?, ?, ?, ?, ?)''',
 (206, "John", "Crack", 1, "Health", "Nursing" ))
conn.commit()
conn.close()
```

Updating Records in SQLite

If an existing record in the database needs to be changed, the **UPDATE** statement is used. You specify the table name, the column(s) to update, the new values, and a condition (WHERE) to select which rows should be updated.

Syntax

```
UPDATE table_name
SET column1 = new_value1, column2 = new_value2
WHERE condition;
```

Example,

```python
import sqlite3

conn = sqlite3.connect("datafile.db")
cursor = conn.cursor()

cursor.execute(
    '''
    UPDATE student SET year = ?  WHERE firstname = ?
    ''',
    ( 4, "John")                #updates year to 4, for student with firstname = "John"
)

cursor.execute(
    '''
    UPDATE student SET firstname = ?, lastname =? WHERE id = ?
    ''',
    ("Marrie","Bridge", 205)     #updates firstname and lastname to Marrie and Bridge
)

conn.commit()      # Save changes
conn.close()
```

Deleting Records from the Database

Sometimes, records stored in a database may contain errors, become outdated, or no longer be relevant to the application. SQL provides a simple and powerful command to delete such records from a table.

Syntax

```
DELETE FROM table_name;          #Empties the table (removes all rows)

DELETE FROM table_name WHERE condition;
```

Example,

```python
import sqlite3

conn = sqlite3.connect("datafile.db")
cursor = conn.cursor()

# Delete a student record with index 101
cursor.execute("DELETE FROM student WHERE index = ?", (206,))

# Delete a student record with lastname Crack
cursor.execute("DELETE FROM student WHERE lastname = ?", ("Crack",))

# Save changes
conn.commit()
conn.close()
```

Key Points:

- DELETE FROM specifies the table where the record should be removed.
- WHERE ensures only matching rows are deleted.
- Omitting WHERE deletes **all** rows from the table - use with caution.
- Always commit your changes using conn.commit() after deleting records.

Fetching Data from a Database

Fetching data refers to retrieving records stored in a database for use within a program. This process is essential, as most applications rely on stored data for displaying information, applying configurations, providing feedback, and general application logic. Depending on the requirement, you can retrieve all records at once, a specified number of records, or just a single record.

Syntax

```
records = cursor.fetchall()          # Fetches all rows from the last executed query
records = cursor.fetchmany(size)     # Fetches the next 'size' number of rows
record  = cursor.fetchone()          # Fetches the next single row
```

Key Points

- These methods are used after executing a **SELECT** query with cursor.execute().
- fetchall() retrieves all results at once and stores them in a list of tuples.
- fetchmany(size) retrieves the next set of rows (as specified by size) and is memory-efficient for large datasets.
- fetchone() returns the next single row and is useful when expecting only one result or reading results one at a time.
- If no more rows are available, fetchone() and fetchmany() return None and an empty list respectively.

SQL Commands for Fetching Records

SQL provides several commands for retrieving data from a database. These commands fall under the **Data Query Language (DQL)** category and are mainly used with the **SELECT** statement. Below are grouped and described commands commonly used for fetching records:

① Basic SELECT Commands

Commands	Description
SELECT * FROM table_name;	Fetches all columns and rows from the specified table.
SELECT column1, column2 FROM table_name;	Fetches specific columns from the table.
SELECT DISTINCT column FROM table_name;	Fetches unique (non-duplicate) values from a column.

Example 1, Fetches all columns and rows from the specified table.

</> Python

```python
import sqlite3

conn = sqlite3.connect("myfile.db")
cursor = conn.cursor()
cursor.execute("SELECT * FROM student ")
records  = cursor.fetchall()
print(records)
```

```
#Output
[(205, 'Marrie', 'Bridge', 2, 'Health', 'Optometry'), (206, 'John', 'Crack', 1, 'Health', 'Nursing'), (207, 'Bob', 'Orwell', 1, 'Computing', 'Cybersecurity'), (208, 'Derrick', 'Rich', 4, 'Engineering', 'Electrical'), (209, 'Winifred', 'Smith', 1, 'Engineering', 'Aerospace'), (301, 'Williams', 'White', 3, 'Computing', 'Computer Science'), (303, 'Kelvin', 'Wood', 3, 'Health', 'Nursing')]
```

Deep

The results returned from an SQL query in Python are typically presented as a list of tuples. While these results can be used for various purposes in your program, they may not be visually appealing when printed directly. To improve readability and present the data in a clean, table-like format, you can use the tabulate module.
You can install it using the command: pip install tabulate

Example 2, Tabulated results with the *tabulate module*

```python
import sqlite3
from tabulate import tabulate

conn = sqlite3.connect("myfile.db")
cursor = conn.cursor()
cursor.execute("SELECT * FROM student ")
records  = cursor.fetchall()

#retrieving individual records
print(records[1])
print(records[2][1])

#tabulating the results
header = ["id", "+
", "lastname", "year", "department", "course"]
print(tabulate( records, headers=header, tablefmt="grid") )
```

#Output

(206, 'John', 'Crack', 1, 'Health', 'Nursing')
Bob

id	firstname	lastname	year	department	course
205	Marrie	Bridge	2	Health	Optometry
206	John	Crack	1	Health	Nursing
207	Bob	Orwell	1	Computing	Cybersecurity
208	Derrick	Rich	4	Engineering	Electrical
209	Winifred	Smith	1	Engineering	Aerospace
301	Williams	White	3	Computing	Computer Science
303	Kelvin	Wood	3	Health	Nursing

Example 3, Fetches specific columns from the table.

```
</> Python
import sqlite3
from tabulate import tabulate

conn = sqlite3.connect("myfile.db")
cursor = conn.cursor()

cursor.execute("SELECT firstname, lastname, course FROM student ")
records  = cursor.fetchall()

header = ["id", "firstname", "lastname", "year", "department", "course"]
print(tabulate( records, headers=header, tablefmt="grid") )
```

#Output

firstname	lastname	course
Marrie	Bridge	Optometry
John	Crack	Nursing
Bob	Orwell	Cybersecurity
Derrick	Rich	Electrical
Winifred	Smith	Aerospace
Williams	White	Computer Science
Kelvin	Wood	Nursing

② SELECT with Conditions (Filtering Data)

Commands	Description
SELECT * FROM table_name WHERE condition;	Fetches rows that meet a specified condition.
SELECT * FROM table_name WHERE column = value;	Fetches rows where the column matches a value.

SELECT * FROM table_name WHERE column LIKE pattern;	Fetches rows using pattern matching (e.g., 'A%' for names starting with 'A').
SELECT * FROM table_name WHERE column IN (val1, val2);	Fetches rows where column matches any value in a list.
SELECT * FROM table_name WHERE column BETWEEN val1 AND val2;	Fetches rows with values within a range.

Example 1, Fetches rows that meet a specified condition.

</> Python

```
cursor.execute("SELECT * FROM student WHERE  id >= ? ", (300, ))
```

#Output

id	firstname	lastname	year	department	course
301	Williams	White	3	Computing	Computer Science
303	Kelvin	Wood	3	Health	Nursing

Example 2, Fetches all columns and rows from the specified table.

</> Python

```
cursor.execute("SELECT * FROM student WHERE  department =  ? ", ('Engineering', ) )
```

#Output

id	firstname	lastname	year	department	course
208	Derrick	Rich	4	Engineering	Electrical
209	Winifred	Smith	1	Engineering	Aerospace

Example 3, Fetches rows using pattern matching.

```python
cursor.execute("SELECT * FROM student WHERE  course  LIKE  ?  ", ('C%', ) )
```

#Output

id	firstname	lastname	year	department	course
207	Bob	Orwell	1	Computing	Cybersecurity
301	Williams	White	3	Computing	Computer Science

Example 4, Fetches rows where column matches any value in a list.

```python
cursor.execute("SELECT * FROM student WHERE  year  IN  (?, ?) ", (2, 4))
```

#Output

id	firstname	lastname	year	department	course
205	Marrie	Bridge	2	Health	Optometry
208	Derrick	Rich	4	Engineering	Electrical

③ SELECT with Sorting and Limiting

Commands	Description
SELECT * FROM table_name ORDER BY column ASC;	Fetches data sorted by a column in ascending order.
SELECT * FROM table_name ORDER BY column DESC;	Fetches data sorted by a column in descending order.

SELECT * FROM table_name LIMIT number;	Limits the number of rows returned. Useful for pagination or previewing results.

Example 1, Fetches rows where column matches any value in a list.

</> **Python**

```
cursor.execute("SELECT * FROM student ORDER BY  id  DESC  ")
```

#Output

id	firstname	lastname	year	department	course
303	Kelvin	Wood	3	Health	Nursing
301	Williams	White	3	Computing	Computer Science
209	Winifred	Smith	1	Engineering	Aerospace
208	Derrick	Rich	4	Engineering	Electrical
207	Bob	Orwell	1	Computing	Cybersecurity
206	John	Crack	1	Health	Nursing
205	Marrie	Bridge	2	Health	Optometry

Note

In the examples above, we used cursor.execute() both with and without parameters. It can be tricky when passing a single string as a parameter. If a comma (,) is not included at the end of the string, it may raise an error because Python does not recognize it as a tuple.

```
cursor.execute("SELECT * FROM student WHERE lastname = ?", ("Smith",))
```

Note the comma after "Smith" — without it, the value is treated as a string, not a tuple, which can lead to unexpected behavior or errors.

④ SELECT with Aggregates (Summarizing Data)

Commands	Description
SELECT COUNT(*) FROM table_name;	Returns the total number of rows.
SELECT MAX(column) FROM table_name;	Returns the maximum value in a column.
SELECT MIN(column) FROM table_name;	Returns the minimum value in a column.
SELECT AVG(column) FROM table_name;	Returns the average value of a column.
SELECT SUM(column) FROM table_name;	Returns the sum of a numeric column.

</> Python

```python
cursor.execute("SELECT COUNT(*) FROM student ")
print(f"Count: {cursor.fetchall()[0][0]}")

cursor.execute("SELECT MIN( year ) FROM student ")
print(f"Minimum Year: {cursor.fetchall()[0][0]}")

cursor.execute("SELECT MAX( year ) FROM student ")
print(f"Maximum Year: {cursor.fetchall()[0][0]}")

cursor.execute("SELECT SUM( id ) FROM student ")
print(f"Total ID: {cursor.fetchall()[0][0]}")

cursor.execute("SELECT AVG( id ) FROM student ")
print(f"Average: {cursor.fetchall()[0][0]}")
```

#Output

```
Count: 7
Minimum Year: 1
Maximum Year: 4
Total ID: 1639
Average: 234.14285714285714
```

⑤ SELECT with Grouping (Grouped Data Analysis)

Commands	Description
SELECT column, COUNT(*) FROM table_name GROUP BY column;	Groups records and applies aggregate functions.
SELECT column, COUNT(*) FROM table_name GROUP BY column HAVING COUNT(*) > 1;	Filters groups using aggregate condition (like WHERE but for groups).

Example 1, Groups records and applies aggregate functions.

</> Python

```
cursor.execute("SELECT  COUNT(*), department FROM student GROUP BY department" )
```

#Output

COUNT(*)	department
2	Computing
2	Engineering
3	Health

Chapter 19

Text-to-Speech (pyttsx3)

After you have studied this chapter, you should be able to:

- Understand what pyttsx3 is and its use for text-to-speech conversion
- Utilize text-to-speech methods to convert text into spoken words
- Start and control the pyttsx3 speech engine
- Get and set properties such as voice, rate, and volume
- Save spoken text as an audio file

Text to Speech (pyttsx3)

Text-to-speech (TTS) has become an essential feature in mobile, web, and desktop applications, offering accessibility, user convenience, and automation. This functionality is based on the concept of converting written text into spoken audio. Its counterpart, speech-to-text, converts spoken words into written text and typically relies on machine learning or AI-powered models.

In Python, **pyttsx3** is a popular offline module used for text-to-speech conversion. Unlike cloud-based solutions, pyttsx3 works without an internet connection, making it ideal for local applications.

Installation

The pyttsx3 module is not included in the standard Python library. You can install it via pip:

```
$ pip install pyttsx3
```

Why Use Text-to-Speech in Applications

- Enhances accessibility for visually impaired users.
- Improves user interaction through voice-enabled responses.
- Useful in virtual assistants and chatbots.
- Can generate audio for learning tools or audiobooks.
- Allows dynamic content to be voiced without pre-recorded audio.
- Supports multiple voices and adjustable speech rate for customization.
- Works offline, ensuring privacy and speed in local applications.

Text-to-Speech Methods

Methods	Description
pyttsx3.speak(text)	Method to queue text to be spoken
pyttsx3.init()	Function used to initialize the TTS engine
pyttsx3.engine	Controls voice, speech rate, volume, and queues text for speaking
pyttsx3.driver	Manages speech synthesis under the hood (e.g., 'sapi5', 'espeak', 'nsss')
pyttsx3.weakref	Used internally in pyttsx3 for memory management without affecting object lifecycle

pyttsx3.speak(text)

pyttsx3.speak(text) takes the provided text and converts it into spoken audio using the system's speech engine.

```python
import pyttsx3 as sp

text = "Hello Pythonist!, do you want some coffee?"
speech = sp.speak(text)
```

```
#Output
🎶
```

Note

The above code generates either a male or female voice that reads the text aloud when executed. The speech can be heard through your device's speakers.

pyttsx3.init()

The init() function initializes the text-to-speech engine and returns an engine object. This object can be used not only to generate speech from text, but also to customize the speech experience—such as changing the voice, adjusting the pitch and volume, saving audio to a file, and more.

The init() Methods

Methods	Description
connect()	Registers a callback function for specific engine events like started-utterance
disconnect()	Unregisters a callback from the event loop
endLoop()	Ends the event loop started by startLoop()
getProperty()	Gets properties such as 'rate', 'volume', or 'voice'
isBusy()	Returns True if the engine is still processing speech
iterate()	Yields the next event (used internally in async speech synthesis)
proxy()	Internal use for proxying engine method calls (less commonly used directly)
runAndWait()	Starts speech processing and waits for all queued commands to finish
save_to_file()	Saves spoken text to an audio file (e.g., .mp3 or .wav)
say()	Queues text to be spoken
setProperty()	Sets speech properties like 'rate', 'volume', or 'voice'
startLoop()	Starts a non-blocking event loop for speech synthesis
stop()	Stops current speech and clears the queue

say(**text**)

</> Python

```
import pyttsx3 as sp

engine = sp.init()
text = "There is nothing much better than coding in peace"
engine.say(text= text)
```

```
print(engine.isBusy())
engine.runAndWait()
```

```
#Output
True
🎶
```

📌 **runAndWait()** → Runs the speech engine until all commands are processed.

📌 **isBusy()** → Returns True if the engine is currently speaking.

Getting Properties

The getProperty() method in pyttsx3 allows you to access different attributes of the speech engine. These include voice settings, speech rate, and volume, among others.

① Voices

getProperty(**"voices"**)

</> Python

```
import pyttsx3 as sp

engine = sp.init()
voices = engine.getProperty("voices")
print(voices)

print(f"first_voice_name = {voices[0].name}")
print(f"second_voice_name = {voices[1].name}")
print(f"first_voice_id = {voices[0].id}")
print(f"second_voice_id = {voices[1].id}")
```

```
#Output
[<pyttsx3.voice.Voice object at 0x000001E2500F67B0>, <pyttsx3.voice.Voice object at 0x000001E25007F750>]

first_voice_name = Microsoft David Desktop - English (United States)

second_voice_name = Microsoft Zira Desktop - English (United States)

first_voice_id =
HKEY_LOCAL_MACHINE\SOFTWARE\Microsoft\Speech\Voices\Tokens\TTS_MS_EN-
US_DAVID_11.0

second_voice_id =
HKEY_LOCAL_MACHINE\SOFTWARE\Microsoft\Speech\Voices\Tokens\TTS_MS_EN-
US_ZIRA_11.0
```

This returns a list of available voice objects on the system. Each voice has properties such as id, name, languages, and gender. On Windows, pyttsx3 typically comes with two default voices: one male and one female (e.g., Microsoft David and Microsoft Zira).

② Volume

getProperty("volume")

```
</> Python
import pyttsx3 as sp

engine = sp.init()
volume = engine.getProperty("volume")
print(f" volume level :{volume}")
```

```
#Output
volume level :1.0
```

This returns the current volume level of the speech engine. Volume is a floating-point number between 0.0 (mute) and 1.0 (maximum).

③ Rate

getProperty(**"rate"**)

```python
import pyttsx3 as sp

engine = sp.init()
rate = engine.getProperty("rate")
print(f" rate :{rate}")
```

```
#Output
rate :200
```

This returns the current speech rate (words per minute). The default value typically ranges between 150 and 200.

Setting Properties

After retrieving the engine's properties using getProperty(), you can customize them using engine.**setProperty(**name, value**)**

setProperty(**name, value**)

```python
import pyttsx3 as sp


engine = sp.init()

# Set voice
voices = engine.getProperty("voices")
engine.setProperty("voice", voices[1].id)
```

```
# Set volume
engine.setProperty("volume", 0.9)

# Set rate
engine.setProperty("rate", 180)

# Speak
engine.say("Hello, this is a customized voice!")
engine.runAndWait()
```

```
#Output
🎶
```

Saving Speech to an Audio File

pyttsx3 allows you to convert text to speech and save the spoken audio directly to a file. This is useful for generating voice messages, narrations, or offline audio files from written content.

Supported Audio Formats

pyttsx3 typically supports **WAV** format by default, as it uses the underlying text-to-speech engine of the system (such as SAPI5 on Windows). Other formats like **MP3** or **OGG** are not natively supported directly by pyttsx3. If you need other formats, consider saving as .wav and converting later using external libraries like **pydub** or **ffmpeg**.

save_to_file(**text, filename**)

</> Python

```
import pyttsx3

engine = pyttsx3.init()

text = "Heya! Hope you're loving it. Keep Pythonizing."

# Save speech to WAV audio file
engine.save_to_file( text, "output.wav")

engine.runAndWait()
```

📌 Always call engine.runAndWait() after save_to_file() to ensure the audio is properly written.

Chapter 20

QR Code

After you have studied this chapter, you should be able to:

- Understand what a QR code is and how it functions
- Identify the benefits and applications of QR codes
- Generate QR codes using Python
- Customize QR codes with colors and styles

QR Code

A **QR Code (Quick Response Code)** is a type of matrix barcode (or two-dimensional barcode) that stores information as a pattern of black-and-white squares. While the pattern may look random, it is a structured visual code that can hold various types of data such as:

- URLs or website links
- Text messages
- Contact details (vCards)
- Wi-Fi login credentials
- Emails and phone numbers
- Calendar events
- Geolocation (latitude and longitude)
- App download links
- Product or payment information

This information can be quickly retrieved by scanning the QR Code using a smartphone camera, QR scanner, or barcode reader. Python provides a handy library called **qrcode** to easily generate QR codes from custom content.

Installation

```
$ pip install qrcode
```

Why Use QR Codes?

- To embed URLs or web links
- To store and share plain text messages
- For secure authentication (e.g., two-factor authentication codes)
- To share Wi-Fi network credentials without typing
- To store contact information (e.g., name, phone number, email)
- For event invitations or calendar scheduling
- In product packaging for more information or support
- For quick app downloads or installation instructions

The qrcode Methods

Methods	Description
qrcode.make(data)	A shortcut function that takes data (string) and returns a QR Code image. Useful for quick QR code generation.
qrcode.image	Provides different backends for generating image outputs like PIL (Pillow). You can subclass it to use a custom image factory.
qrcode.main	The primary module with user-friendly functions like make() that simplifies creating QR codes with just one line of code.
qrcode.run_example()	A built-in demonstration function that generates a sample QR code when run. Useful for testing and seeing default behavior.
qrcode.base	Contains the core QRCode class used for creating and configuring QR codes. It handles the data input, version, error correction level, box size, and border.
qrcode.compat	Provides compatibility functions between Python 2 and 3. This is mainly used internally and not commonly accessed directly.
qrcode.constants	Holds constants used by the QRCode generator such as error correction levels (e.g., ERROR_CORRECT_L, ERROR_CORRECT_M, ERROR_CORRECT_Q, ERROR_CORRECT_H).
qrcode.exceptions	Defines custom exceptions used in the QR code process. Helps catch specific QR code generation-related errors.
qrcode.util	Contains utility functions used internally like matrix creation, bit buffer handling, and version checks. Typically not used directly by most users.

qrcode.make()

The make() method is a high-level convenience function provided by the qrcode module. It is used to quickly generate a QR code from simple data such as a string, URL, or message. This method is ideal when you don't need to customize the QR code's appearance or settings extensively. It automatically chooses the best-fit version and error correction level for the data.

Parameters

data	→	The main content (text, URL, etc.) to encode into the QR code. This is a required parameter.
image_factory	→	*(Optional)* A custom image factory used to generate the image. For example, qrcode.image.pil.PilImage (default) or SVG-based factories.

version	→	*(Optional)* Specifies the size/version of the QR code. Ranges from 1 to 40. If not provided, it's auto-calculated.
error_correction	→	*(Optional)* Sets the error correction level. Values can be qrcode.constants.ERROR_CORRECT_L, M, Q, or H.
box_size	→	*(Optional)* The number of pixels for each box of the QR code grid. Affects the image resolution.
border	→	*(Optional)* The thickness of the border (number of boxes thick). Default is 4, which is the minimum required.

Example 1,

</> Python

```
import qrcode

image = qrcode.make("https://google.com")
image.save("mycode.png")
```

#Output

Example 2, Changing size of the box

</> Python

```
import qrcode

image = qrcode.make("Hello, fellow Pythonist - this is my page", box_size= 50)
image.save("mycode.jpg")
```

```
#Output
```

Adding Colors to the Image

Example ,

</> Python

```python
import qrcode

data = "https://www.example.com"

# Create a QRCode object
qr = qrcode.QRCode(
    version=1,
    box_size=10,
    border=5
)

qr.add_data( data )
qr.make(fit=True)

# Generate an image with custom fill and background colors
img = qr.make_image(fill_color="orange", back_color="white")

# Save the image
img.save("myqrcode.jpg")
```

#Output

- fill_color → The color of the actual QR code (default is black).
- back_color → The background color (default is white).
- You can use color names ("red", "green"), hex codes ("#ff5733"), or RGB tuples ((255, 0, 0)).

Chapter 21

Yagmail Python Email

After you have studied this chapter, you should be able to:

- Understand what Yagmail is and its purpose in automating email tasks
- Explore the main features of Yagmail
- Send emails programmatically using Python
- Attach files and include content in emails

Yagmail

Yagmail is a powerful and easy-to-use Python library for sending emails. It simplifies the process of composing and delivering emails by wrapping around Python's built-in smtplib, making it ideal for developers who want to send text, HTML content, or files like PDFs and images without dealing with low-level configurations.

Installation

Yagmail can be installed using pip, just like most other Python libraries

```
$ pip install yagmail
```

Key Features of Yagmail

✏ **Easy Email Sending**
Send emails with a few lines of Python code.

✏ **Rich Content Support**
Supports plain text, HTML, and mixed content emails.

✏ **File Attachments**
Easily attach files like PDFs, images, or documents.

✏ **Multiple Recipients**
Send emails to one or multiple recipients at once.

✏ **Secure Authentication**
Uses keyring for secure credential storage or supports login per session.

✏ **Inline Images**
Embed images directly in the email body.

✏ **Readable Syntax**
Clean, Pythonic syntax that's beginner-friendly.

✏ **SMTP Configuration**
Easily connect to Gmail, Outlook, or any custom SMTP server.

✏️ **Auto-Signature Support**
Supports default signatures and reusable templates.

Yagmail Methods

Methods	Description
yagmail.SMTP	The main class for initializing an email session and sending messages. It wraps around the standard SMTP protocol with added convenience.
yagmail.compat	Handles compatibility between different Python versions to ensure smooth operation.
yagmail.dkim	(DomainKeys Identified Mail) Handles cryptographic email verification for enhanced email authentication.
yagmail.error	Contains custom exceptions and error handling specific to Yagmail operations.
yagmail.headers	Manages and formats email headers such as Subject, From, To, etc.
yagmail.inline	Allows embedding images or other media within the body of the email (inline attachments).
yagmail.logging	Internal logging module used for debugging and tracking email sending activity.
yagmail.message	Constructs the email content including body, subject, attachments, etc.
yagmail.oauth2	Provides OAuth2-based authentication support (especially for Gmail or Google Apps users).
yagmail.password	Manages and retrieves stored passwords securely from the system's keyring or other sources.
yagmail.raw	Sends raw email content directly, used for more customized or low-level email structures.
yagmail.register	Used to register user credentials with Yagmail (especially to use stored credentials via keyring).
yagmail.sender	Handles sending logic for messages, used internally by the SMTP object.
yagmail.utils	Utility functions that support parsing, formatting, and general tasks.
yagmail.validate	Validates email addresses, parameters, and content before sending.

Note

Gmail and other email providers often require enhanced security when accessing email through third-party apps or programs. Instead of using your actual email password, you should enable Two-Factor Authentication (2FA) and generate an App Password specifically for the application.

For Gmail users, you can generate an App Password by visiting:
https://myaccount.google.com/apppasswords
Use this App Password when registering your email with Yagmail instead of your regular email password.

Sending Messages with Yagmail

yagmail.SMTP()

To send emails using Yagmail, you start by creating an instance of the SMTP class:

Parameters

user	→	The email address you want to send from. This can also be an alias registered with Yagmail via yagmail.register().
password	→	(Optional) The password for the email account. If not provided, Yagmail will try to fetch it securely from the system keyring.
host	→	(Optional) The SMTP server host (e.g., smtp.gmail.com). If not specified, Yagmail auto-detects based on the email domain.
port	→	(Optional) The SMTP port number. Default is 587 for TLS, or 465 for SSL.
smtp_starttls	→	(Optional) Set to True or False to enable or disable STARTTLS encryption.
smtp_ssl	→	(Optional) Set to True to connect via SSL. Typically used when port 465 is set.
smtp_set_debuglevel	→	(Optional) Sets debug output level. 0 = silent, 1 = verbose logging.
encoding	→	(Optional) Sets the character encoding. Default is 'utf-8', which supports international characters.
smtp_skip_login	→	(Optional) If True, skips the SMTP login step. Useful if authentication is not required.

Basic Email Sending

Syntax

```
yag = yagmail.SMTP("username@mail.com", "app_password")

yag.send(
    to = "recipient@mail.com",
    subject = "email subject",
    contents = "your message"
)
```

Other Parameters of the send() Method

In addition to the required fields like **to**, **subject**, and **contents**, the send() method in Yagmail supports several optional parameters to enhance functionality:

- **attachments**: Any – Files to be attached to the email.
- **cc**: Any – Carbon copy recipients.
- **bcc**: Any – Blind carbon copy recipients.
- **preview_only**: bool – If set to True, the email will be printed to the console instead of being sent.
- **headers**: Any – Additional custom headers for the email.
- **prettify_html**: bool – If True, formats HTML content for better readability.
- **message_id**: Any – Custom message ID for the email.
- **group_messages**: bool – Allows grouping of similar messages to reduce duplication.

Example1,

</> Python

```python
import yagmail

yag  = yagmail.SMTP("alice@gmail.com", "ali_xyz")

yag.send(
        to = "john@gmail.com",
        subject = "Greetings",
        contents = "Hello John, how is your morning?"
)
```

Example2,

</> Python

```python
import yagmail

email = "oliviabridge@gmail.com"
password = "gen_pass_from_google"
message = '''
                Hello Irene,
                I just wanted to check up on you.
                Have a blessed day.

                Best regards,
                Olivia Bridge.
                '''
yag  = yagmail.SMTP( email,  password)

yag.send(
        to = "irene@outlook.com",
        subject = "Friends Duty",
        contents = message
)
```

Sending Email With Attachments

Example1 ,

```python
import yagmail

yag  = yagmail.SMTP("bob@gmail.com",  "my_gen_app_pass_google")

image = "pictures/birthday_image.png"
yag.send(
        to = "gloria@gmail.com",
        subject = "Birthday Wishes",
        contents = "Happy Birthday Buddy.!",
        attachements = image
)
```

Example1 , Sending Multiple Files

```python
import yagmail

yag  = yagmail.SMTP("steve@gmail.com",  "pass_google_app_pass")

attach = ["pictures/site.png", "project.pdf", "credentials.docx"]
yag.send(
        to = "director@gmail.com",
        subject = "Agenda",
        contents = "Attached are copies of received documents.",
        attachements = attach
)
```

Sending Email With HTML Content

Example ,

```python
import yagmail

yag = yagmail.SMTP("marrie@gmail.com", "mar_@_r")

html_content = "<h1>Hello</h1><p>This is a <b>HTML</b> email</p>"
yag.send(
    to = "buddy@gmail.com",
    subject = "HTML Message",
    contents = html_content
)
```

Sending Email With Inline Image

Example,

```python
import yagmail

yag = yagmail.SMTP("steve25@gmail.com", "gen_google_app_pass")

yag.send(
    to = "director@gmail.com",
    subject = "Agenda",
    contents = [
        "Hi Boss, check out this image: ",
        yagmail.inline("doc/site_plan.jpg"),
    ]
)
```

Chapter 22

Faker -Generating Fake Data

After you have studied this chapter, you should be able to:

- Understand what the Faker library is
- Recognize the importance of generating fake data for testing
- Use Faker methods to generate various kinds of data (names, emails, addresses, etc.)
- Create realistic dummy data for development and testing purposes

Faker – Generating Fake Data

In programming and software testing, it is often necessary to generate large amounts of sample data. Manually creating this data can be tedious and error-prone. The **faker** module in Python provides a convenient way to generate realistic fake data such as names, email addresses, phone numbers, addresses, dates, CSV data, and much more.

It is especially useful for:

- Testing databases
- Creating mock APIs
- Prototyping applications
- Populating UI elements with realistic-looking data

Installation

To install **Faker**, use the following command:

```
$ pip install faker
```

Why Use Faker?

Using **Faker** offers several advantages during development, testing, and prototyping. Here are some key reasons to use it:

Eases Data Guesswork
No need to manually guess or create fake data — Faker generates it instantly.

Provides Templated Data
Faker follows consistent templates for generating realistic data, such as emails, phone numbers, names, etc.

Speeds Up Development
Quickly populate your app or database with mock data to test logic and UI.

Serves as Placeholders
Use generated data as temporary placeholders until real data is available.

Faker Methods

Methods	Description
Faker	Main class used to generate fake data. You typically instantiate this class (Faker()) to access all fake data methods (like .name(), .email())
Factory	Internal utility used to create and manage Faker instances. It handles locale settings and initializes the Faker environment.
Generator	The core engine behind data generation. It manages the actual logic and calls to data providers. Developers rarely use this directly.
config	Contains configuration settings for Faker, such as default locales or seeding options.
decode	Handles decoding operations (e.g., Unicode or encoded content). Typically used internally.
exceptions	Manages all exception classes used in Faker, such as UnsupportedLocaleError.
factory	Similar to Factory, this module assists in creating Faker instances, usually invoked behind the scenes.
generator	The module containing the Generator class. Handles the actual mechanics of how data is randomly selected from providers.
providers	This is where all the fake data providers live — name, address, email, job, etc. You can even add custom providers here.
proxy	Used for dynamic attribute access. Supports lazy loading of certain components.
typing	Contains type hints and annotations to help with static type checking (introduced for better code clarity and IDE support)
utils	A helper module with utility functions like string formatting, randomizers, and helper tools used by providers and core components.

Generating Faker Data

The faker module offers a wide range of pre-defined methods through the Faker() class that can be used to generate various types of fake data — such as names, addresses, emails, jobs, and more. These methods are extremely useful for testing, prototyping, or populating databases with placeholder data.

Some of these methods accept optional parameters to customize the output (e.g., locale, gender, or formatting), while others work perfectly without any arguments.

Below is a list of some commonly used methods available in the Faker() class:

binary	add_provider	administrative_unit	building_number
boolean	date_between	date_time_between_dates	ascii_email
bothify	date_this_century	rgb_color	ascii_free_email
ssn	date_this_decade	domain_word	ascii_safe_email
csv	date_this_month	android_platform_token	bank_country
currency	date_this_year	ascii_company_email	country_code
address	future_datetime	image	company_suffix
century	generator_attrs	image_url	credit_card_full
chrome	get_arguments	year	company_email
city	get_formatter	zip	color_rgb_float
city_prefix	get_providers	basic_phone_number	cache_pattern
city_suffix	get_words_list	domain_name	catch_phrase
color	ipv4	country_calling_code	currency_code
color_hsl	suffix	postcode_in_state	currency_name
color_hsv	ipv4_private	credit_card_expire	currency_symbol
color_name	ipv4_public	texts	current_country
color_rgb	ipv6	credit_card_number	date_time_between
file_path	isbn10	credit_card_provider	ipv4_network_class
company	isbn13	credit_card_security_code	date_time_this_century
coordinate	profile	cryptocurrency	date_time_this_decade
country	provider	cryptocurrency_code	date_time_this_month
am_pm	providers	cryptocurrency_name	date_time_this_year
bban	psv	current_country_code	passport_full
date	pybool	random_digit_above_two	passport_gender
dsv	pydecimal	random_digit_not_null	passport_number
ean	pydict	mac_address	passport_owner
ean13	pyfloat	random_digit_or_empty	password
ean8	pyint	random_element	past_date
ein	pyiterable	random_elements	past_datetime
email	pylist	free_email	phone_number
emoji	pyobject	free_email_domain	port_number
enum	pyset	future_date	postalcode
factories	state	hex_color	state_abbr
day_of_week	state_abbr	hexify	street_address
del_arguments	street_address	random_elements	street_name
items	street_name	random_digit_above_two	street_suffix
itin	street_suffix	first_name	paragraphs
job	suffix	first_name_female	suffix_female
job_female	suffix_female	first_name_male	suffix_male
job_male	suffix_male	first_name_nonbinary	suffix_nonbinary
json	suffix_nonbinary	month_name	file_extension
language_code	name	sentence	text
language_name	name_female	sentences	time
last_name	name_male	state	passport_dates
last_name_female	license_plate	swift	passport_dob

Deep

You can explore even more by running:

```
>>> from faker import Faker
>>> fake = Faker()
>>> print( dir(fake) )    # List all available methods
...... [...........]
```

Example 1, Generating fake emails and words

</> Python

```
>>> import faker
>>> fake =  fake.Faker()
>>> email = fake.email(domain = "gmail.com")
>>> print(email)
...... 'elizabethburke@gmail.com'

>>> email = fake.email(domain = "outlook.com")
>>> print(email)
...... 'matthew25@outlook.com'

>>> sentence = fake.sentence()
>>> print(sentence)
...... 'Begin sport ten by activity run really heart.'

>>>>>> emoji = fake.emoji()
>>> print(emoji)
...... '🤪'
>>>
```

Example 2, Generating fake addresses

```
</> Python
>>> from faker import Faker
>>> fake =  Faker()
>>> address = fake.address()
>>> print(address)
...... '66584 Spence Squares Suite 139
       Johnhaven, PR 26380'

>>> address = fake.address()
>>> print(address)
...... '98567 Mccormick Lodge
       Lake Ashleyland, VT 04829'
```

```
</> Python
>>> fake.state()
...... 'Florida'
>>> fake.zipcode()
...... '76665'
>>> fake.street_name()
...... 'Bradley Highway'
>>> fake.street_address()
...... '9227 Galloway Landing'
>>> fake.postalcode()
...... '58553'
>>> fake.phone_number()
...... '914-209-0864'
```

Example 3, Generating fake identity

```
</> Python
>>> import faker
>>> fake =  fake.Faker()
>>> name = fake.name()
>>> print(name)
......  'Colleen Williams'

>>> fake.name_female()
...... 'Sabrina Higgins'
>>> fake.password()
...... '$4X(RXyiFb'
>>> fake.city()
...... 'South Barbaraton'
>>> fake.currency()
...... ('AED', 'United Arab Emirates dirham')
>>> fake.company()
...... 'Reid LLC'
```

```
</> Python
>>> fake.country()
...... 'Switzerland'
>>> fake.ssn()
...... '330-84-1846'
>>> fake.passport_number()
...... '955631232'
>>> fake.passport_dob()
...... datetime.date(1955, 9, 28)
>>> fake.passport_owner()
...... ('Rebecca', 'Hamilton')
>>> fake.ipv4()
...... '143.13.3.56'
>>> fake.credit_card_number()
...... '6011167979221760'
>>> fake.credit_card_provider()
...... 'Mastercard'
```

Chapter 23

Emoji

After you have studied this chapter, you should be able to:

- Understand the importance and use cases of emojis in software
- Use different emoji methods for generating emojis in text
- Retrieve emojis by name
- Get emoji names from emoji symbols

Emoji

Human communication is multifaceted, encompassing text, speech, visuals, gestures, images, symbols, and more. While visual communication—such as images—can often convey meaning more effectively than plain text, it's not always practical. For example, when dealing with small-sized messages or limited bandwidth, sending full images becomes less feasible.

This is where emojis come in. Emojis are compact, expressive text-based visuals formed using Unicode characters. They allow users to convey emotion, context, or tone quickly and efficiently—without needing large files or complex graphics.

In Python, the emoji module provides functionality for:

- Converting text or keywords into emojis
- Converting emojis back to their names
- Handling Unicode emoji characters programmatically

Installation

You can install the emoji module using pip:

```
$ pip install emoji
```

Why the Need for Emojis in Programming?

Emojis aren't just for fun—they serve practical purposes in programming as well:

Enhance User Interface
Emojis can make UIs (especially chat apps, dashboards, and notifications) more expressive and engaging.

Convey Emotions & Context
Emojis help convey the tone of a message without extra text.

✏️ **Reduce Text Length**
A single emoji can replace several words (e.g., 👍 instead of "I agree").

✏️ **Improve Readability**
They break monotony in long texts or logs and highlight key points.

✏️ **Placeholders in Testing**
Useful in testing emoji-related features or generating placeholder text.

✏️ **Cross-Platform Consistency**
Unicode-based emojis look similar across systems and devices.

Emoji Methods

Methods	Description
emojize(text)	Converts emoji names (e.g., :smile:) to actual emojis.
demojize(text)	Converts emojis in the given text to their descriptive names (e.g., '😊' → ':smile:').
config	Contains configuration settings for the emoji module.
core	Core internal functions used by the module (not often used directly).
distinct_emoji_list(text)	Returns a list of unique emojis found in the text.
emoji_count(text)	Returns the number of emojis in a given string.
emoji_list(text)	Returns a list of all emojis found in the text along with their positions.
get_emoji_by_name(name)	Returns the emoji corresponding to a name like 'thumbs_up'.
is_emoji(text)	Returns True if the character is a valid emoji.
load_from_json(file)	Loads custom emoji data from a JSON file.
purely_emoji(text)	Checks whether a string consists only of emojis.
replace_emoji(text, replace)	Replaces all emojis in the text with the given replacement.
tokenizer(text)	Tokenizes the text into emojis and words for analysis.
unicode_codes	Contains mappings between emoji names and Unicode points.
version	Returns the version of the emoji module being used.

Emoji Names in Python

Each emoji can be referenced either by its **Unicode character** or by a **descriptive name** wrapped in colons (e.g., :smile:). Using Unicode directly works in many environments, but using the **emoji name** is more readable and maintainable—especially in dynamic or multilingual applications.

Python's emoji module provides a powerful function called **emojize()** that converts emoji names into actual emojis.

Using emoji.emojize()

The emojize() function takes in a string containing emoji names in a specific format and returns a string with the corresponding emojis.

Example1

</> Python

```python
import emoji

# Basic usage with default delimiters (: :)
print(emoji.emojize("Python is fun :snake:"))
```

```
#Output
Python is fun 🐍
```

Example2

</> Python

```python
import emoji

# Using alias names (like `:thumbsup:` instead of `:thumbs_up:`)
print(emoji.emojize("I'm great :thumbsup:",  language='alias'))
```

```
#Output
I'm great 👍
```

Example 3

```python
import emoji

# Specifying a text-based emoji variant (some platforms support this)
print(emoji.emojize("planet :sun_with_face: :ringed_planet:", variant="text_type"))
```

```
#Output
planet 🌞 🪐
```

Example 4

```python
import emoji

# Specifying an emoji variant (default is usually emoji-style)
print(emoji.emojize("Congrats :party_popper: :fireworks:", variant="emoji_type"))
```

```
#Output
Congrats 🎉 🎆
```

Example 5

```python
import emoji

# Using custom delimiters, like curly braces
print(emoji.emojize("Sports is life:{basketball}{soccerball}", delimiters=("{" , "}")))
```

```
#Output
Sports is life: 🏀 ⚽
```

Key Points

- **Default delimiters** are : for both sides (e.g., :rocket:).
- language='alias' allows common names like :thumbsup:, :smile:, etc.
- variant='text_type' may return text-style emojis, depending on the emoji and platform.
- Custom **delimiters** let you use any other character (e.g., {}) if : conflicts with your data.

Available Emoji Names and Their Unicode Characters

Emojis are standardized by the Unicode Consortium, each assigned a unique name and Unicode character. Below is a selection of commonly used emojis with their names and Unicode representations:

Emoji	Name	Unicode	Emoji	Name	Unicode
😀	grinning_face	U+1F600	🖐	hand with fingers splayed	U+1F590
😃	grinning_face_with_big_eyes	U+1F603	🤙	call me hand	U+1F919
😄	grinning_face_with_smiling_eyes	U+1F604	✍	writing hand	U+270D
😁	beaming_face_with_smiling_eyes	U+1F601	🧠	brain	U+1F9E0
😆	grinning_squinting_face	U+1F606	🫀	anatomical heart	U+1FAC0
🤣	rolling_on_the_floor_laughing	U+1F923	🧑	person	U+1F9D1
😂	face_with_tears_of_joy	U+1F602	👴	old man	U+1F474
😉	winking face	U+1F609	🙆	person gesturing OK	U+1F646
🤩	star-struck	U+1F929	🤷	person shrugging	U+1F937
🤑	money-mouth face	U+1F911	🧑‍⚕️	health worker	U+1F9D1
🥸	disguised face	U+1F978	👩‍⚖️	woman judge	U+1F469
🤠	cowboy hat face	U+1F920	🧑‍✈️	pilot	U+1F9D1
🤡	clown face	U+1F921	🧑‍🚀	astronaut	U+1F9D1
👹	ogre	U+1F479	🎅	Santa Claus	U+1F385
😺	grinning cat	U+1F63A	🤶	Mrs. Claus	U+1F936
😹	cat with tears of joy	U+1F639	🧛	vampire	U+1F9DB
🙈	see-no-evil monkey	U+1F648	🐶	dog face	U+1F436
🙉	hear-no-evil monkey	U+1F649	🐺	wolf	U+1F43A
💘	heart with arrow	U+1F498	🐭	mouse face	U+1F42D
💞	revolving hearts	U+1F49E	🐼	panda	U+1F43C

💔	broken heart	U+1F494	🐻	bear	U+1F43B
💋	kiss mark	U+1F48B	🐧	penguin	U+1F427
💯	hundred points	U+1F4AF	🏵	rosette	U+1F3F5
💥	collision	U+1F4A5	🍁	maple leaf	U+1F341
💫	dizzy	U+1F4AB	🍓	strawberry	U+1F353
👋	waving hand	U+1F44B	🥕	carrot	U+1F955
🍔	hamburger	U+1F354	🏠	house	U+1F3E0
🍕	pizza	U+1F355	🚑	ambulance	U+1F691
🍲	pot of food	U+1F372	🚁	helicopter	U+1F681
🍩	doughnut	U+1F369	🚀	rocket	U+1F680
🌍	globe showing Europe-Africa	U+1F30D	🌤	sun behind small cloud	U+1F324
🏈	american football	U+1F3C8	🎓	graduation cap	U+1F393
🎲	game die	U+1F3B2	📢	loudspeaker	U+1F4E2

Table 15.0 : List of Emoji

📝 Note

This is a partial list. For a complete and up-to-date list of all emojis, please refer to the Unicode Full Emoji List

🚀 Deep

You can use Unicode characters to generate emojis in Python. For example:

```
>>> print("\U0001F349")
...... 🍉
>>> print("\U0001F3AF")
...... 🎯
>>> print(chr(0x1F380))
...... 🎀
>>> print(chr(0x1F381))
...... 🎁
```

Converting Emojis to Unicode Names

The Python emoji module provides a convenient method called demojize() that converts emojis into their respective Unicode names. This is particularly useful when you need to process or analyze text containing emojis. The **demojize()** function replaces each emoji in the text with its corresponding Unicode name, enclosed in colons.

Example 1

```
</> Python

import emoji

text = 'I love Python! 😍 🐍'
converted_emoji = emoji.demojize( text )
print(converted_emoji )
```

```
#Output
I love Python! :smiling_face_with_heart-eyes::snake:
```

Example 2

```
</> Python

import emoji

text = 'Happy Birthday buddy 🎁 🎉 🎈 🎊 '
converted_emoji = emoji.demojize( text )
print(converted_emoji )
```

```
#Output
Happy Birthday buddy :wrapped_gift::party_popper::balloon::confetti_ball:
```

Chapter 24

HTTP Server

After you have studied this chapter, you should be able to:

- Understand what an HTTP server is
- Identify various alternative HTTP servers available in Python
- Recognize the reasons and use cases for running a local HTTP server
- Set up a computer as a local server using Python

HTTP Server

Python isn't just a programming language—it also comes with powerful built-in modules that can transform your computer into a local server. Using the **http.server** module, you can serve files over a network, making them accessible to other devices on the same network or beyond, depending on configuration.

This functionality can be incredibly useful for quick file sharing, testing websites locally, or hosting static content during development.

Although it's not intended for production use, the **http.server** module is lightweight, easy to set up, and highly customizable by extending its classes.

Alternative Python Server Modules

While http.server is great for basic tasks, Python also offers **powerful frameworks** for building full-featured web servers and APIs:

Framework	Description
Flask	Lightweight and flexible for small-to-medium web applications
FastAPI	High-performance, async-ready framework for APIs
Django	Full-stack web framework with ORM, admin panel, and more
Tornado	Asynchronous networking library with web server capabilities
aiohttp	Async HTTP client/server framework
Bottle	Minimalist micro-framework ideal for small apps

Table 24.0: Some Python Servers

Why Use an HTTP Server?

Here are some common reasons to set up a basic HTTP server using Python:

- **Quick file sharing** between devices on the same network
- **Download files** without using third-party apps or services
- **Serve static websites** during development
- **Test frontend interfaces** before backend integration
- **Share folders in classrooms or teams** over Wi-Fi
- **Learn basic client-server concepts** using Python

Steps to Turn Your Computer into a Local Server

Turning your computer into a server using Python is both simple and powerful for local file sharing, development, or testing. Here's a step-by-step guide to get you started.

① Establish a Network Connection

Before your computer can function as a server, it must be connected to the same network as the client devices that will access it.

How to Create a Local Network

The key is to ensure both the **host (server)** and **clients** are on the **same local network**. This can be achieved in several ways:

1. **Connect all devices to the same Wi-Fi network**
2. **Share a mobile hotspot** from the server computer and connect clients to it
3. **Use an Ethernet cable** for a LAN (Local Area Network) setup
4. **Enable Wi-Fi Direct** if supported by the devices
5. **Use a home router to interconnect wired and wireless devices**
6. **For Virtual Machines (VMs)**, use **bridged or NAT networking** to simulate a shared network

Note

If you are hosting to virtual machines installed on the same computer, a physical network is not required. Most VMs use internal virtual network bridges that allow access to the host automatically.

② Start the Python HTTP Server

Once the network is ready, it's time to start the server on the **host computer**.

On the Host Computer (Server)

Open your terminal (macOS/Linux) or PowerShell/Command Prompt (Windows) and navigate to the folder you wish to share.

Run one of the following commands:

Runs on localhost(domain) with default port (8000)

```
$ python -m  http.server
```

Custom port

```
$ python -m  http.server  2000
```

This launches a basic HTTP server, serving the current directory's files.

③ Accessing the Server from a Client Device

Now, from any client computer connected to the same network:

On the Client Device

1. Open a **web browser** (Chrome, Edge, Firefox, etc.)
2. In the address bar, type the server address based on the host configuration:
    - If using the host's IP address:
      http://192.168.0.105:2000 *(replace with actual host IP)*
    - If accessing from the same machine (for testing):
      http://localhost:8000 or http://127.0.0.1:8000

3. You'll now see a file explorer-style view of the server directory—these are your **server resources**!

Deep

Finding the Server IP Address

If you're unsure of your host IP address (for client access), you can find it with:

On Windows

```
PS D:\Python> ipconfig
```

On Linux/macOS

```
$ ifconfig
$ ip a
```

Key Points

- Ensure all devices are on the same network.
- Use python -m http.server [port] to start the server.
- Access via browser using http://host_ip:port.

Chapter 25

Turtle

After you have studied this chapter, you should be able to:

- Understand what the Turtle module is and its applications
- Explore the features provided by the Python Turtle library
- Perform basic turtle operations
- Control turtle movement and positioning
- Manage pen behavior and styles
- Change turtle appearance and shape
- Draw basic and complex shapes
- Control the turtle screen and window properties

Turtle

The Python Turtle module is a powerful tool for drawing geometric shapes, animations, and patterns by moving the turtle (cursor) in different directions on the screen. The turtle follows a set of programmed instructions, allowing users to create intricate designs. This module is pre-packaged in Python and can be imported using the import turtle statement.

Turtle graphics are widely used in educational environments to introduce programming concepts in a fun and interactive way. It helps beginners understand loops, functions, and event-driven programming by visually representing code execution.

Features of Python Turtle

✎ Cursor as a Drawing Tool

The turtle acts as a pen or cursor controlled by user-defined commands. It draws shapes or patterns as it moves on the screen.

✎ Directional Movement

The turtle can move forward, backward, left, and right, each defined with a specific length or angle.

✎ Customizable Appearance

Users can change the turtle's color, shape, and size. Some predefined shapes include arrow, classic, square, triangle, and circle.

✎ Drawing Geometric Shapes

By combining movement commands and loops, users can create polygons, fractals, spirals, and stars, among other complex patterns.

✎ Animation Capabilities

Animations can be created by adjusting the speed, timing, and using loops to control the turtle's motion.

Methods

done	goto	home	penup
mainloop	setx	undo	pendown
forward	sety	pencolor	teleport
fd	setheading	color	getshapes
backwards	seth	bgcolor	shape
bk	setpos	fillcolor	shapesize
right	setposition	begin_fill	hideturtle
rt	position	end_fill	hd
left	pos	pensize	showturtle
lt	clone	width	st
bye	write	stamp	speed
clear	reset	begin_poly	delay
clearscreen	resetscreen	end_poly	circle
title	exitonclick	bgpic	dots
tracer	clearstamp	pu	isdown
textinput	clearstamps	pd	isinvisible
back	numinput	up	turtlesize
distance	addshape	update	towards

Deep

To discover additional methods and attributes in the turtle module, use the dir() function

```
>>> import turtle
>>> tut = turtle.Turtle()
>>> dir(turtle)
```

Note

After drawing shapes with Turtle, you can save everything on the screen as an **.eps** file using **getcanvas()** and **postscript(file)**. This .eps file can later be converted to an image. For example:

```
>>> from PIL import Image
>>> turtle.circle(100)
>>> tscreen = turtle.getscreen()
>>> tscreen.getcanvas().postscript(file = "shape.eps")
```

```
>>>
>>> img = Image.open("shape.eps")
>>> img.save("drawing.png")
```

① Basic Turtle Operations

done() and mainloop()

After drawing a shape, the screen normally closes immediately. The following methods prevent the screen from closing automatically after the drawing is completed:

- turtle.done(): Keeps the window open until manually closed.
- turtle.mainloop(): Similar to turtle.done(), keeps the turtle graphics window active.

```python
import turtle
turtle.done()
turtle.mainloop()
```

bgcolor(color):

bgcolor() defines the background color of the turtle graphics window.
Colors can be specified in two formats:

- Named colors such as **"red"**, **"blue"**, **"purple"**, etc.
- Hexadecimal format **"#rrggbb"**, where **r**, **g**, and **b** are values from 0-9 or A-F.

```python
import turtle
turtle.bgcolor("#443E46")
turtle.mainloop()
```

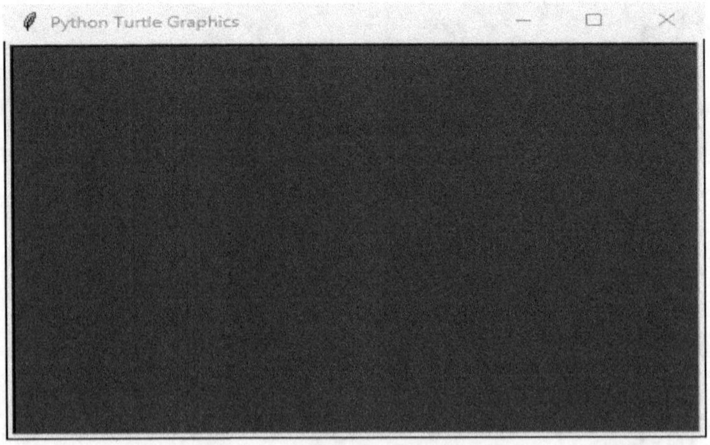

② Movement and Positioning

foward(float) and fd(float)

Moves the turtle forward by the specified distance.

```python
import turtle
turtle.forward( 250 )
turtle.mainloop()
```

backward(float) and bk(float)

Moves the turtle backward by the specified distance.

```python
import turtle
turtle.bk( 100 )
turtle.mainloop()
```

right(angle) and rt(angle)

Rotates the turtle clockwise by the specified angle.

```python
import turtle
turtle.fd( 200 )
turtle.right( 90 )        #rotates by 90 degrees clockwise
turtle.fd( 200 )
turtle.mainloop()
```

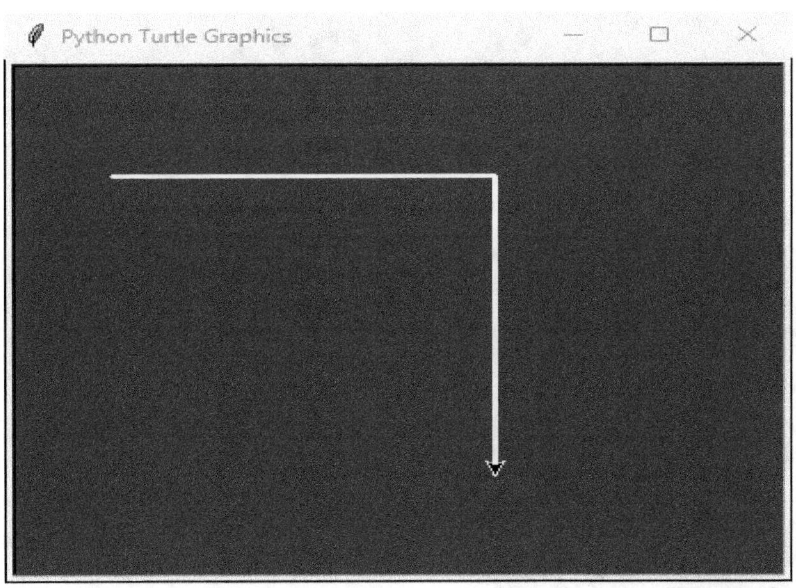

left(angle) and lt(angle)

Rotates the turtle counterclockwise by the specified angle.

```python
import turtle
turtle.forward( 200 )
turtle.left( 45 )          #rotates by 45 degrees counterclockwise
turtle.mainloop()
```

goto(x, y)

Moves the turtle to the specified (x, y) coordinates.

```python
import turtle
turtle.goto( 50, 100 )        #moves turtle to 50 on x-axis and 100 on y-axis
turtle.goto( 100, 0 )
turtle.goto( 150, 0 )
turtle.goto( 200, 0 )
turtle.goto( 200, 0 )
turtle.goto( 150, -100 )
turtle.goto( 200, -200 )
turtle.goto( 50, -150 )
turtle.goto( 0, -200 )
turtle.mainloop()
```

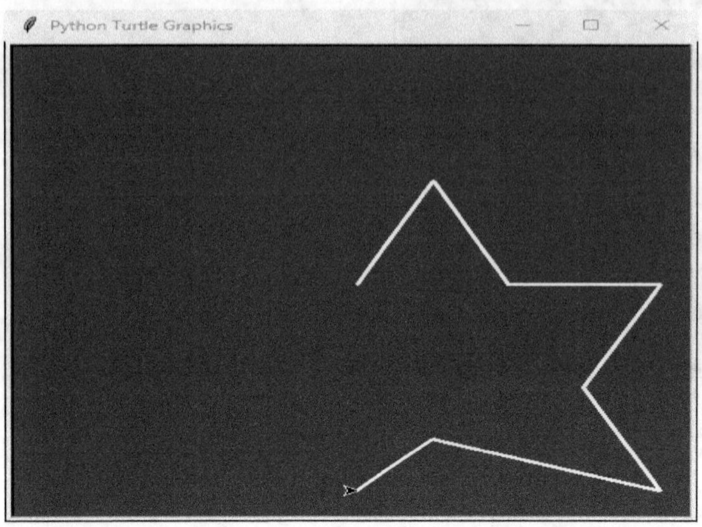

setx(x) and sety(y)

setx(x): Moves the turtle to a specific x-coordinate while keeping the y-coordinate constant.
sety(y): Moves the turtle to a specific y-coordinate while keeping the x-coordinate constant.

</> Python

```
import turtle
turtle.setx( 20 )      #set x coordinate to 20
turtle.sety( 45 )      #set y coordinate to 45
turtle.mainloop()
```

setheading(angle) and seth(angle)

Sets the turtle's heading to the specified angle.

</> Python

```
import turtle
turtle.forward( 100 )
turtle.setheading( 90 )      #turns to 90 degrees
turtle.forward( 50 )
turtle.done()
```

setposition(x, y) and setpos(x, y)

Moves the turtle to the specified (x, y) coordinates and begins drawing from that point.

</> Python

```
import turtle
turtle.setposition( 0, 100 )
turtle.setposition( 200, 100 )
turtle.setpos( 200, 0 )
turtle.setpos( 0, 0 )
turtle.done()
```

position( ) and pos( )

Returns the current (x, y) coordinates of the turtle.

</> Python

```
import turtle
coord = turtle.position( )
print( coord )                #output : (0.00, 0.00)
```

Think about it ?

- clone(): Creates a duplicate instance of the turtle at the current position.
- home(): Moves the turtle to the origin (0,0) and resets the heading to 0 degrees.
- undo(): Removes the last action performed by the turtle, such as a drawn line.

③Pen Control

pencolor(color) and color(color)

These set the line color for drawing. It accepts:

- Named colors: **"red"**, **"green"**, **"blue"**, etc.
- Hexadecimal format "**#rrggbb**", where **r**, **g**, and **b** are values from 0-9 or A-F.

</> Python

```
import turtle
turtle.color("orange")    #line color is set to red

for width in [200, 100, 200, 100]:
    turtle.forward( width )
    turtle.right( 90 )
turtle.done()
```

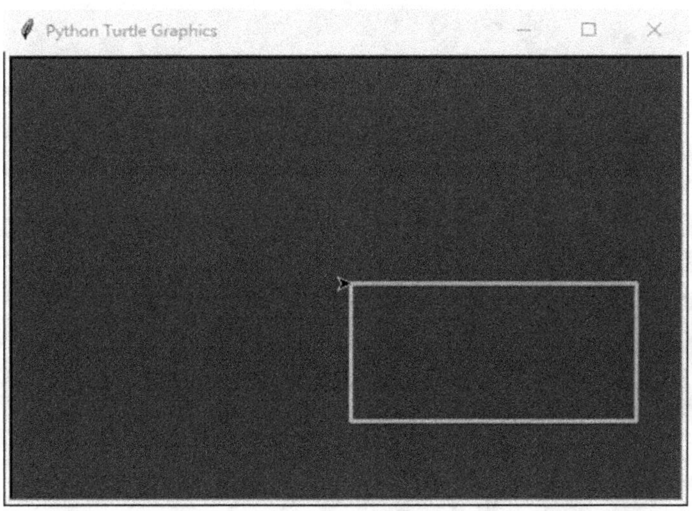

fillcolor(color), begin_fill(color) and .end_fill(color),
The fillcolor defines the fill color for closed shapes.
begin_fill(): Marks the start of filling.
end_fill(): Completes and fills the drawn shape.
Colors can be specified in two formats:

- Named colors such as **"red"**, **"blue"**, **"purple"**, etc.
- Hexadecimal format **"#rrggbb"**, where **r**, **g**, and **b** are values from 0-9 or A-F.

</> Python

```
import turtle

tut = turtle.Turtle()
tut.fillcolor("#209010")    #fill color is set to green
tut.begin_fill()

for i in range( 4 ):
    tut.forward( 200 )
    tut.right( 90 )

tut.end_fill()
turtle.done()
```

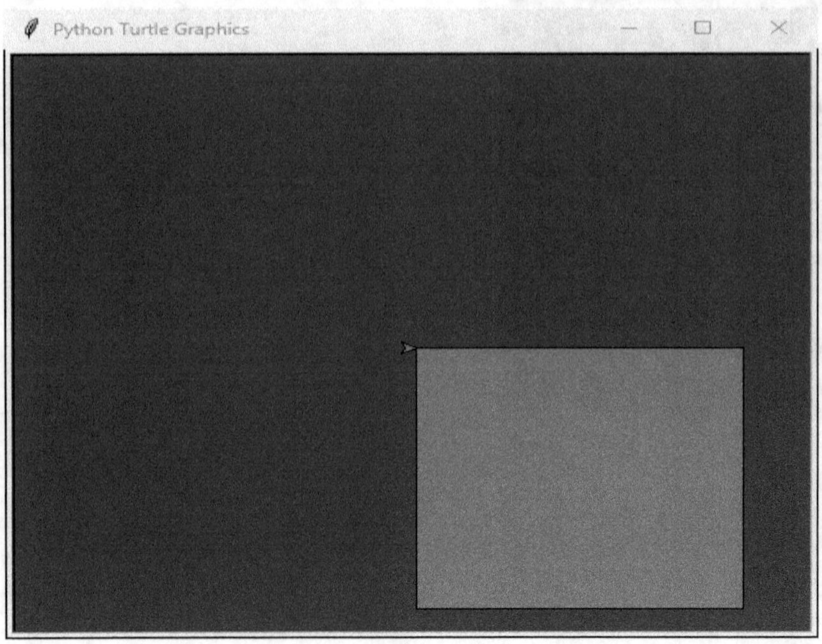

penup( ) or pu( ) and pendown( ) or pd( )

turtle.penup() or turtle.pu() lifts the pen so the turtle moves without drawing.
turtle.pendown() or turtle.pd() lowers the pen so the turtle resumes drawing.

</> Python

```
import turtle

turtle.goto( 50, 100 )
turtle.goto( 100, 0 )
turtle.goto( 0, 0 )

turtle.penup( )
turtle.goto( -200, 0 )
turtle.pendown( )

for i in range( 4 ):
    turtle.forward( 100 )
    turtle.right( 90 )

turtle.done()
```

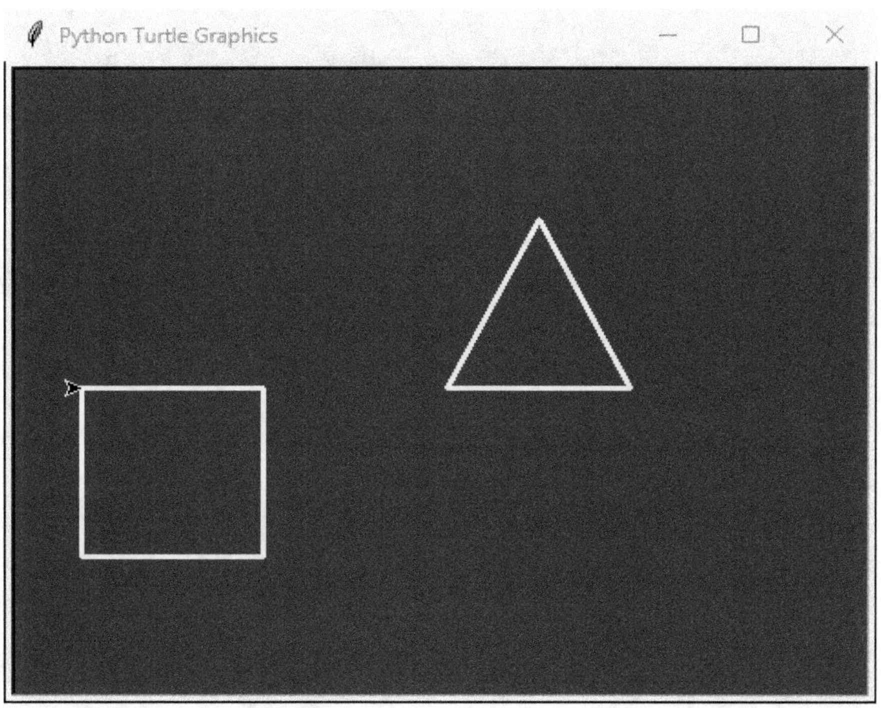

Think about it ?

- turtle.teleport(x, y):

Moves the turtle to a new position without drawing, similar to **penup()** and **pendown()** but with specified coordinates.

- What will the appearance be without using **penup()** and **pendown()**

pensize(float) and width(float)

turtle.pensize(): Defines the thickness of the drawing line.

turtle.width(): Functions the same as pensize(), adjusting the pen thickness.

</> Python

```
import turtle
turtle.pensize( 20 )
turtle.done()
```

④ Appearance and Shape Control

hideturtle( ) or ht( ) and showturtle( ) or st( )

The hideturtle() or ht() hides the turtle cursor from the screen.

The showturtle() or st() makes the turtle visible after hiding.

</> Python

```
import turtle
turtle.showturtle( )
turtle.hideturtle( )
turtle.done()
```

shape(shape) , shapesize(stretch_wid, stretch_len, outline) and getshapes( )

The shape() sets the shape of the turtle cursor.
The shapesize() modifies the shape's width, length, and outline thickness.
The getshapes() returns a list of all available shapes. The following are available shapes.
"arrow", "blank", "circle", "classic", "square", "triangle", "turtle"

Shape	Icon	Shape	Icon
arrow		triangle	
square		turtle	
circle		blank	
classic			

Table 25.0: Some available turtle shapes

</> Python

```
import turtle
shapes = turtle.getshapes( )
print( shapes )          #output: ['arrow', 'blank', 'circle', 'classic', 'square', 'triangle', 'turtle']

turtle.shape("turtle" )
turtle.shapesize( stretch_wid= 10, stretch_len= 20,  outline = 2  )
```

speed(int) and delay(number)

The speed() sets the drawing speed from 0 (slowest) to 10 (fastest). Accepts strings: **"slow"**, **"normal"**, **"fast"**.
The delay() defines the time delay between turtle movements.

</> Python

```
import turtle
turtle.speed( 5 )
turtle.delay(  3.5 )
turtle.done()
```

⑤ Drawing Shapes

circle(radius, extent=None, steps=None)

The circle() method allows the turtle to draw a circle with the specified radius.

extent → (float) [Optional]: Defines the length of the circumference to be drawn.

steps → (int) [Optional]: Specifies the number of points to form an enclosed polygon. Using steps, you can draw different polygons instead of a perfect circle.

</> Python

```
import turtle
turtle.shape("turtle" )
turtle.color(  "purple", "orange")
turtle.begin_fill()
turtle.circle( radius = 100 )
turtle.end_fill()

turtle.mainloop()
```

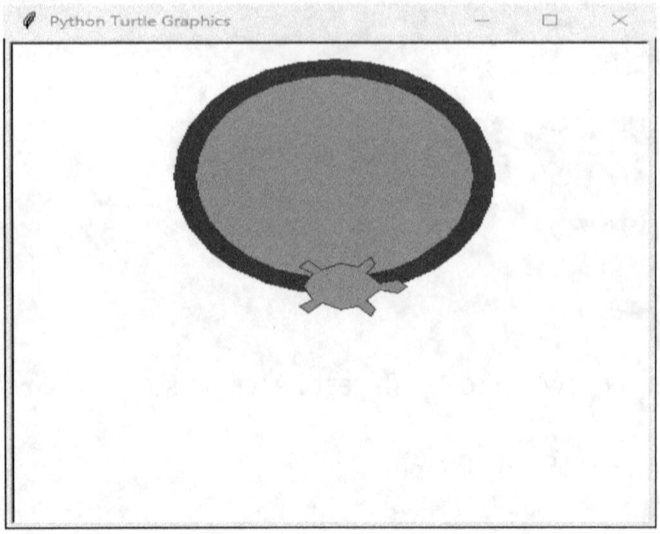

Think about it ?

How can the **circle()** method be used to draw polygons?


```python
turtle.pensize( 5 )
turtle.shape( 'turtle' )
turtle.color("purple", "orange")
turtle.begin_fill()
turtle.circle(radius=100, steps= 3 )          #polygon with 3 sides (triangle)
turtle.teleport(x=-150, y= 100)
turtle.color("pink", "cyan")
turtle.circle(radius=100, steps= 4 )          #polygon with 4 sides (square)
turtle.teleport(x= 200, y= 50)
turtle.color("teal", "yellow")
turtle.circle(radius=100, steps= 5 )          #polygon with 5 sides (pentagon)
turtle.teleport(x= 50, y= -200)
turtle.color("red", "green")
turtle.circle(radius=100, steps= 6 )          #polygon with 6 sides (hexagon)
turtle.teleport(x= -150, y= -160)
turtle.color("purple", "orange")
turtle.circle(radius=100, steps= 7 )          #polygon with 7 size (heptagon)
turtle.end_fill()

turtle.mainloop()
```

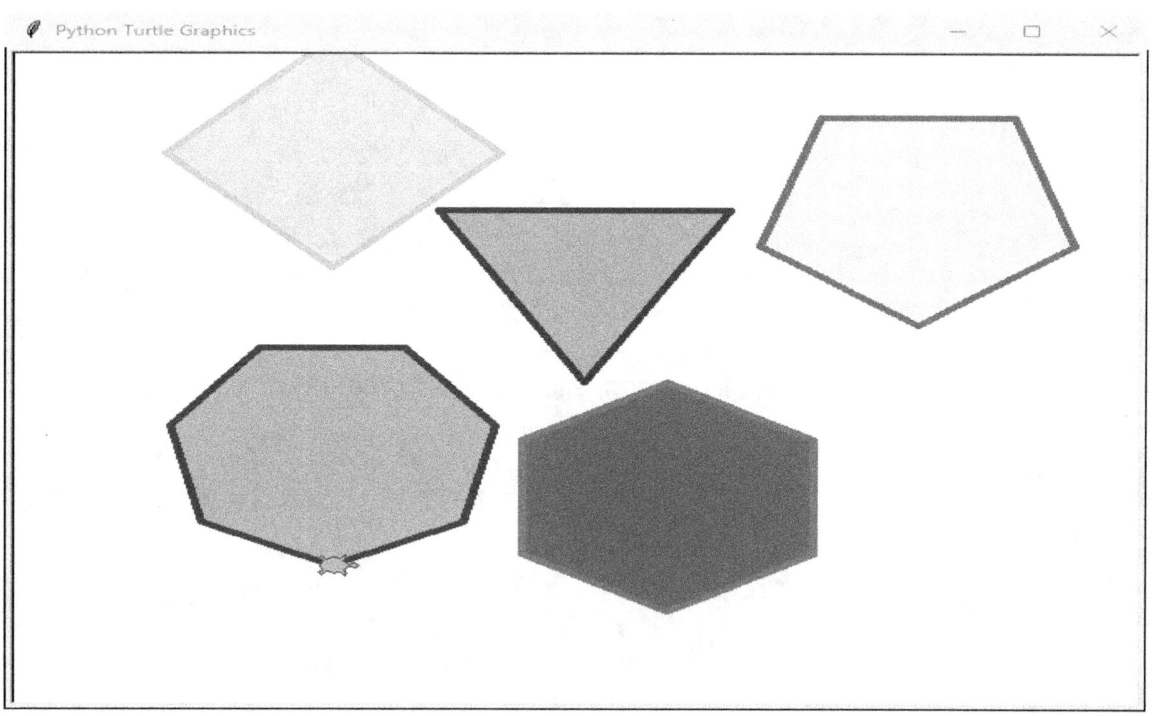

dot(size)

The dot() method creates dots on the screen with a specified size (integer).

```python
import turtle
import random

colors = ["red", "orange", "green", "purple", "blue"]
for i in range(1, 500):
    turtle.pencolor(colors[random.randint(0,len(colors) -1)])
    turtle.dot(size=10)
    turtle.teleport(x=random.randint(-i, i), y=random.randint(-i, i))

turtle.mainloop()
```

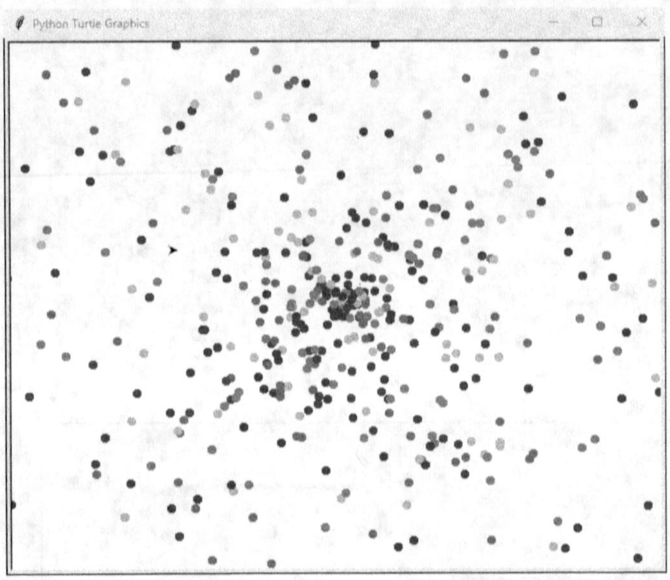

begin_poly( ) and end_poly( )

The begin_poly() marks the start of a polygon, allowing you to define custom shapes. The end_poly() marks the completion of the polygon.

```python
import turtle
turtle.begin_poly( )
turtle.end_poly( )
```

write(arg, move, align, font)

The write() method prints text onto the screen with customizable options.

arg → Can be a string, number, list, dictionary, set, tuple, boolean, or bytes.

move → (bool) [Optional]: If True, the turtle moves by the length of the text. Default is False.

align → (string) [Optional]: Defines text alignment ("left", "center", or "right"). Default is "left".

font → (tuple) [Optional]: Defines the text appearance:

- Font Family (str) – Example: "Arial", "Consolas", "Times New Roman", "Tahoma", "Georgia".
- Font Size (int) – Defines the text size.
- Font Style (str) – "normal", "bold", "italic", or "underline"

</> Python

```
import turtle
turtle.bgcolor("orange")
turtle.color("white")
turtle.shape('turtle')
turtle.teleport(x=-30, y=50)
turtle.write(arg="Cracky Code", font=("tahoma", 25, "bold"))
turtle.teleport(x=-200, y=0)
turtle.write(arg="Awesome Python!😊", font=("Georgia", 30))
turtle.teleport(x=-30, y=-50)
turtle.write(arg="Just get me a coffee", align="center", font=("Georgia", 25, "italic"))
turtle.done()
```

Think about it ?

The **stamp()** method leaves an impression of the turtle's shape at its current position on the screen. Does it works the same way as the stamps used in letters?

⑥ Screen and Window Control

bye( ), reset( ), cleaerscreen( ), and clear( )

The bye() closes the turtle window immediately.
The reset() resets the screen and clears all drawings.
The clearscreen() clears all shapes drawn by the turtle.
The clear() clears only the currently drawn object.

</> Python

```
import turtle
turtle.bye( )
turtle.reset( )
turtle.clearscreen( )
turtle.clear( )
```

title(title) and exitonclick()

The title() sets the window title.
The exitonclick() closes the window when clicked.

</> Python

```
import turtle
turtle.title( "My Title" )
turtle.exitonclick( )
```

Examples of Shapes Created Using Turtle

1. Flower with Spiral Petals

```python
import turtle
import math

t = turtle.Turtle()
t.speed(0)
turtle.bgcolor("#F5F8FA")
t.pensize(1)
t.pencolor("red")

# Function to draw a spiral flower
def flower(petals, angle_step, size_factor):
    for i in range(petals):
        t.forward(math.sqrt(i) * size_factor)
        t.left(angle_step)

# Draw the flower
flower(360, 65, 10)

turtle.done()
```

```python
import turtle
import math

t = turtle.Turtle()
t.speed(0)
turtle.bgcolor("#F5F8FA")
t.pensize(1)
t.pencolor("purple")

# Function to draw a spiral flower
def flower(petals, angle_step, size_factor):
    for i in range(petals):
        t.forward(math.sqrt(i) * size_factor)
        t.left(angle_step)

# Draw the flower
flower(360, 100, 20)

turtle.done()
```

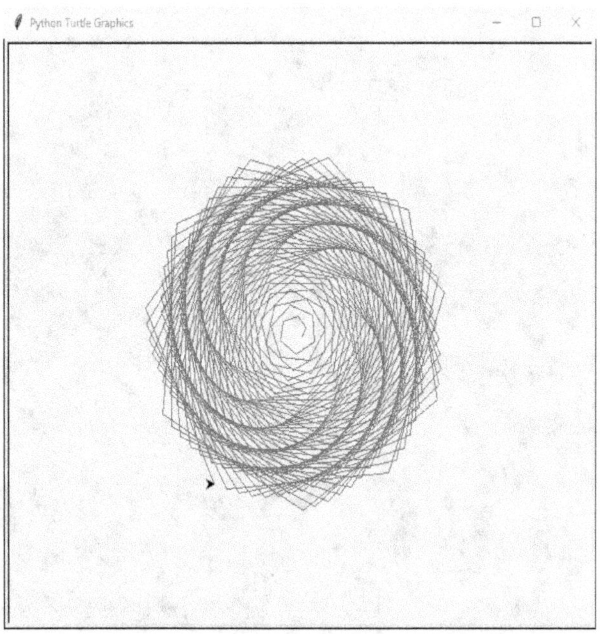

2. Colorful spiral flower

```python
import turtle
import random

t = turtle.Turtle()
t.speed(0)
turtle.bgcolor("#14171A")
t.pensize(1)
colors =
["red","yellow","green","blue","orange","purple"]

# Function to draw a spiral flower
def flower(petals, angle_step):
    for i in range(petals):
        t.pencolor(random.choice(colors))
        t.forward( i )
        t.left(angle_step)

# Draw the flower
flower(360, 59)

turtle.done()
```

```python
import turtle
import random

t = turtle.Turtle()
t.speed(0)
turtle.bgcolor("#14171A")
colors =
["red","yellow","green","blue","orange","purple"]

# Function to draw a spiral flower
def flower(petals, size, angle):
    for i in range(petals):
        t.pencolor(random.choice(colors))
        t.circle( size )
        t.left(angle)

# Draw the flower
flower( 72, 100, 10)

turtle.done()
```

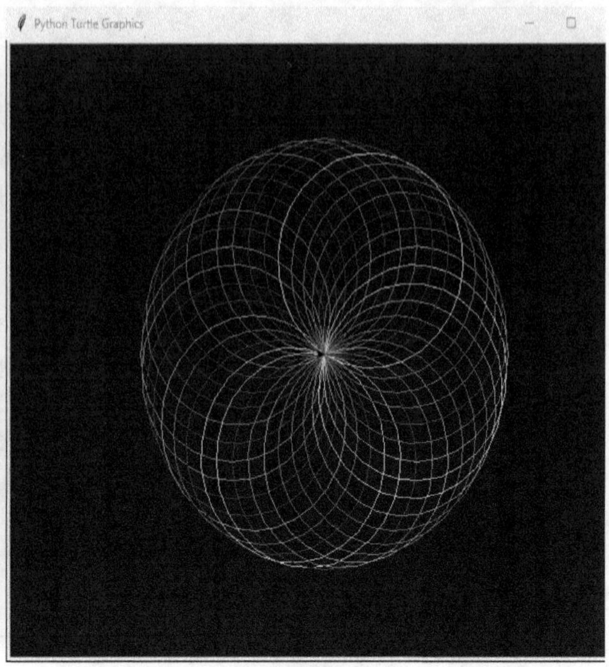

2. Colorful square flower

```python
import turtle
import random

t = turtle.Turtle()
t.speed(0)
turtle.bgcolor("#14171A")
colors =
["red","yellow","green","blue","orange","purple"]

def create_square(size):
   for i in range(4):
      t.forward( size )
      t.right(90)

def flower(repeat, size, angle):
   for i in range(repeats):
      t.pencolor(random.choice(colors))
      create_square(size )
      t.right(angle)

flower(72, 100, 10)
turtle.done()
```

```python
import turtle

t = turtle.Turtle()
t.speed(0)
turtle.bgcolor("#14171A")
colors =
["red","yellow","green","blue","orange","purple"]


for i in range( 100 ):
     t.pencolor( colors[ i % len(colors)])
     t.forward( i * 5 )
     t.right( 91 )

turtle.done()
```

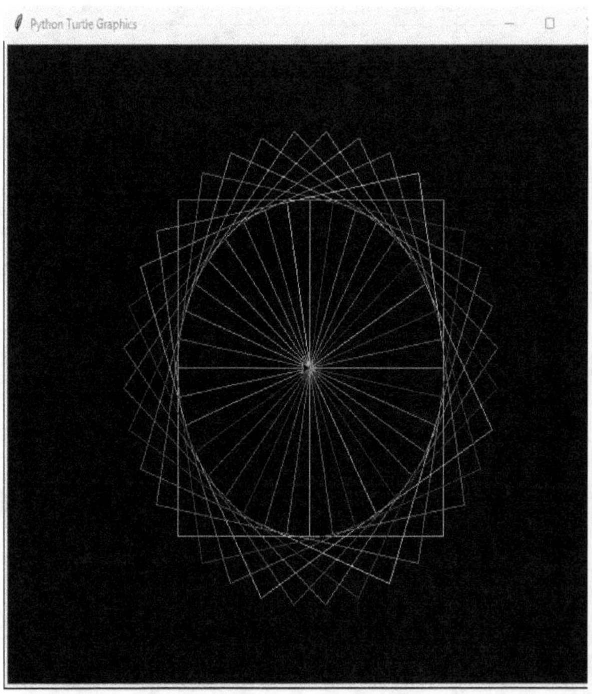

2. Colorful hexagonal flower

```python
import turtle

t = turtle.Turtle()
t.speed(0)
turtle.bgcolor("#14171A")
colors = ["red","yellow","green",
"blue","orange","purple"]

for i in range( 6 ):
    t.pencolor( colors[ i % len(colors)])
    for _ in range( 6 ):
        t.forward( 100 )
        t.right( 60 )
    t.right( 60 )


turtle.done()
```

```python
import turtle

t = turtle.Turtle()
t.speed(0)
turtle.bgcolor("#ffffff")


for i in range( 100 ):
    for _ in range( 3 ):
        t.forward( i * 4 )
        t.right( 140 )
    t.right( 5 )


turtle.done()
```

Chapter 26

Pillow (PIL)

After you have studied this chapter, you should be able to:

- Understand what Pillow is and its significance in image processing
- Explore key features of the Pillow library
- Work with various image file formats
- Use the Image module for opening, editing, and saving images
- Save images in different formats and perform format conversion
- Create animated images
- Apply geometric transformations (e.g., rotation, cropping, resizing)
- Draw shapes and text using ImageDraw
- Enhance images using ImageEnhance
- Apply image filters using ImageFilter
- Manipulate images using ImageChop
- Capture screenshots using ImageGrab

Pillow (PIL)

Pillow, also known as **PIL (Python Imaging Library),** is a core Python module for loading, manipulating, enhancing, and processing images in various formats. It provides a wide range of image-processing capabilities that allow developers to modify images programmatically. Pillow enables tasks such as image resizing, cropping, rotating, filtering, and format conversion, making it an essential tool for applications that involve image processing.

Features and Functionalities

Loading, Showing, and Printing Images

Pillow allows users to load images from different file formats and display them directly. Additionally, it provides the capability to print image details such as size, mode, and format.

Creating Images from Scratch

Developers can generate images from scratch using Pillow, defining colors, sizes, and shapes as needed. This feature is particularly useful for creating placeholders, patterns, or visual data representations.

Image Rotation

Pillow provides built-in methods to rotate images at various angles. This feature is useful in applications requiring image orientation adjustments, such as correcting tilted photos.

Image Cropping

Images can be cropped to extract specific areas of interest. This feature is commonly used in applications requiring face detection, object recognition, or automated document processing.

Scaling Images

Resizing images while maintaining aspect ratio is an essential function in many applications. Pillow enables users to scale images to fit different screen sizes or optimize them for various platforms.

Image Filtering

Pillow provides filtering capabilities to enhance images, including sharpening, blurring, and edge detection. These features improve image quality and can be used for artistic effects or pre-processing in machine learning applications.

Image File Format Conversion

Pillow supports converting images from one file format to another. This functionality is useful for optimizing images for different use cases, such as converting a high-resolution PNG to a more storage-efficient JPEG.

Color Transformation

The library allows changing an image's color mode, such as converting an image from RGB to grayscale. This is useful for reducing file size, improving contrast, or preparing images for further analysis.

Resizing Images

Pillow provides methods to resize images while preserving quality. This feature is particularly useful for creating thumbnails or optimizing images for web applications.

Retrieving Image Statistics

The library includes a histogram method that allows users to analyze pixel distribution within an image. This feature is commonly used in image recognition, segmentation, and color analysis applications.

Installation and Compatibility

While Pillow is often pre-installed with Python, some environments may require manual installation. It is important to ensure that PIL is not installed alongside Pillow, as they may not coexist properly.

Note

In case of compatibility issues, it is recommended to uninstall PIL before installing Pillow.

- pip uninstall PIL
- pip install pillow

Pillow remains a powerful and versatile tool for image processing in Python, supporting a wide range of functionalities suitable for beginners and advanced users alike. Whether for simple tasks such as resizing and cropping or complex operations like filtering and transformation, Pillow provides a robust solution for handling images programmatically.

Image File Formats

Pillow (PIL) is a powerful image processing library capable of handling various image file formats across different operating systems. It allows seamless conversion between formats while preserving image quality. An image can be loaded in one format, processed, and saved in another without loss of essential details.

Supported Image Formats and Platforms

Pillow supports a wide range of image file formats commonly used across multiple platforms:

Format	Extension(s)	Description	Platforms
JPEG / JFIF	.jpg, .jpeg	Common image format, lossy compression	Windows, macOS, Linux
JPEG 2000	.jp2, .j2k, .jpx	Advanced JPEG format with better compression	Windows, macOS, Linux
PNG	.png	Portable Network Graphics, supports transparency	Windows, macOS, Linux
TIFF	.tif, .tiff	Tagged Image File Format, used in professional photography	Windows, macOS, Linux
ICO	.ico	Windows icon format	Windows
ICNS	.icns	macOS icon format	macOS
GIF	.gif	Graphics Interchange Format, supports animation	Windows, macOS, Linux
PPM/PGM/PBM	.ppm, .pgm, .pbm	Portable Pixmap/Graymap/Bitmap	Unix-based systems
SGI	.sgi, .rgb, .rgba, .bw	Silicon Graphics Image format	Windows, macOS, Linux
MSP	.msp	Microsoft Paint format (old versions)	Windows
PCX	.pcx	Paintbrush image format	Windows
BMP	.bmp	Bitmap image format	Windows, macOS, Linux
DDS	.dds	DirectDraw Surface, used in game textures	Windows, macOS, Linux
DIB	.dib	Device-independent bitmap	Windows
EPS	.eps	Encapsulated PostScript	Windows, macOS, Linux
IM	.im	A format used by LabEye and other applications	Windows, macOS, Linux

WEBP	.webp	Modern web image format with better compression	Windows, macOS, Linux
TGA	.tga	Truevision TGA, used in 3D graphics and gaming	Windows, macOS, Linux
XPM	.xpm	X PixMap, used in X11 applications	Unix-based systems
XBM	.xbm	X Bitmap, used in X11 GUI systems	Unix-based systems
SPIDER	.spi	Multi-image format used in electron microscopy	Windows, macOS, Linux
PFM	.pfm	Portable Float Map, used in high-precision images	Windows, macOS, Linux
FITS	.fli, .flc	Flexible Image Transport System, used in astronomy	Windows, macOS, Linux
CUR	.cur	Windows cursor format	Windows
MIC	.mic	Microsoft Image Composer format	Windows
PSD	.psd	Adobe Photoshop format	Windows, macOS, Linux
WMF, EMF	.wmf, .emf	Windows Metafile / Enhanced Metafile, used for vector graphics	Windows

Table 26.0: Supported Image File Formats in Pillow

Deep

With Pillow's image file conversion capabilities, you can easily convert an image from one format to another, including converting images to PDF.

The PIL Modules

Pillow (PIL) consists of several modules, each designed to provide specialized classes and methods for handling different aspects of image processing. These modules focus on various functionalities such as image filtering, color manipulation, special effects, image composition, painting, 2D graphics, and other advanced graphic features. Each class within these modules offers distinct methods that enable efficient image and graphic processing.

Some essential Pillow modules

- **Image Module (PIL.Image)**
  - Provides the core functionality for opening, creating, and saving images.
  - Supports multiple image formats.
- **ImageChops Module (PIL.ImageChops)**
  - Supports image arithmetic and logical operations.
  - Used for blending, compositing, and enhancing images.
- **ImageEnhance Module (PIL.ImageEnhance)**
  - Provides methods to adjust brightness, contrast, sharpness, and color balance.
- **ImageFilter Module (PIL.ImageFilter)**
  - Offers predefined filters such as BLUR, CONTOUR, DETAIL, EDGE_ENHANCE, SHARPEN, etc.
- **ImageDraw Module (PIL.ImageDraw)**
  - Allows drawing shapes, lines, and text onto images.
- **ImageFont Module (PIL.ImageFont)**
  - Handles different font styles for rendering text on images.
- **ImageGrab Module (PIL.ImageGrab)**
  - Captures screenshots (Windows and macOS only).

Note

Pillow includes many modules, some of which extend beyond the scope of this book. The modules listed above are essential for graphic design.

Deep

There are four simple ways to utilize the modules or classes provided by PIL:

1. Importing a single module by its name from PIL.
   ```
   >>> from PIL import Image
   ```
2. Importing multiple modules from PIL at once.
   ```
   >>> from PIL import Image, ImageDraw, ImageFilter
   ```

3. Importing all classes using the * wildcard.
   ```
   >>> from PIL import *
   ```

4. Importing PIL and creating instances of classes when needed.
   ```
   >>> import PIL
   >>> img = PIL.Image.open('mypicture.jpg')
   ```

The Image Module

The **Image** module in Pillow provides a class with various methods, each offering unique functionalities for handling images. This module allows you to open, load, display, rotate, create, crop, and retrieve image information seamlessly.

Methods

open	show	blend	core
close	save	alpha_composite	deprecate
new	merge	annotation	effect_noise
frombyte	split	atexit	enum
frombuffer	math	builtins	eval
module	abc	cast	fromarray
fromqimage	fromqpixmap	getmodebans	getmodebase
getmodetype	init	io	is_path
item	linear_gradient	logger	logging
preint	os	radia_gradient	re
isImageType	register_extensions	register_save	register_open
tempfile	register_mime	register_save_all	register_extensions

show( )

Displays the image using the system's default image viewer. It creates a temporary file to preview the image.

new(mode, size, color)

The new() method creates a new image from scratch by specifying its mode, size, and color.
mode →(string): Defines the type of color bands (e.g., "RGB", "RGBA", "L", or "CMYK").
size → (float,float): A 2-tuple (width, height) representing the image dimensions.
color → *(Optional)*: Defines the image color as:

- A single integer (e.g., 156).
- An RGB or RGBA tuple (red, green, blue, alpha).
- A string representing a color name (e.g., "red").
- A hex color name (e.g., "# F5F8FA").

</> Python

```
from PIL import  Image
img =  Image.new( mode = "RGBA", size = (600, 800), color = "#1DA1F2")
img.show( )
```

open(path, mode, format)

This method loads an image from a specified path.

path → (string): The file location (as a string or bytes).

mode → (string) [Optional]: Specifies read 'r' (default) or write 'w'.

format → (Optional): Defines the format if not inferred from the file.

Methods and Attributes of an Open Image

height	custom_mimetype	format	getexif	save
app	decoderconfig	fp	getextrema	seek
applist	decodermaxblock	frombytes	getim	show
histogram	get_format_mimetype	entropy	getpalette	size
bits	effect_spread	filename	getpixel	split
close	get_child_images	getbands	getprojection	tell
convert	has_transparency_data	getchannel	getxmp	thumbnail
copy	apply_transparency	getcolors	load_djpeg	tile
crop	alpha_composite	getdata	load_prepare	tobitmap
draft	format_description	filter	quantization	transform
icclist	putpalette	load_read	quantize	transpose
info	putpixel	point	readonly	verify
layer	palette	putalpha	reduce	width
mode	paste	putdata	remap_palette	resize
rotate				

Table 26.1: Some Available Methods of an Open Image

Deep

To retrieve the methods and attributes of an image opened with **Image.open()**, use the **dir()** function on the image object.

```
>>> img = Image.open("path/to/image.jpg")
>>> dir(img)
```

Think about it ?

The **close()** method closes the image and frees up system resources, such as memory and file handles, that were allocated when the image was opened for editing. What other specific resources does it release?

```python
from PIL import Image
img = Image.open(“flower_girl.jpg”)
img.show( )
```

Saving Images and File Conversion

save(fp, format, save_all, append_images, loop, duration, quality, disposal, transparency, interlace)

The save() method in Pillow plays a crucial role in saving and converting images. It provides multiple functionalities depending on the file format used. For instance, saving an image as a GIF requires parameters that might not be applicable when saving as a JPEG.

Key Functions of save()

- Saving an edited or manipulated image as a new file.
- Converting an image from one format to another.
- Stacking multiple images into a single file.
- Creating animated images such as GIFs.

Parameters

fp →(str) [required]: The filename or file path to save the image. The file extension must be included (e.g., "myimage.jpg").

format →(str) [Optional]: Specifies the file format (e.g., "JPEG", "PNG", "GIF"). If omitted, the format is inferred from fp.

save_all →(bool) [Optional]: If True, saves all frames of a multi-frame image (e.g., GIF). Default is False, which saves only the first frame.

append_images →(list of Image objects) [Optional]: A list of additional images to be appended, useful for stacking images or creating animations.

loop →(int) [Optional, GIF-specific]: Specifies how many times an animated image should loop. 0 means infinite looping.

duration →(int) [Optional, GIF-specific]: Sets the display duration (in milliseconds) for each frame in an animated image.

quality →(int) [Optional, JPEG-specific]: Determines the quality of the saved image (1 to 95). Higher values yield better quality. Default is 75.

disposal →(int)[Optional, GIF-specific]: Determines how the previous frame is handled in animations. Default is 0.

transparency →(int or None)[Optional, GIF/PNG-specific]: Defines a transparency color index.

interlace →(bool)[Optional, PNG-specific]: If True, enables interlacing for progressive loading.

</> Python

```
from PIL import  Image
img =  Image.open("flower_girl.jpg")
img.save( "new_image.jpg" )
```

Deep

You can convert an image to a different format by changing the file extension in the filename.

```
>>> from PIL import  Image
>>> img =  Image.open("image.jpg")
>>> img.save( "myimage.png" )        # conversion from JPG to PNG
```

Creating GIFs or Animated Images

</> Python

```
from PIL import  Image
img1 = Image.open("image1.jpg").resize(size=(600, 800))
img2 = Image.open("image2.jpg").resize(size=(600, 800))
img3 = Image.open("image3.jpg").resize(size=(600, 800))

imgs = [ img2, img3]

img1.save(fp="animate.gif", save_all= True, append_images= imgs, duration= 5, loop=0)
```

Creating PDFs

```python
from PIL import Image
pic1 = Image.open("picture1.jpg").resize(size=(600, 800))
pic2 = Image.open("picture2.jpg").resize(size=(600, 800))
pic3 = Image.open("picture3.jpg").resize(size=(600, 800))

imgs = [ pic2, pic3]

pic1.save(fp="sample.pdf", format="PDF", save_all= True, append_images= imgs)
```

Think about it ?

A multi-frame image is a single file that contains multiple images, allowing for animation or layered content. Formats that support multi-frame images include **GIF** and **TIFF**, which can store multiple frames within one file. What other formats support multi-frame images?

Color Conversion and Filters

Pillow provides various methods for converting colors, applying filters, and manipulating image color channels. These functions help in changing image modes, adjusting transparency, and processing pixel values.

convert(mode, colors)

The **convert()** method is used to change an image from one color mode to another.

mode →(string)[optional] : Specifies the target color mode. Common modes include:

- RGB – Red, Green, Blue
- CMYK – Cyan, Magenta, Yellow, Black
- L – Luminance (grayscale)
- RGBA – RGB with an Alpha (transparency) channel
- LAB, HSV, P, 1, I, F – Other modes for various image types

colors →(optional): An integer (0–256) specifying the number of colors when using the Palette.ADAPTIVE mode.

</> Python

```
from PIL import  Image
img =  Image.open("flower_girl.jpg")

gray_image = img.convert( mode = "L" )
img.show( )                  # showing the original image
gray_image.show( )           # showing a gray image
```

Note

In grayscale conversion, the formula used is:
L=(R×299/1000)+(G×587/1000)+(B×114/1000)L = (R \times 299/1000) + (G \times 587/1000) + (B \times 114/1000)L=(R×299/1000)+(G×587/1000)+(B×114/1000)
Where: R = Red, G = Green, B = Blue

putalpha(alpha)

This method adjusts the transparency (alpha) of an image.

alpha →(int): An integer that defines the transparency level. Lower values increase transparency. A value of **1** makes the image almost completely invisible.

</> **Python**

```
from PIL import  Image
img =  Image.open("flower_girl.jpg")
copied = img.copy( )          # creates a copy of the image
img.putalpha( alpha = 100 )
copied.putalpha( alpha = 20 )
img.show( )                   # showing first image with alpha 100
copied.show( )                # showing second image with alpha 20
```

point(lut)

It applies a function to modify pixel values across all bands in the image.

lut →(function): A required function that takes a single argument and returns a new pixel value.

</> Python

```
from PIL import  Image

img =  Image.open("africa.jpg")
inverted = img.point( lut = lambda x: 255 - x )  # this function inverts each pixel's value

img.show( )          # showing the original image
inverted.show( )     # showing an inverted image (dark areas become white and white area, dark)
```

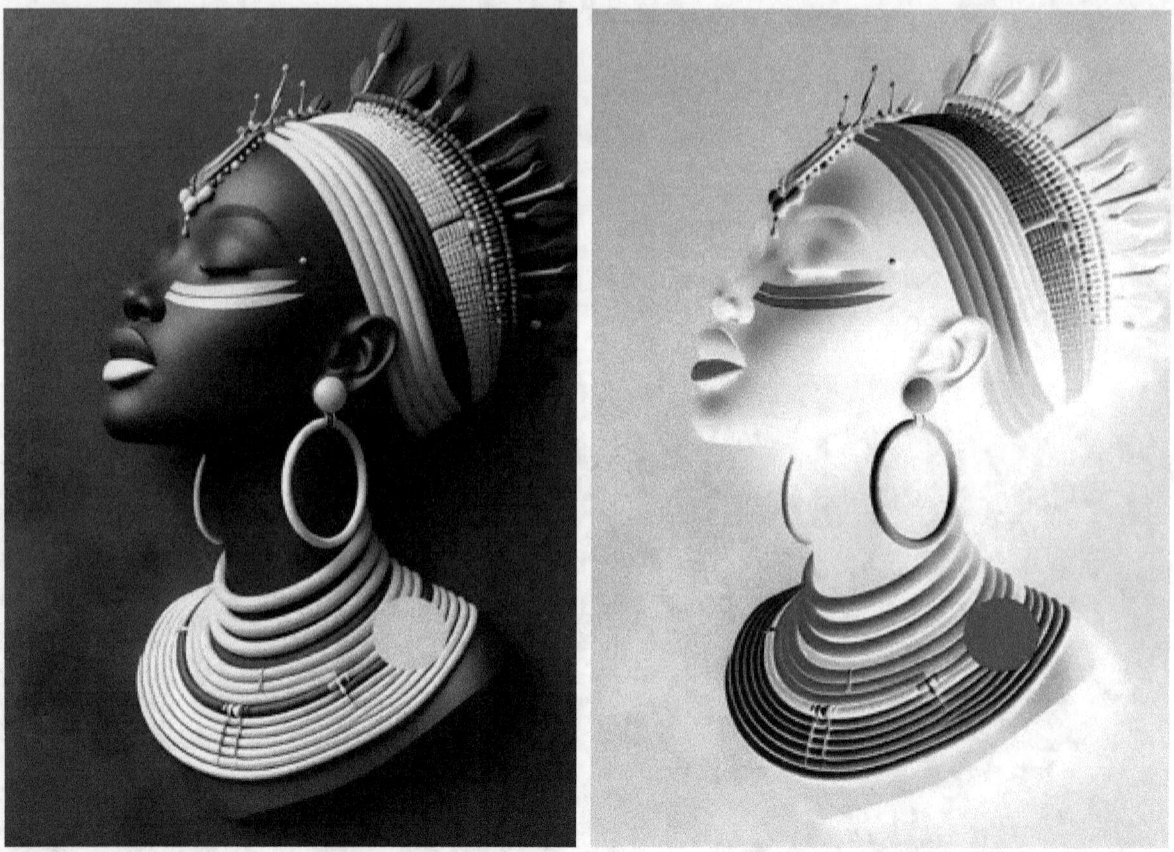

split( ) and merge(mode, bands)

The *splits()* divides an image into individual color bands. This is useful for processing specific channels separately. For example,
Splitting an RGB image results in three separate images for Red, Green, and Blue.

The *merge()* combines individual image bands into a single image.
mode : The target mode for merging, such as "RGB" or "CMYK".
bands : A sequence of images, each representing a single color channel.

```python
from PIL import Image

img = Image.open("africa.jpg")
r, g, b = img.split( )          # splitting image into 3 color bands ( red, green, blue)
r.show( )
g.show( )
b.show( )

merged_img = Image.merge( mode= "RGB" , bands = [ r, g, b] )     # merging the color bands
merged_img.show( )
```

Red color band

Green color band

Blue color band

Merged color bands (bands = [r, g, b])

Merged color bands (bands = [b, g, r])

Merged color bands (bands = [g, b, r])

Think about it ?

1. Why do the images above show only slight differences in their color bands?
2. Why do the images appear in grayscale even in the red, green, and blue color bands?
3. Can you identify the subtle differences between them?

Geometric Transformations

Image Transformation refers to modifying an image's structure, size, orientation, or content without altering its core data. Pillow provides various transformation methods such as resizing, rotating, cropping, and pasting images. These transformations allow precise control over how images appear and are processed.

resize(size, box, resample)

The resize() method is used to scale an image up or down, modifying its width and height.

size → (width, height): A required 2-tuple defining the new dimensions.

box → (left, top, right, bottom): An optional 4-tuple specifying the region to be scaled.

resample: Defines the resampling filter (e.g., Image.Resampling.NEAREST, Image.Resampling.BILINEAR, Image.Resampling.BICUBIC).

</> Python

```
from PIL import  Image

img =  Image.open("bird.jpg")
resized = img.resize(size= (600, 800 ) )
resized_with_box = img.resize(size= (600, 800 ), box =(0, 0, 400, 600 ) )

resized.show( )
resized_with_box.show( )
```

reduce(factor, box)

The reduce() method scales down an image by a given factor while preserving quality.
factor →(int or 2-tuple) : Required parameter defining the reduction ratio.
box → (left, top, right, bottom): Optional 4-tuple specifying a region to be reduced.

</> Python

```
from PIL import  Image

img =  Image.open("bird.jpg")
reduced = img.reduce( factor= 5 )
img.show( )
reduced.show( )
```

Deep

The thumbnail(size, resample) method resizes an image to fit within a bounding box while maintaining its aspect ratio.

- size: *(width, height)* — A 2-tuple defining the maximum size.
- resample: Defines the resampling filter (same as resize).

rotate(angle, center, fillcolor, resample, expand, translate)

The **rotate()** method rotates an image by a given angle around a specified center point.

angle → (float): Rotation angle in degrees.

center → (x, y): Optional 2-tuple defining the pivot point.

fillcolor → (int or tuple): Optional color for the empty areas.

expand → (bool): If True, resizes the output to fit the entire rotated image.

translate → (x, y): Optional 2-tuple shifting the image.

resample: Defines the resampling filter (same as resize). The available filters include,

Resampling.NEAREST	Resampling.BILINEAR	Resampling.BICUBIC
Resampling.BOX	Resampling.HAMMING	Resampling.LANCZOS

</> Python

```
img =  Image.open("bird.jpg")

rotation_180 = img.rotate( angle=180)
rotation_90=img.rotate( angle=90, expand=True, resample=Image.Resampling.BICUBIC)
rotation_45 = img.rotate( angle= 45, expand= True, fillcolor="red")
rotation_135 = img.rotate( angle= 135, expand= True, center= (300,300))

rotation_180.show()
rotation_90.show()
rotation_45.show()
rotation_135.show()
```

180° rotation

90° rotation

45° rotation

135° rotation

Note

Image.Resampling.BOX is not supported for rotation.

transpose(method)

The transpose() method provides predefined rotation and flipping options: The available defined rotation methods are,

Methods	Description
Image.Transpose.ROTATE_90	Rotates 90° counterclockwise.
Image.Transpose.ROTATE_180	Rotates 180°.
Image.Transpose.ROTATE_270	Rotates 270°.
Image.Transpose.FLIP_LEFT_RIGHT	Flips the image horizontally.
Image.Transpose.FLIP_TOP_BOTTOM	Flips the image vertically.
Image.Transpose.TRANSVERSE	Rotating 90° counterclockwise, then flipping horizontally
Image.Transpose.TRANSPOSE	Rotating 90° clockwise, then flipping vertically.

Table 26.2 : Defined rotation methods

```python
from PIL import Image
img = Image.open("bird.jpg")

transpose = img.transpose( Image.Transpose.TRANSPOSE)
transverse = img.transpose( Image.Transpose.TRANSVERSE)
transpose_90 = img.transpose( Image.Transpose.ROTATE_90)
transpose_180 = img.transpose( Image.Transpose.ROTATE_180)
transpose.show()
transverse.show()
transpose_90.show()
transpose_180.show()
```

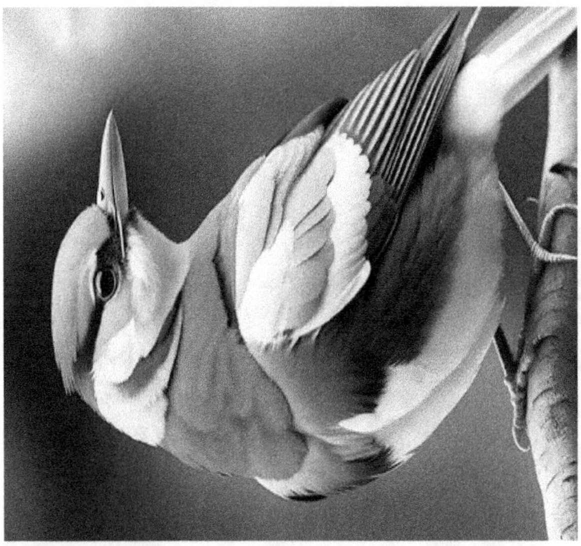
TRANSPOSE

TRANSVERSE

ROTATE_90

ROTATE_180

crop(box) and paste(image, box, mask)

The **crop()** extracts a rectangular region from an image.

box →(left, top, right, bottom): A 4-tuple defining the region to extract.

The **paste()** pastes or places an image onto another image at a specified position.

image: The source image to paste.

box → (left, top): Optional coordinates for positioning.

mask →(Image or None): An optional mask for transparency.

</> Python

```python
from PIL import  Image
puppy1 = Image.open("puppy1.jpg")
puppy2 = Image.open("puppy2.jpg")

puppy1.show()
puppy2.show()

cropped = puppy1.crop(box= (200, 200, 600,1000) )    # extracting a region from puppy1
puppy2.paste(im= cropped, box = (10, 500) )
puppy2.show()
```

Puppy1

Puppy2

puppy1 pasted into puppy2

Image Attributes

Pillow provides several attributes for retrieving essential information about an image. These attributes help in understanding the image's format, size, color composition, and more.

filename and format

The *filename* returns the full name of the image file, including its extension.
The *format* returns the image file format, such as "JPEG", "PNG", or "GIF". This corresponds to the file extension of the image.

```python
>>> from PIL import  Image
>>> img =  Image.open("flower_girl.jpg")
>>> img.filename
'flower_girl.jpg'
>>> img.format
'JPEG'
>>>
```

width, height and size

The *width* returns the width of the image in pixel.
The *height* method returns the height of the image in pixel.
The size() returns the width and height of the image as a tuple (width, height).

```python
>>> from PIL import  Image
>>> img =  Image.open("flower_girl.jpg")
>>> img.width
736
>>> img.height
920
>>> img.size
(736, 920)            # (width, height)
>>>
```

getpixel(xy) and histogram(maxcolors)

The *getpixel()* returns the pixel value at a specific (x, y) coordinate. The returned value format depends on the image mode.

The *histogram*() method returns a histogram of the image, representing pixel intensity distribution. This is useful for analyzing image contrast and color composition.

```python
>>> from PIL import  Image
>>> img =  Image.open("flower_girl.jpg")
```



```
>>> img.getpixel( xy = (10, 20))
(190, 190, 182)
>>> img.histogram()
[.........]                # List of pixels
>>>
```

mode, getbands() and getcolors()

The *mode* returns the color mode of the image, defining the number and type of color bands. Common modes include:

- **RGB** – Red, Green, Blue
- **CMYK** – Cyan, Magenta, Yellow, Black
- **L** – Luminance (grayscale)
- **RGBA** – RGB with an Alpha (transparency) channel
- **LAB**, **HSV**, **P**, **1**, **I**, **F** – Other modes for various image types

The *getbands()* returns a tuple listing the names of each color band in the image. For an **RGB** image, it returns ('R', 'G', 'B').

The *getcolors()* returns a list of colors used in the image, limited to the specified maxcolors (default: 256). Returns None if the color count exceeds the limit.

```
</> Python
>>> from PIL import  Image
>>> img =  Image.open("pictures\\cat.jpg")
>>> img.mode
'RGB'
>>> img.getbands()
('R', 'G', 'B')
>>>
```

The ImageDraw Module

The **ImageDraw** module in the Python Imaging Library (PIL) provides methods for drawing 2D graphics, including shapes, geometric figures, and text, onto images. It is used alongside the Image module to create and manipulate images.

Methods

Any	Draw	ModuleType	annotations
AnyStr	Image	Outline	cast
Callable	ImageColor	Sequence	deprecate
Coords	ImageDraw	Union	floodfill
getdraw	math	struct	

Deep

Use dir(ImageDraw) to list all the methods and attributes available in the **ImageDraw** module.

```
>>> from PIL import ImageDraw, Image
>>> dir(ImageDraw)
[.........]
>>>
>>> img = Image.open("picture.ico")
>>> draw = ImageDraw.Draw(im = img)
>>> dir(draw)
[.........]
>>>
```

Draw(im, mode)

The **Draw()** class is crucial for adding graphics to images. It provides numerous functions for drawing geometric shapes and applying text.
im →(Image)[required]: A required parameter that specifies the image to be drawn on.
mode → (string)[optional]: Specifies the color mode, such as "RGB", "L", or "CMYK".

Methods and Attributes of Draw

arc	ellipse	im	multiline_textbbox	rectangle
bitmap	fill	ink	palette	regular_polygon
chord	font	line	pieslice	rounded_rectangle
circle	fontmode	mode	point	shape
draw	getfont	multiline_text	polygon	text
textbbox	textlength			

Table 26.3: Some methods of Draw()

text(xy, text, fill, font, fill, spacing, align, direction, stroke_width, stroke_fill, embedded_color)

The **text()** method is used to add text to an image.
xy →(tuple (x, y)): Specifies the coordinates where the text should appear.
text →(string): The actual text to be displayed.
font →(ImageFont) [optional]: Defines the font style. Example: ImageFont.truetype("path/to/font.ttf", size).
fill → (int/str/tuple) [optional]: Defines the text color.
spacing →(float) [optional]: Sets the space between lines in multiline text.
align → (string) = ("left", "right", "center"): Controls text alignment.
direction → (string) = ("ltr", "rtl", "ttb"): Specifies text direction.
stroke_width →(float) [optional]: Sets the stroke thickness.
stroke_fill →(color) [optional]: Defines the stroke color.
embedded_color →(bool)[optional]: Determines whether to use font-embedded color glyphs.

</> Python

```python
from PIL import Image, ImageDraw, ImageFont

img  = Image.new(mode="RGB", size=(600,800), color="#324D34")
draw = ImageDraw.Draw(im=img)

font = ImageFont.load_default(size=50)
mytext = "Awesome Python!\nGraphics"
draw.text(text=mytext, xy=(100, 350), font=font, align= "center" )
img.show()
```

Deep

The **ImageFont** module in PIL is used for customizing fonts.

The **ImageFont.load_default(size)** method adjusts the default font size. To use a custom font, **ImageFont.truetype(font, size, index)** is used, where **font** specifies the font file, **size** defines the font size, and **index** indicates the font face to load.

```
>>> from PIL import ImageFont
>>> font = ImageFont.truetype( font= "san_serif.ttf", size = 20)
```

>>>
You can explore and download fonts from Google Fonts.

</> Python

```
from PIL import Image, ImageDraw, ImageFont

smile  = Image.open("smile.jpg")
draw = ImageDraw.Draw(im=smile)
font = ImageFont.truetype(font="font.ttf", size=50)
text = "smile with love"
draw.text(text=text, xy=(50, smile.height-200), font=font, align= "center", fill="#D86350" )

eagle  = Image.open("eagle.jpeg")
draw = ImageDraw.Draw(im=eagle)
font = ImageFont.truetype(font="arvo.ttf", size=60)
text = "The power of courage!"
draw.text(text=text, xy=(20, 500), font=font, align= "center", stroke_fill="#ff6700", stroke_width=50)

smile.show()
eagle.show()
```

Deep

Multiline Text

The **multiline_text()** method has the same parameters as text(), but it is specifically designed to render text containing newline characters (\n).

Drawing Shapes

line(xy, fill, width, joint)

The **line()** method draws a line by connecting coordinate points.

xy →(list of (x, y) tuples): Points defining the line path.

width →(float) [optional]: Line thickness.

fill →(color)[optional]: Line color.

</> Python

```
from PIL import Image, ImageDraw

line  = Image.new(mode="RGB", size=(800, 600), color="#3a6ea5")
draw = ImageDraw.Draw(im=line)
draw.line(xy= [(100,300), (400, 200), (450, 400), (750, 300)], width= 5, fill="#ebebeb")
line.show()
```

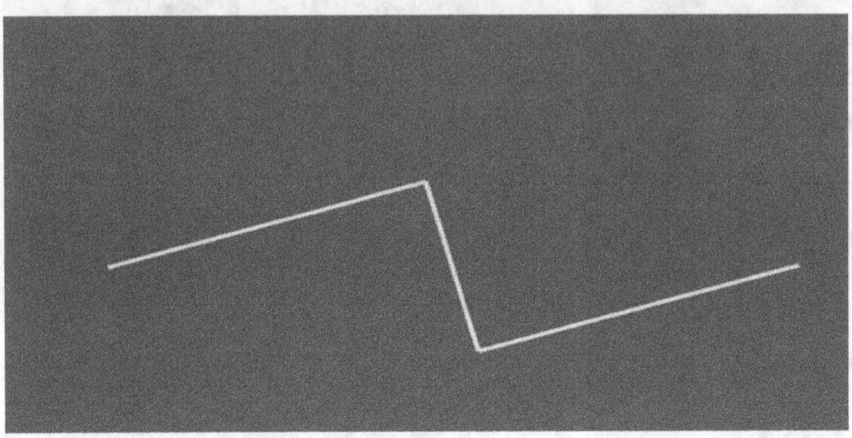

rectangle(xy, fill, outline, width)

The **rectangle()** method is used to draw a rectangular shape on an image.

xy →(tuple or list of tuples (x, y, width, height)): Defines the rectangle coordinates.

fill →(color)[optional]: Background color.

outline →(color) [optional]: Border color.

width →(float)[optional]: Border thickness.

Note

The **rectangle()** method can also be used to draw squares. This can be achieved by ensuring that the coordinates define equal side lengths.

</> Python

```
from PIL import Image, ImageDraw

rectangle  = Image.new(mode="RGB", size=(500,500), color="#3a6ea5")
draw_rec = ImageDraw.Draw(im=rectangle)
draw_rec.rectangle(xy= (100,100, 400, 300), width= 2, fill="#ebebeb")

square  = Image.new(mode="RGB", size=(500,500), color="#3a6ea5")
draw_sq = ImageDraw.Draw(im=square)
draw_sq.rectangle(xy= (100,100, 400,400), width= 5, outline="#ebebeb")

rectangle.show()
square.show()
```

rectangle

square

rounded_rectangle(xy, fill, outline, width)

The **rounded_rectangle()** method is used to draw a rectangle with rounded corners.

radius →(float): Defines corner rounding.

xy →(tuple or list of tuples (x, y, width, height)): Defines the rectangle coordinates.

fill →(color)[optional]: Background color.

outline →(color)[optional]: Border color.

width →(float)[optional]: Border thickness.

</> Python

```
from PIL import Image, ImageDraw
round_rec = Image.new(mode="RGB", size=(500,500), color="#324D34")
draw = ImageDraw.Draw(im=round_rec)
draw.rounded_rectangle(radius= 25, xy= (100,150, 400, 300), width= 2, fill="#ebebeb")

round_rec_pic = Image.open("girl.jpeg")
draw2 = ImageDraw.Draw(im=round_rec_pic)
xy = (100,100, round_rec_pic.width-100, round_rec_pic.height-100)
draw2.rounded_rectangle( radius= 20, xy= xy, width= 5, outline="#c57284")
round_rec.show()
round_rec_pic.show()
```

circle(xy, radius, outline, width, fill)

The **circle()** method is used to draw a circle with a defined radius and center point.

xy →(x, y) [required]: Defines the center coordinates of the circle.

radius →(float) [required]: Specifies the radius of the circle.

width → (float)[required]: Determines the thickness of the circle's outline.

outline → (int or "string" or "#hex" or (red, green, blue))[optional]: Specifies the boundary color of the circle.

fill → (int or "string", "#hex" or (red, green, blue))[optional]: Defines the background color of the circle. It is transparent by default.

</> Python

```
from PIL import Image, ImageDraw

circle  = Image.new(mode="RGB", size=(500,500), color="#151419")
draw = ImageDraw.Draw(im=circle)
draw.circle(radius= 100, xy = (250,250,), width= 5, fill="#EB5E28")

circle_pic  = Image.open("potrait.jpg")
draw2 = ImageDraw.Draw(im = circle_pic)
draw2.circle( radius= 200, xy =  (370,300) , width= 10, outline="#EB5E28")

circle.show()
circle_pic.show()
```

ellipse(xy, width, outline, fill)

The **ellipse()** is used to draw circles by specifying a bounding box.

xy → (x, y, width, height) [required]: Defines the center coordinates of the circle.

width → (float)[optional]: Determines the thickness of the circle's outline.

outline → (int, "string", "#hex" or (red, green, blue)) [optional]: Specifies the boundary color of the circle.

fill → (int, "string", "#hex" or (red, green, blue)) [optional]: Defines the background color of the ellipse. It is transparent by default.

</> Python

```python
from PIL import Image, ImageDraw

img  = Image.new(mode="RGB", size=(500,500), color="#3A6EA5")
draw = ImageDraw.Draw(im=img)
draw.ellipse(xy= (100, 100, 400, 400), width= 20, outline="#0D2137", fill="#ebebeb")
draw.ellipse(xy= (150, 150, 350, 350), width= 10, fill="red")
img.show()
```

arc(xy, start, end, width, fill)

The **arc()** method draws an incomplete circle or a portion of a circle outline..

xy → (x, y, width, height) [required]: Defines the center coordinates of the circle.

start , end → (float) [required]: Define the start and end angles of the arc.

width → (float) [optional]: Determines the thickness of the circle's outline.

fill → (int, "string", "#hex" or (red, green, blue)) [optional]: Defines the background color of the arc. It is transparent by default.

</> Python

```
from PIL import Image, ImageDraw

arc  = Image.new(mode="RGB", size=(500,500), color="#3A6EA5")
draw = ImageDraw.Draw(im=arc)
draw.arc(xy= (50, 50, 350, 350), start=10, end=150, width= 10, fill="#EBEBEB")

arc.show()
```

chord(xy, start, end, width, fill, outline)

The chord() method draws an arc whose ends are connected by a line.

xy → (x, y) [required]: Defines the center coordinates of the circle.

start , end → (float) [required]: Define the start and end angles of the arc.

width → (float) [optional]: Determines the thickness of the arc's outline.

fill → (int, "string", "#hex" or (red, green, blue)) [optional]: Defines the background color of the chord. It is transparent by default.

</> Python

```python
from PIL import Image, ImageDraw

chord  = Image.new(mode="RGB", size=(500,500), color="#3A6EA5")
draw = ImageDraw.Draw(im=chord)
xy = (50, 50, 400, 400)
draw.chord(xy= xy, start= 10, end=200, width= 15, fill="#ff6700", outline="#0D2137")

chord.show()
```

polygon(xy, width, fill, outline)

The **polygon()** method is used to draw a polygon by connecting multiple coordinate points.

xy → ([(x1, y1), (x2, y2), (x3, y3), ...]) [required]: – A list of coordinate points that define the vertices of the polygon.

width → (float) [optional]: Determines the thickness of the polygon's outline.

fill → (int, "colorname", "#hex" or (red, green, blue)) [optional]: Defines the background color of the polygon. It is transparent by default.

</> Python

```
from PIL import Image, ImageDraw

poly  = Image.new(mode="RGB", size=(500,500), color="#3A6EA5")
draw = ImageDraw.Draw(im=poly)
xy = [(150, 450),(350, 450),(450, 250),(250, 50),(50, 250),]
draw.polygon(xy= xy, width= 10, outline="#ebebeb")

poly.show()
```

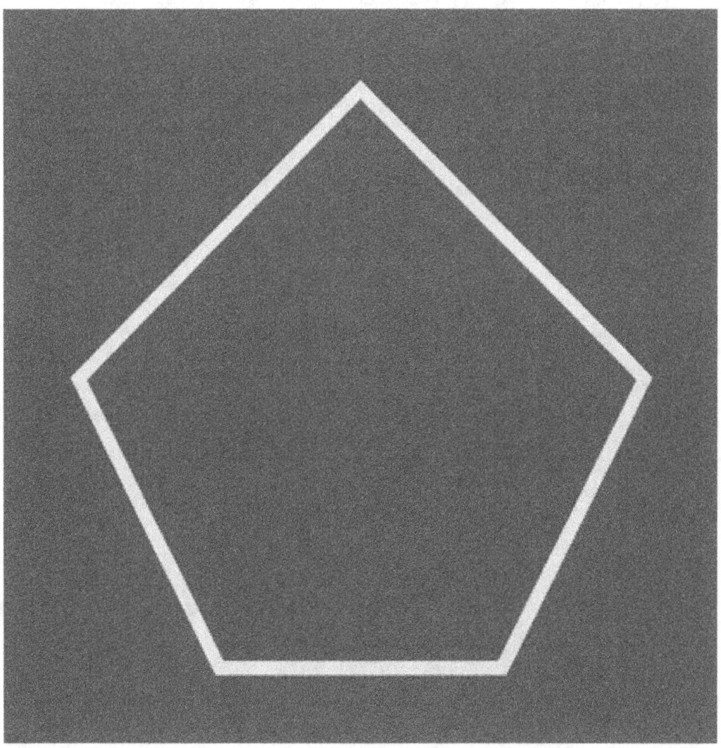

The ImageEnhance Module

The **ImageEnhance** module provides various classes for enhancing images by adjusting their **color**, **contrast**, **brightness**, and **sharpness**. These classes take an image as a parameter and modify its appearance using an enhancement factor, typically ranging from **0.0** to **1.0**, where **1.0** represents the original image.

Methods

Brightness	Contrast	ImageFilter	Sharpness
Color	Image	ImageStat	annotations

Deep

To explore the available methods and attributes of the **ImageEnhance** module, use the dir() function.

```
>>> from PIL import  ImageEnhance
>>> dir(ImageEnhance)
```

The ImageEnhance module provides **three key objects** for each enhancement class:

image
Represents the input image and provides methods for manipulation and data retrieval.

degenerate
This generates the **least enhanced version** of the image, often used as a reference for scaling enhancements.

enhance(factor)
Applies the enhancement effect to the image based on the specified factor, where 1.0 represents the original image.

Brightness(image)

The **Brightness()** class controls the light intensity of an image:

- A factor of **0.0** results in a completely dark image.
- A factor of **1.0** preserves the original brightness.
- A factor above **1.0** increases the brightness.

</> **Python**

```
from PIL import Image, ImageDraw
img  = Image.open("girl.jpeg")
enhanced1 = ImageEnhance.Brightness(image=img).enhance(factor=0.3)
enhanced2 = ImageEnhance.Brightness(image=img).enhance(factor=2)
enhanced3 = ImageEnhance.Brightness(image=img).enhance(factor=5)

img.show()
enhanced1.show()
enhanced2.show()
enhanced3.show()
```

Original image

brightness factor: 0.3

brightness factor: 2

brightness factor : 5

Contrast(image)

The **Contrast()** class adjusts the difference between the darkest and lightest parts of an image:

- A factor of **0.0** results in a completely gray image.
- A factor of **1.0** maintains the original contrast.
- A factor above **1.0** increases contrast.

</> Python

```
from PIL import Image, ImageDraw
img  = Image.open("girl.jpeg")
img.show()
ImageEnhance.Contrast(image=img).enhance(factor=0.6).show()
ImageEnhance.Contrast(image=img).enhance(factor=2) .show()
ImageEnhance.Contrast(image=img).enhance(factor=4) .show()
```

original image

contrast factor : 0.6

contrast factor : 2

contrast factor : 4

Color(image)

The **Color()** class manages the **saturation** or **intensity** of colors in an image:

- A factor of **0.0** converts the image to black and white.
- A factor of **1.0** keeps the original colors.
- A factor above **1.0** increases color vibrancy.

</> Python

```
from PIL import Image, ImageDraw
img  = Image.open("parrot.jpeg")
enhanced1 = ImageEnhance.Color(image=img).enhance(factor=0.
enhanced2 = ImageEnhance.Color(image=img).enhance(factor=0.4)
enhanced3 = ImageEnhance.Color(image=img).enhance(factor=3)

img.show()
enhanced1.show()
enhanced2.show()
enhanced3.show()
```

Original image

color factor : 0.0

color factor : 0.4

color factor : 3.0

Sharpness(image)

The **Sharpness()** class controls the **clarity of edges and fine details** in an image:

- A factor of **0.0** results in a completely blurred image.
- A factor of **1.0** maintains the original sharpness.
- A factor above **1.0** enhances the sharpness.

</> Python

```
from PIL import Image, ImageDraw
img  = Image.open("snow_trip.jpeg")
img.show()
ImageEnhance.Sharpness(image=img).enhance(factor= -10.0 ).show()
ImageEnhance.Sharpness(image=img).enhance(factor= 0.0) .show()
ImageEnhance.Sharpness(image=img).enhance(factor=15.0) .show()
```

Original image

sharpness factor : -10.0

sharpness factor : 0.0

sharpness factor : 15.0

The ImageFilter Module

Image filtering enhances an image's appearance by modifying pixel values using predefined functions. The ImageFilter module in PIL provides various classes for applying different filtering effects.

Predefined Filters in Pillow
Pillow includes several built-in filters:

Filter Name	Effect
SMOOTH	Applies a subtle smoothing effect
SMOOTH_MORE	Enhances the smoothing effect
BLUR	Softens the image
SHARPEN	Enhances image sharpness
FIND_EDGES	Highlights edges in the image
CONTOUR	Creates a contour-like effect
DETAIL	Enhances fine details
EDGE_ENHANCE	Enhances image edges
EDGE_ENHANCE_MORE	Stronger edge enhancement
EMBOSS	Creates an embossed effect

Table 26.4: Predefined Filters

Deep

To explore the available methods and attributes of the **ImageFilter** module, use the dir() function.

```
>>> from PIL import  ImageFilter
>>> dir(ImageFilter)
[........]
>>>
```

```python
from PIL import Image, ImageFilter
img  = Image.open("orange_love.png")
img.show()
img.filter( ImageFilter.BLUR ).show()
img.filter( ImageFilter.CONTOUR ).show()
img.filter( ImageFilter.SMOOTH_MORE ).show()
img.filter( ImageFilter.EMBOSS ).show()
img.filter( ImageFilter.FIND_EDGES ).show()
img.filter( ImageFilter.DETAIL ).show()
img.filter( ImageFilter.SHARPEN ).show()
```

Original image

BLUR

CONTOUR

SMOOTH_MORE

EMBOSS

FIND_EDGES

DETAIL

SHARPEN

ImageFilter Classes

RankFilter(size, rank)

Sorts all pixels in a window of the specified size and returns the rankth value.

size → (int)[required]: The kernel size in pixels.

rank → (int)[required]: The pixel value to pick.

- 0 → Minimum filter
- size*size/2 → Median filter
- size*size - 1 → Maximum filter

</> Python

```
from PIL import Image, ImageFilter
img  = Image.open("orange_love.png")
img.filter( ImageFilter.RankFilter( size = 7, rank= 2) ).show()
```

MinFilter(size)

Selects the lowest pixel value in a given window size.

size → (int)[required]: Kernel size in pixels.

MaxFilter(size)

Selects the highest pixel value in a given window size.

size → (int)[required]: Kernel size in pixels.

MedianFilter(size)
Selects the median pixel value in a given window size.
size → (int)[required]: Kernel size in pixels.

ModeFilter(size)
Selects the most frequent pixel value in a given window size. Pixels that appear only once or twice are ignored.
size → (int)[required]: Kernel size in pixels.

MultibandFilter
Used for filtering multi-band images.

BoxBlur(radius)
Blurs the image by averaging pixel values in a square box extending radius pixels in each direction.
radius → (float or list of floats)[required]: Defines the blur area.

- radius = 0 → No blur applied

</> Python

```
from PIL import Image, ImageFilter
img  = Image.open("orange_love.png")
img.filter( ImageFilter.BoxBlur( radius = 10) ).show()
```

GaussianBlur(radius)
Blurs the image using a Gaussian kernel approximation with extended box filters.
radius → (float or list of floats)[required]: Defines the standard deviation of the Gaussian kernel.

The ImageChops Module

The **ImageChops** module in Pillow provides a collection of channel operations ("chops") for performing arithmetic image manipulations. These operations are useful for image comparison, blending, masking, and logical operations.

Methods

add	composite	duplicate	logical_and
add_modulo	constant	hard_light	logical_or
annotations	darker	invert	logical_xor
blend	difference	lighter	multiply
offset	overlay	screen	soft_light
subtract	subtract_modulo		

Deep

Use the dir() function to explore the available methods and attributes of the ImageChops module.

```
>>> from PIL import  ImageChops
>>> dir(ImageChops)
[........]
>>>
```

add(image1, image2, scale, offset)

This method **adds** one image to another with an optional **scale** and **offset**.

image1→ (PIL.Image) : First image.

image2 → (PIL.Image): Second image.

scale → (float)[optional- default=1.0]: The resulting image is divided by this scale factor.

offset → (int)[optional- default=0]: A value added to the result to adjust brightness.

</> Python

```
from PIL import Image, ImageChops

img1 = Image.open("freshview.jpeg")
img2 = Image.open("warmview.jpeg")
img1.show()
img2.show()
ImageChops.add(image1=img1, image2=img2, scale=3, offset=10).show()
```

add_modulo(image1, image2, scale, offset)

This method **adds** two images without applying a scale factor, meaning pixel values wrap around (modulo 256).

image1→ (PIL.Image) : First image.

image2→ (PIL.Image) : Second image.

◇ **Use Case**: Prevents image values from clipping when they exceed the maximum pixel value.

subtract(image1, image2, scale, offset)

Subtracts image2 from image1 and divides by a **scale** factor, with an optional **offset**.

image1 → (PIL.Image): First image.

image2 → (PIL.Image): Second image.

scale → (float)[optional- default=1.0]: Controls the degree of subtraction.

offset → (int)[optional- default=0]: Adjusts the resulting image brightness.

◇ **Use Case**: Used to detect changes between images.

```python
from PIL import Image, ImageChops

img1 = Image.open("freshview.jpeg")
img2 = Image.open("warmview.jpeg")
img = ImageChops.subtract(image1=img1, image2=img2, scale=3, offset=10)
img.save("new_image.jpg")
```

subtract_modulo(image1, image2)

Subtracts image2 from image1 without clipping pixel values (wraps around if values go negative).

image1→ (PIL.Image): First image.

image2→ (PIL.Image): Second image.

- **Use Case**: Works well for periodic images where wrapping pixel values is desired.

difference(image1, image2)

Computes the **absolute difference** between two images, pixel by pixel.

- **Use Case**: Commonly used in image comparison and detecting changes between two images.

```python
from PIL import Image, ImageChops
img1 = Image.open("girl_with_orange.jpeg")
img2 = Image.open("girl_with_glass.jpeg")
img1.show()
img2.show()
ImageChops.difference(image1=img1, image2=img2).show()
```

lighter(image1, image2)

Creates an image where each pixel is the **lighter** value of the two images.

- **Use Case**: Useful for highlighting bright areas.

</> Python

```
from PIL import Image, ImageChops
img1 = Image.open("girl_with_orange.jpeg")
img2 = Image.open("girl_with_glass.jpeg")
ImageChops.lighter(image1=img1, image2=img2).show()
```

hard_light(image1, image2)

This method applies the **Hard Light** blending mode, which enhances contrast by either multiplying or screening the pixel values of two images based on the brightness of the top image.

◇ **Use Case**: Used for adding dramatic lighting effects by intensifying highlights and shadows

</> Python

```
img1 = Image.open("girl_with_orange.jpeg")
img2 = Image.open("girl_with_glass.jpeg")
ImageChops.hard_lighter(image1=img1, image2=img2).show()
```

invert(image)

This method **inverts** an image, meaning dark areas become bright and vice versa.

- **Use Case**: Used for negative effects.

```
</> Python
img = Image.open("dark_girl.jpeg")
img.show()
ImageChops.invert(image = img).show()
```

multiply(image1, image2)

Multiplies pixel values of two images, making dark areas **darker** and bright areas **brighter**.

image1→ (PIL.Image): First image.

image2→ (PIL.Image): Second image.

- **Use Case**: Often used for shadow effects.

screen(image1, image2)

This method **blends two inverted images** and superimposes them.

image1→ (PIL.Image) - First image.

image2→ (PIL.Image) - Second image.

- **Use Case**: Used in graphics editing for soft light effects.

overlay(image1, image2)

Applies the **Overlay blending mode**, enhancing contrast by mixing highlights and shadows.

image1→ (PIL.Image): First image.

image2→ (PIL.Image): Second image.

- **Use Case**: Used in photo filters and color correction.

blend(image1, image2, alpha)

Blends two images with a constant **transparency weight** (alpha).

image1→ (PIL.Image): First image.

image2→ (PIL.Image): Second image.

alpha→ (float)[required]: A value between 0.0 (fully transparent) and 1.0 (fully visible).

- **Use Case**: Used in fading effects.

constant(image1, image2, value)

This method fills a channel with a given **gray level**.

image1→ (PIL.Image): First image.

image2→ (PIL.Image): Second image.

value → (int)[required]: Level of gray (0-255).

- **Use Case**: Used for background manipulation.

The ImageGrab Module

The **ImageGrab** module in Pillow is primarily used for capturing screenshots of the entire computer screen or retrieving content from the clipboard. It provides two key functions: one for taking screenshots and another for extracting clipboard content.

Taking Screenshots

grab(bbox, include_layered_window, all_screens, xdisplay)

The **grab()** function captures a screenshot of the screen. If no bounding box (bbox) is specified, it captures the entire screen.

bbox → (tuple)[optional]: Defines the region of the screen to capture in the format (x, y, width, height).

x, y → Coordinates of the top-left corner.

width, height → Dimensions of the region to capture.

include_layered_windows → (bool)[optional]: If True, captures layered windows (Windows-only).

all_screens → (bool)[optional]: If True, captures all screens in a multi-monitor setup (Windows-only).

xdisplay → (string): Specifies the display to capture (Linux-only).

</> Python

```python
from PIL import Image, ImageGrab

img  = ImageGrab.grab()
img.show()
img.save("screenshot.png")
```

Capturing Clipboard Content

grabclipboard()

The **grabclipboard()** function retrieves the current clipboard content if available.

Return Values:

- If an image is stored in the clipboard, it returns a PIL.Image object.
- If file paths are stored, it returns a list of filenames.
- Returns None if the clipboard is empty or contains unsupported data.

</> Python

```python
from PIL import Image, ImageGrab

content  = ImageGrab.grabclipboard()
print( content )
```

Think about it ?

1. Is there any other class in the ImageGrab module besides grab() and grabclipboard()?
2. How does the computer's print screen function differ from ImageGrab.grab()?

Remarks

Thank you so much for taking the time to read this book. I sincerely appreciate your support, and I pray that the Almighty God replenishes every penny you have spent on this book. May you be blessed abundantly.

Ouereila Publishing House is continuously growing, and we acknowledge that we are not yet perfect. Your feedback is invaluable in helping us improve and refine our work. If you have any suggestions, comments, or insights, please feel free to share them with us at oueneila@gmail.com or through this feedback form. Your input will contribute to the betterment of not only this book but also future publications.

Acknowledgment

First and foremost, I extend my deepest gratitude to the Almighty God for guiding me through this journey and giving me the strength to complete this work.

A special thanks goes to my dear mother, **Irene**, for her unwavering love, encouragement, and belief in me. Her support has been a cornerstone of my journey, and I pray she continues to live a long and fulfilling life.

Additionally, I extend my gratitude to everyone who has supported me in any way—whether through words of encouragement, constructive feedback, or simply believing in this vision. Your contributions, big or small, have played a role in bringing this book to life.

May this book serve as a stepping stone for those eager to explore the world of Python.

With appreciation,
Williams Asiedu

About the Author

Williams Asiedu is a software engineer, entrepreneur, and philanthropist recognized for his commitment to technological innovation and community development. He earned his Master's degree from the Illinois Institute of Technology, a prestigious academic institution in the United States, where he honed his skills in computer science and software engineering. Today, he works as a software engineer and applies his expertise to cutting-edge projects in the field of digital technologies.

Beyond his professional career, Williams is also an accomplished author and editor. He has published several books on computer science, programming, and new technologies, allowing him to share his knowledge with a wide audience, from students to seasoned professionals. His writing style is distinguished by its clarity, pedagogy, and ability to make complex concepts accessible. His publications, translated and distributed to an international readership, contribute to democratizing technical knowledge and training a new generation of developers. His role as editor has also allowed him to collaborate with other authors and experts, thus strengthening the quality and diversity of the content he makes available to the community. Through his books, courses, and editorial initiatives, he positions himself as an influential voice in the field of technology education and knowledge sharing.

At the same time, Williams Asiedu is actively involved in philanthropy. Driven by a deep desire to give back to society, he supports various social and educational projects aimed at improving the living conditions of disadvantaged communities. His philanthropic work goes beyond simple financial support: he is directly involved in training, mentoring, and community development programs, encouraging young people to believe in their potential and pursue careers in science and technology.

His career perfectly illustrates the balance between professional expertise, intellectual commitment, and social responsibility. Through his work, writings, and initiatives, Williams Asiedu continues to inspire and support future engineers, entrepreneurs, and innovators. His vision, fueled by a passion for technology and a deep sense of humanity, helps build a future where knowledge and innovation serve the common good.

www.ingramcontent.com/pod-product-compliance
Lightning Source LLC
LaVergne TN
LVHW080014210926
848481LV00011B/3023